Gone South

Gone South

CANADIAN FOOTBALL 1983-1994

FRANK COSENTINO

This is the third in a series about Canadian football. The objective in the set is to trace the development of competition for the Grey Cup beginning in 1909. Three themes predominate: Rule changes, style of play, and, the trend from amateur to professional with emphasis on the Americanization of the game. Canadian Football 1983-1994: Gone South is the title of this book. It leans heavily on the original publication A Passing Game: A History of the CFL which was published in 1996 by Bain & Cox of Winnipeg as an imprint of Blizzard Publishing. The Copyright owner was the author, Frank Cosentino. Blizzard has since left the publishing business. This publication relies heavily on minutes of meetings made available to the author. This work is a companion to another effort published under the title Canadian Football 1969-1982: CLOSED DOORS & Alberta Crude. Photos are included in these new publications. An earlier work, entitled Canadian Football: The Grey Cup Years, and was published in 1969 will also become available again in the near future. The fourth book in the series Canadian Football 1995-2014 Home Again has already been published and is available. Books can be ordered through the website <valleyoldtimers.com> also <Lulu. com> or from Frank Cosentino, Box 316, Eganville, Ontario, Canada

Copyright © Frank Cosentino

Players' cards courtesy of JOGO

ISBN: 978-1-365-65196-0

Printed by Lulu Press

Contents

Dedication and Thanks.

My special thanks to my parents, Vincenzo Cosentino and Maria Annunziata Sisinni who traveled the road from San Giorgio Morgeto in their native Calabria to give their children opportunity. They arrived in Hamilton Ontario where I met my wife of now 57 years, Sheila, always my love and support. We have been blessed with 4 children, 12 grand children and one great grand child. This book is dedicated to Sheila, my bride of 57 years, my support and the love of my life.

Thanks and much appreciation also to Bayberry Lane Designs and especially Ms Kelly Klinck.

Foreword

When the forward pass was adopted in 1931 by the Canadian Rugby Union (CRU), the governing body for football in Canada, the Montreal Amateur Athletic Association (MAAA) unveiled Warren Stevens as its quarterback. Stevens was an American from Syracuse University who had come to McGill to do graduate work and to learn about hockey, which he considered to be the game of the future. The CRU had expected that all teams in Canada would develop their proficiency with the new rule equally; it was new to all Canadians even though the forward pass had been used in the west and the Grey Cup game of 1929. Stevens was far advanced in the use of the new tactic; the MAAA was undefeated and won the Grey Cup in 1931.

As a result, there was a search for American talent in an attempt to gain an edge, particularly at the quarterback position. It wasn't so much that players were recruited with contracts, football in Canada was still "amateur" by and large, but players were enticed with jobs in the communities. The Sarnia Imperials, for example, won Grey Cups in two of three appearances in the thirties. Many of their players, Americans as well as Canadians, were attracted to the team with the promise of a job during the Depression. And, when the Winnipeg Blue Bombers won the Grey Cup for the west for the first time in 1935, they did so with nine Americans they had recruited from the northern United States at a cost of $7400.

The CRU reacted. It wanted to ensure that a football team was representative of individuals who lived in its area by extending its "residency rule." Ever since 1909, players for a team were required to have lived in the area where they played football (universities were exempted). Most believed that Winnipeg would repeat as the west's representatives in 1936. The new rule would not affect them retroactively, but when Saskatchewan won the west, their Americans were not eligible for the CRU sponsored Grey Cup. Consequently, the 1936 Grey Cup game was won by Sarnia when it defeated the Ottawa Rough Riders 26-20. A categorization of players occurred: There were Canadians, often known as "homebrews", and Americans. There followed Canadians, Canadian-Americans (those Americans who had been in the country five years and therefore qualified as Canadians for football purposes) and Americans. With the phasing out of these Canadian Americans after 1965, a new distinction of Designated Imports was introduced. There were Imports, Designated Imports and Non-imports (Canadians). By 1993, then Commissioner Larry Smith stated that the CFL could be receptive to unlimited imports, (i.e.) no import/non-import restrictions with the beginning of the 1995 season. It was a period in time when expansion of the CFL to the United States was a reality, albeit on shaky ground. The Southern exposure ended after the 1995 season after which the terms Internationals (Americans) and Nationals (Canadians) were in vogue.

The purpose of these books, Canadian Football 1969-1982: Closed Doors & Alberta Crude followed by Canadian Football 1983-1994: Gone South is to trace the leagues which competed for the Grey Cup beginning in 1909 and the development of Canadian football's rules, style of play as well as the trend from amateur to professional and the move towards the Americanization of the Canadian game. Each volume will stand on its own, as an extension of my book Canadian Football: The Grey Cup Years (1909-1968) or as a lead-in to Canadian Football: 1995-2014 Home Again.

Frank Cosentino
Eganville, Ontario
August 15, 2016

Chapter One

Much of the football news of 1983 emanated from the far west where Canada's first functioning dome stadium was built in time for the 1983 football season. It was the home of "Crazy George", the Lions "Cheerleader", and the site of the "wave" formed by spectators standing and sitting in sections simulating movement around the seating perimeter of the dome. And B.C. Place was not for sensitive ears. The noise reverberated to the point that it was deafening. Visiting teams especially had difficulty in hearing the quarterback's signal; hand movements became a means of communicating with wide receivers.

The stadium officially opened June 19, 1983. An exhibition game was played four days later: B.C. defeated Calgary 41–19. The first regular season CFL game there was between the B.C. Lions and Saskatchewan, the Lions winning 44–28. Mervyn Fernandez scored after only 57 seconds of play with a 30 yard pass from Roy Dewalt.

B.C. Place was an amazing structure: "The world's largest air supported dome in terms of area, because of the size required to host Canadian football".[1] Ten acres were covered by the building, a maximum width of 623 feet, maximum length of 760 feet, and a maximum height of 200 feet. The roof, made of Teflon-bonded fibreglass, covered 40,000 square yards. Its 46 ton weight was "supported by air pressure inside that is six points per square foot above outside atmospheric pressure".[2] Total cost of the facility was $126 million.

Previous to B.C. Place, the largest crowd to witness a B.C. Lions game was in 1965 when 36,704 saw the Lions and Stampeders play in Empire Stadium. In 1964 when the Lions won the Grey Cup a record attendance of 260,039 fans had been attracted. B.C. Place erased all of that. A total of 448,857 watched the Lions in '83; B.C.'s first pre season game attracted 53,472. A regular season record of 56,852 watched B.C. and Winnipeg on August 12, 1983. A capacity crowd of 59,409 saw the same two teams in the Western final of 1983.[3]

The B.C. Lions were the envy of every team in the CFL in 1983. Not only did they play in what some considered to be the most outstanding stadium in North America, their training facilities were similarly outstanding. The Club opened its own private office and practice complex in nearby Surrey, B.C. Ticket offices, dressing rooms, storage area weight training equipment, laundry capability, a sauna, whirlpool and shower along with athletic therapy areas were all part of the new headquarters. All of this was on the ground floor; four meeting rooms for simultaneous sessions were also available; the practice field was immediately outside "only a matter of stepping out the back door".[4] Administrative offices were located on the upper floor of the two storey building.

B.C. Place was not only affecting the League attendance wise, it was responsible for removing a one hundred year tradition in Canadian football. There had always been end zones of 25 yards depth. Throughout the course of play, adjustments had been made in individual parks if they couldn't meet the specifications. For example, Delormier Downs in Montreal could only support 10 yard end zones in early Alouette days long before the Alouettes moved to McGill University and Molson Stadium. Similarly, corners might have been rounded and fenced such as at Taylor Field in the sixties or the chalk lines extended from the field to the surrounding track in order to get the full 25 yards past the goal line. When the matter of B.C. Place and its 20 yard end zones came up during a pre season meeting of the CFL Management Council, Calgary's Jack Gotta proposed that other stadiums be made to conform. His motion was too radical, barely. It was defeated 5–4 but Edmonton's Norm Kimball suggested that the proposal was more of a rules committee matter. He would consider submitting a proposal for the 1984 season.[5] It did not in fact receive approval until January of '86 in time for the 1986 season but the reason for the change was directly attributable to the building of B.C. Place in 1983.

There were other standardizations. Television and video equipment was making its presence felt in the League. The Football Reporters of Canada requested that television monitors be placed in the press box's main print area. The League was only too pleased to concur since, as Norm Kimball advised, "very little cost is involved because the equipment is usually supplied either by a sponsor or by the television network".[6] They also asked that "each radio broadcast booth be equipped with a signal light activated by the game time keeper to indicate when time has been called for a commercial". While both of these suggestions were incorporated for the upcoming season, there was some delay over another recommendation. The installation of twenty second clocks was suggested but a decision deferred until the May meeting. In 1982, Ottawa, Saskatchewan and Montreal had the clocks in their stadium. B.C. Place would have them in 1983. The other five were at various stages in the decision making process; new Winnipeg General Manager Paul Robson thought the lack of uniformity among teams in the matter to be very "unprofessional".[7]

The Designated Import rule continued to be discussed in the CFL boardrooms but for another reason other than the typical one. During the 1982 season, a team had put its designated import quarterback into a blocking back position on a third down punt. It was a classic case of coaches attempting to stretch the rules. The argument was made that the snap could still be made to the quarterback even though he was not in the traditional under-the-centre position. Norm Kimball "argued that it was never intended that a designated quarterback could line up at another position. However, he could see permitting a direct snap to another player while another quarterback is operating in his normal position".[8] While there was much discussion about the situation at the January meeting, a final decision was made at the Management Council meeting of February 15. There, it was decided that "the provision would be interpreted to mean that the player would be deemed to be playing at quarterback if at the instant the ball is snapped he is in a position to receive the ball directly from the centre, whether or not he actually receives the ball.[9]

Discussion of imports and non-imports was always a topic for CFL meetings. Those in 1983 were no exception. By 1983, all the so-called "grandfather clauses" which were enacted in order "to avoid making legislation retro-active" in 1965, were unnecessary. "All the players who had been protected by these transitional provisions were no longer active in the league". The grandfather clauses were therefore eliminated. Non-imports could now "be a player who was physically resident in Canada for an aggregate period of seventeen years prior to his attaining the age of 21 years".[10]

If Harold Ballard had his way, the whole notion of non-imports would be swept away. Ballard stated: "I'm a Canadian but I believe we have to do something to improve our product. Sure you can look at it from the Canadian point of view but you've also got to look at it as a business and I'm not going to sell any more seats the way it stands now".[11] For whatever reason, Ballard did not communicate his preference to Tiger Cat General Manager, Joe Zuger. The latter voted against Montreal's proposal that the number of imports be increased from 15 to 18, the designated restrictions to apply to the eighteenth; rosters be increased to 38, the number of non-imports be 20. Only Montreal, its vote cast by Sam Etcheverry voted in favour while arguing that the money spent on the (to be abolished) 4 man taxi squad would fund the increased roster and improve the calibre of play.

There were other instances where the individual clubs chose to act in that manner as opposed to a League approach. Property rights, logos, trade marks, team names and the such could not be vested in the League in Canada until the current rights in Toronto and Montreal expired. A plan was approved to merchandise them in the U.S. through a firm called West Nally Inc. of New York. The period would not go beyond December 31, 1984 and in return the League was to receive a guarantee of sixty per cent of the profits or a minimum of $15,000.[12]

From time to time, the media requested information from the League offices about players' options and which players' contracts were due to expire. Gaudaur, noting that "the NFL issues press releases on the subject" asked for guidance on the matter. The Clubs preferred to handle it individually.[13] They took a similar approach with a scouting combine. There was a League operation but the Ottawa, Toronto, Hamilton and Calgary clubs acted on their own. Calgary's Jack Gotta spoke for the four when he stated that his club "feels it could do a better job on its own".[14] With such an individualistic approach among League members, it was only natural that there were continuous strains on the CFL as it sought to speak and act with one voice.

Expansion of the CFL to the Maritime region was also anticipated. The name of the team was to be the Schooners, a reference to the famous "Bluenose" which adorned the Canadian ten cent piece. It was also the name of a popular beer; so there was prestige and the possibility of corporate sponsorship tie-in as well.The move had been approved but there were sceptics. The League gave the Schooners a May 1983 deadline "to prove beyond a doubt they will be able to field a team for the 1984 season".[15] The Schooners' General Manager-in-waiting J.I. Albrecht, who held similar positions with the Alouettes and Argonauts, sought to soothe any fears: "Sure there are sceptics and cynics but if you had to depend on sceptics and cynics nothing would get done. I've just come back after spending 11 days in Halifax/Dartmouth and everything down there is favourable. We've got season ticket orders coming out of our ears".[16]

That didn't deter the League from deciding that the Schooners would not be part of the 1984 schedule. Its May meeting identified three major shortcomings with the Maritime expansion franchise: There was not a clear financing picture of the proposed $6.5 million stadium; a failure to clearly spell out the breakdown of shareholders in the Maritime Professional Football Club Ltd.; the absence of required statements of undertaking from their principal owner, R.B. Cameron".[17] Perhaps even more critically, however, "the group didn't bring along the required $900,000 of the $1.5 million franchise fee".[18] The Schooners were given until June 17 to "get their ship out of dry dock and be up to specifications"... otherwise they would "be sent to the bottom for good".[19] And they were! Expansion to the Maritimes came close but was ruled out when the June 17 deadline arrived and passed without the League being assured that a viable franchise was possible under the arrangements of the time.

The League also announced its Grey Cup game prices. All seats at B.C. Place would be $30 "regardless of location".[20] Eighty-five percent of all the tickets were allocated to the west for the game which was certain to attract record revenue for the League and its Clubs. The 1982 play-offs and Grey Cup yielded $514,714 and $624,761 respectively for a total of $1,139,475 to be distributed among the nine clubs as follows:[21]

Club	Percent	Amount
Edmonton	13.0	$148,131
Toronto	12.0	136,736
Winnipeg	11.5	131,040
Ottawa	11.5	131,040
Calgary	11.0	125,342
Hamilton	11.0	125,342
B.C.	10.0	113,948
Saskatchewan	10.0	113,948
Montreal	10.0	113,948
Totals	100.0	1,139,475

The business of football was brought home with Edmonton's end of year statement of finances. Consecutive Grey Cup Champions for five years, the Eskimos offered some sober insights into their operations. They "drew a record 616,000 spectators to their 11 home games, generated $5,136,000 in gate receipts and suffered a $230,000 operating loss". Winnipeg was raising its ticket prices. The 29,000 seats between the goal lines in Winnipeg Stadium were being increased by $2.00 to $16.50 between the 15 yard lines. From the fifteen to the goal line, they were dropping by $2.00 to $12.50. Season tickets at $150 were higher by $5 over 1982, End Zone seats were $1.50 higher at $10. North Stand season tickets were $90, five dollars more than in 1982.[22]

The CFL still had a system of revenue sharing which had been agreed to at the November 20, 1981 meeting and effective through 1983. "The contribution by each club would be 20% of the amount by which its gross gate exceed the League average. This contribution cannot exceed 5% of the club's gross gate for the season.[23] The Clubs had to make a decision as to whether to increase each Club's maximum contribution to $225,000 or "$150,000 times the annual compounded consumer price index factors for 1981, 1982, and 1983 . . . whichever is greater"[24] or to extend the existing provisions beyond the 1983 season".[25] Among the factors to be considered was the knowledge that when the changes were introduced in 1980, the figures were based on the fact that six of the nine clubs either made a profit or broke even. "In 1982, it is understood that at least seven of the nine clubs suffered significant operating losses".[26] Some attempt was made to pinpoint player salaries as the culprit. The player salary and bonus costs had risen to 55% from 47% of the average revenue for all Clubs.[27]

The League also showed its tendency to be pragmatic. When there was a complaint that teams were not adhering to the fifteen minute half-time intermission period, they were more likely to take twenty minutes, the rules committee acted to change the intermission time to 20 minutes and placed the onus on the clubs to have their teams on the field ready for the kick-off "at exactly

20 minutes after the conclusion of the first half".[28] There were to be no exceptions but the League softened its hard-line stance somewhat by adding the rider "the guilty team will be subject to penalty, possibly".[29]

Time was important especially if the CFL wished to improve and maximize its exposure and revenue from the media, particularly television. A subtle balancing act was necessary. Starting times which were ideal for television were not necessarily good for the live gate. At the best of times too, east-west tensions might surface but especially when it appeared that decisions were being made to cater to the eastern markets. Schedules were set in 1983 only after refinement as a result of meetings with Carling O'Keefe representative Mrs. Shirley Slade, CTV's Oliver Babirad and CBC's Bill Sheehan.[30] The three had spoken with each other prior to the meeting and had analyzed the schedule with a view to station availabilities and maximum viewership. Each club was dealt with individually.

Winnipeg was asked whether it would schedule its games of August 13 and September 24 at 8:30 p.m. and its Sunday, October 23 contest at 3:00 p.m. in order "to minimize the overlap with other games on those dates and thus permit all games to be televised". Toronto was asked to reschedule a 7:00 p.m. game on September 24 to 1:30 p.m. Sazio refused but "he would agree to lift the secondary blackout of the Winnipeg game coming into Toronto at 8:30 EDT". Hamilton liked to have its night games start at 7:30p.m. They were requested to move to a 7:00p.m. start and play Saturday evening games on October 1 and 15 in the afternoon. Joe Zuger replied that a 7:00 p.m. start was acceptable but afternoon games on October 1 and 15 were not. Ottawa's dates and times were acceptable as were Montreal's. British Columbia was asked to start its games, "particularly against eastern opponents" at 7:30p.m. General Manager Bob Ackles agreed to do so if all of its games were moved to 7:30p.m. but he stated that a city ordinance prevented an earlier start. Saskatchewan's starting times of 7:00 p.m. and 1:30 p.m. were acceptable except for Sunday October 30. On that date, Standard Time resumed in all areas. The Carling O'Keefe representative requested a 2:30 p.m. start in order "to permit the telecast of two games on that date". Saskatchewan which drew its audience from a wide geographical area, had its doubts that it could accommodate but General Manager Herrera promised to look into the matter and advise.

Edmonton's Norm Kimball turned down a request by CTV's Oliver Babirad for a 7:00 p.m. start, as opposed to 7:30 p.m., because "the city transit systems provide 600 buses for home games and a 7:00 p.m. start would be too close to the evening rush hour to permit bus service at that earlier time. He supported his contention by advising that an earlier start "had been tried on a previous occasion and was found to be unsatisfactory".

When Calgary's Jack Gotta requested a later starting time on Sunday July 31 because of a conflict with the World Student Games, the 7:30 p.m. start was ruled out because of previous television time commitments.

CTV had "some interest in Sunday evening games in July and August, but not thereafter". Five clubs felt that Sunday summer games merited consideration. They were Winnipeg, Calgary, Ottawa, Hamilton and Edmonton. The whole process was then repeated with reference to the lifting of blackouts, allowing games to be telecast into areas where games were being played that same day. It was an exercise in balancing off individual club interests with League requirements accepting as an article of faith that a sacrifice for the common good would result in increased revenues in the long run even though attendance might fall.

The co-operation paid off. The League was rewarded with the highest television contract in its history. Carling O'Keefe Breweries paid a record $33 million to televise the CFL games in 1984, '85, and '86. There were probably some very good reasons for the deal. Carling O'Keefe owned the Argonauts who competed with the Toronto Blue Jays for the entertainment dollar. At the same time, the baseball team was owned by Labatt's. The two breweries were fighting for a larger share of the Southern Ontario market. Carling O'Keefe also had ownership interests with the

Quebec Nordiques. Their biggest rival was the Montreal Canadiens who were owned by Molson's. Even with Carling O'Keefe's
sponsorship, however, it was not automatic that other clubs
would stop what promotional affiliations they had with rival beer
companies. The B.C. Lions 1984 Fact Book, under a heading
the "Lions and Labatt's" paid special tribute to their relationship
with the Carling O'Keefe rival: "whose support and assistance
of the B.C. Lions over the past years has been invaluable. Their
contribution to B.C. Lions football, and the overall development
of the sport in our province cannot be measured, but certainly
the people at Labatt's are some of the finest friends the club could
have".[31] Labatt's even sponsored a Canadian Superstars competition. Ten events were included with each competitor having to
compete in seven including the final obstacle course. Canadian
athletes from a wide variety of sports competed including Skiers
Ken Read and Todd Brooker; Swimmer Alex Baumann; Hurdler
Mark McKoy; Ski Jumper Horst Bulau; Basketballer Leo Rautins,
Hockey players Darryl Sittler, Rick Vaive and Lanny McDonald
and Footballers Rocky DiPietro, Paul Bennett and Nick Hebel-
er. Rocky DiPietro, the Ti-Cat slot back won the "$10,000 first
prize plus $100 for each point earned for a total of $14,100. He
quipped: 'This makes up almost all my salary for last year'".[32]

The Montreal legend Sam Etcheverry was replaced by the Concordes for the 1983 season. In a dispute over who was running
the team, Chairman of the Board, L. Edmond Ricard made it
known that if the Concordes wanted to continue to have Imasco
money involved, Etcheverry would have to go. The President and
Chief Operating Officer of Imasco won his showdown; Etcheverr-
ry was replaced with Joe Galat who added the General Manager
position to his coaching duties. Bob Geary was Director of Football Operations. There was a feeling in the CFL and particularly
in the West that the run to the Grey Cup was wide open for the
first time in years. Hugh Campbell had left Edmonton to join the
Los Angeles Express of the United States Football League. After
some delay the Eskimos replaced him with Peter Kettela, more
noted as a film "breakdown" coach with the Green Bay Packers
of the National Football League. There was a flurry of activity as

teams sought to recruit the Eskimo coaching staff. Joe Faragalli had already moved to Saskatchewan where the Roughriders were invigorated. Don Mathews who had served as defensive co-ordinator with the Eskimos and who had been part of the previous six Grey Cup appearing teams, was appointed Head Coach of the Lions in January of 1983. Cal Murphy, Edmonton's line coach and a coaching member of the winning Grey Cup team for the past six consecutive years, replaced Ray Jauch as Head Coach of the Blue Bombers in Winnipeg. It was part of a general re-organization for the Bombers. Ray Jauch was moving the USFL; Earl Lunsford was replaced in the General Manager's position by former player Paul Robson and quarterback Dieter Brock, who had complained about there being nothing to do in Winnipeg but go the zoo, was traded to Hamilton which sent its top quarterback, Tom Clements, west.

Quarterbacks were still a major draw with most teams and there was a wealth of experience and talent at that position in the CFL in 1983. Roy Dewalt and Joe Paopao were in B.C.; a young veteran Warren Moon and a first year Matt Dunigan were in Edmonton; in Calgary, Bernard Quarles and Gerry Dattilio split the assignment. John Hufnagel with Homer Jordan was in Saskatchewan until he was sent to Winnipeg to replace an injured Tom Clements. In the east, Dieter Brock was with the Tiger Cats; Ottawa had Chris Issac and Dave Marler; Montreal, Vince Evans while the Argonauts were led by the veterans Condredge Holloway and Joe Barnes.

During the 1983 season, it soon became obvious that the Edmonton Eskimo dynasty was at an end. Hugh Campbell's successor Pete Kettela lasted less than half a season as head coach. He was replaced by Eskimo legend Jackie Parker. Edmonton still managed an 8–8 record for a third place finish but was defeated in the western semi-final, 49–22, by Winnipeg led by former Edmonton line coach Cal Murphy. The British Columbia Lions, first place finishers and led by former Edmonton defensive co-ordinator Don Mathews defeated the Blue Bombers 39–21 to represent the West in the 1983 Grey Cup game to be played in the familiar surroundings of B.C. Place. Saskatchewan and Calgary finished out of the play-offs, the former with a 5–11 record and Calgary just barely. The Stampeders finished with an identical record to the Eskimos at 8-8, but third place was awarded to the northern Albertans on the basis of the tie breaking formula. The Stampeders were becoming a CFL trouble spot. Their total attendance was falling steadily in the eighties. Almost 40,000 fewer fans attended their games in 1983 than 1982 and average attendance had fallen from more than 30,000 to just over 25,000 in the same year.

In the east, Montreal and Hamilton had the same 5–10–1 record but the Tiger Cats were awarded third place and a play-off spot. Bud Riley's team, quarterbacked by Dieter Brock surprised the second place Ottawa Rough Riders by defeating them 33–31 at Lansdowne Park. The Eastern Final was a classic Toronto-Hamilton match-up, the Argos prevailing by a 41–36 score and qualifying for the Grey Cup game.

Grey Cup week in Canada has always been a mixture of pageantry, fun, business and the game. The first Grey Cup to be played in Vancouver since 1974 was no exception. With "Crazy George" leading the way B.C. Place was described as "a frenzy cauldron of fan mania"[33] during the Lions' defeat of Winnipeg. Preparations received maximum media exposure. The city seemed just as anxious to show off its jewel of a facility as the League was to hype its Grey Cup. The game was called the "most popular show in Canadian television . . . the 1982 game drew a record audience of 7.8 million viewers on the combined CBC, CTV and CBC French networks . . . with CBC attracting 3.8 million or "47% of all viewers in Canada at that time".[34] The CBC was planning to use 17 cameras, 10 more than used in a regular season game. Eleven were to be for the game itself, eight in the stands or on scaffolds; one was to be at each bench, another in the broadcast booth. Two were to be in the dressing rooms, two with host John Wells in the B.C. Place studio, one roaming through the crowd "looking for celebrities and the final camera will be suspended from B.C. Place roof".[35]

John Wells was son of "Cactus Jack" Wells the former Winni-peg broadcaster who also covered Grey Cup games for the CBC. One couldn't help make the comparisons with the growth of the game from that era. The first Grey Cup game to be televised was the 1952 Toronto-Edmonton Contest. The Canadian Rugby Union (CRU) sold the television rights to the Toronto CBC sta-tion for $7500. The announcers for that first game were Norm Marshall, the voice of the Tiger-Cats and Larry O'Brien, a sports-caster from Montreal. They were paid $250 each.[36] It was 1957, during the Hamilton-Winnipeg contest that the first network telecast occurred. "The television rights for that game brought $75,000".[37]

The Schenley Awards had been a tradition in Canada from their inception in 1953 when Billy Vessels was selected the Outstand-ing Player in Canada, the only award presented. Twenty years later, in 1983, another Edmonton player, quarterback Warren Moon, was chosen over Toronto's Terry Greer as the Most Out-standing Player; the Rookie Award was given to Johnny Shep-herd, running back with Hamilton chosen over Willard Reaves of Winnipeg; Paul Bennett of Winnipeg was selected as the Most Outstanding Canadian, the Concordes' Denny Ferdinand, the runner-up; Rudy Phillips of Ottawa was the recipient of the Of-fensive Lineman Award over John Bonk, the Winnipeg centre, Greg Marshall of Ottawa was picked ahead of Calgary's Danny Bass as the Defensive Player.

But it was the Stadium, B.C. Place, which necessitated almost as much in the way of preparation for the opposition as did the Lions. The noise was the major topic of concern among oppo-nents. It was deafening when "Crazy George" whipped up the fans into a screaming frenzy. Toronto's Ralph Sazio suggested that the orchestrated outbursts at strategic times, i.e., when the opposing quarterback was calling signals, was "unsportsmanlike, a remark greeted with a few gentle scoffs on this side of the Rock-ies".[38] Winnipeg Centre John Bonk, who had trouble hearing the quarterback's voice during the noise even from his close proximity, likened the crowd to "a thirteenth and fourteenth man out there".[39]

Hamilton's Dieter Brock who also quarterbacked Winnipeg during its exhibition game in B.C. Place and had played there twice, concurred: "The building is very tough to play in. The noise doesn't trowel out; it just sort of bounces around. You have troubles with the signals and you have trouble with concentration. And then there is the human wave, one of Crazy George's specialities. While no player would admit having a lapse of concentration during a big game, it's hard not to notice when all those people are jumping up and down in their seats".[40]

But the B.C. Lions had much more than a noisy stadium on its side. Lui Passaglia was the leading scorer in the CFL with 191 pts.; Mervyn Fernandez was one of the premier pass receivers with 78 receptions for 1284 yds; Roy Dewalt had matured as a quarterback completing 62.2% of his 442 pass attempts for 22 touchdowns. Defensively, Larry Crawford led the league with 12 interceptions in addition to his outstanding punt returns. The defensive line was anchored by Mack Moore, a Western All-Star in 1983.

It was the Argonauts' second consecutive appearance in the Grey Cup. They had become a dominant team in the League, just what Carling-O'Keefe hoped for when they signed Ralph Sazio away from Hamilton. Some still considered the Argonaut President to be the most astute football man in the country. There were those who criticized his choice of Bob O'Billovich as the Argonaut head coach in 1982, suggesting he was a no-name. But the Argonauts under O'Billovich made it to the Grey Cup game, their first in a decade and the Argonaut coach was selected as winner of the Annis Stukus Trophy as the CFL's Coach of the Year. This was to be his second consecutive appearance in the national final.

The two seemed to work well as a team. Sazio wanted some hands-on involvement; O'Billovich knew who the boss was. When "Mouse" Davis, the architect of the Club's "run and shoot" approach to offensive football in 1982, wanted more money and more authority, neither Sazio nor O'Billovich were willing. They agreed to part company and the Argonaut output still increased in 1983. Sazio also made some astute player moves. Emmanuel Tolbert was claimed on waivers from Saskatchewan; Linebacker William Mitchell was claimed on waivers from Ottawa at the end of the 1982 season. Carl Brazley who had played out his option with Ottawa and was later cut by the Buffalo Bills, was pursued and signed by the Argos. Another defensive back, Leroy Paul, had originally signed with Sazio in Hamilton where after three seasons he played out his option. Toronto signed him after Paul and Hamilton could not agree on a contract. When Saskatchewan's Ken McEachern was dissatisfied with contract negotiations with the Roughriders, Sazio acquired the talented defensive back for a draft choice. Like Brazely, Mitchell and Tolbert, McEachern was selected to the eastern All-Star team for 1983. To cap it all off, the outstanding CFL punter Hank Ilesic, was brought to Toronto in 1983. Unable to resolve a contract dispute with the Eskimos the young kicker, he originally joined the Eskimos as a 17 year old grade 12 student in 1977, brought consistently good punting and field goal kicking to the 1983 team.

The Argonauts had other weapons as well. Quarterbacks Condredge Holloway and Joe Barnes, a receiving corps led by Terry Greer and an inspired defence led the Argos to an 18–17 victory over the B.C. Lions. After trailing 17–7 at half time, the Argonauts defence stiffened; the offence scored the eleven points necessary. It was the first Argonaut Grey Cup victory since 1952; the Lions had not won since 1964. "One drought is over, the other continues" reported the Vancouver Sun.[41] The Argonauts returned to Toronto where "police estimated 40,000 boisterous fans lined the downtown core exorcising 31 years of pent up frustrations". O'Billovich put in his bid for an improved facility: "Last year at this time the city made a promise we were going to get a domed stadium if we promised to go for the Grey Cup. Now it's up to them to keep their part of the bargain".[42]

There was excitement in Toronto and throughout the League with the Grey Cup. The game, played indoors for the first time, attracted a sell-out of 59,345. Every ticket in B.C. Place was priced at $30. It was the first $2 million gate in CFL history and generated receipts of $2,068,385. The League was happy because Toronto appeared to have turned the corner; its franchise was one of the cornerstones of League prosperity.

Along with the Argos' resurrection, there was the resuscitation of the All-Star Game. A group from Hamilton, which included Ti-Cat linebacker John Priestner, sought to capitalize on the newly found fervour in Vancouver and the indoor facility at B.C. Place. It signed a five year agreement with the Players' Association for the revival of the game and negotiated a television contract with Carling O'Keefe. The game was played Saturday December 3, less than one week after the Grey Cup. Fewer than 10,000 fans were in the stands, although "organizers claimed there were 10,500 tickets sold".[43] The CFL Players' Association was to have benefited by receiving $25,000 or 15% of the gate for its pension fund. All of the selected players appeared, encouraged also by the knowledge that there was insurance coverage guaranteeing them $50,000 should an injury occur. "Several players, notably Edmonton quarterback, Warren Moon and defensive back David Shaw purchased additional insurance".[44] "The West defeated the East 25–15 in a game totally lacking in drama or excitement".[45]

There was news of significance in other areas. Jake Gaudaur announced in February that he would not seek another term as commissioner.[46] Although his term ran out in 1985, Gaudaur would step down one year earlier and serve the last year of his contract as a consultant to the new Commissioner. Doug Mitchell replaced Jake Gaudaur as of June 1, 1984, although the latter continued to serve as an "executive consultant" for the last year of his original contract. He would leave his association with the League December 31, 1985. Mitchell's appointment was a surprise. His name had never been mentioned as a possibility. Others touted for the job had been former Argonaut player Mike Wadsworth, Saskatchewan Roughrider President Dick Rendek, Ottawa great Ron Stewart and Ontario Premier Bill Davis.[47] Mitchell's credentials were solid. He was a lawyer, had attended the University of Colorado on a hockey scholarship before transferring to UBC. On graduation he signed with the Lions playing as a centre and middle linebacker in 1960 before being traded to Hamilton in 1961 where he was released. He returned to his native Calgary where he articled and set-up a law practice and immersed himself in the Calgary sport scene. He had wide interests. He was a member of the Hockey Canada Advisory Board, Legal Counsel to the Calgary Flames, had a string of standard bred racing horses, played a key role in Calgary's attaining the 1988 Winter Games, was a co-chairman of the Willy DeWitt Trust Fund and was a colour commentator for Stampeders games on CFCN radio. His wife headed up All-Pro Contracts Limited, the firm which had concession and souvenir rights at McMahon Stadium.[48]

The new Commissioner did not come cheaply. His yearly salary was "$175,000 with annual cost of living adjustment at the annual Consumer Price Index rate, which increments would be payable into a pension or deferred income plan".[49] His contract was for a three year term with a review after two years and an option "to terminate or to renew for a further two years".[50] Mitchell was to have an expense account to cover those expenses "incurred in carrying out his duties and responsibilities as Commissioner", an automobile, memberships at an athletic club and business club and moving expenses covered to a maximum of $35,000".[51] The CFL would have preferred to make the announcement closer to the end of January so as to allow the new head to familiarize himself, through Gaudaur, for a greater period of the pre-season but the announcement was delayed until March 8. Mitchell was committed to being in Sarajevo for the Winter Olympics in order to gain first hand knowledge and experience for the 1988 Calgary games. The League took a "key man" insurance policy in the amount of $250,000 on the Commissioner designate, the CFL being the beneficiary.[52]

When Doug Mitchell took over as Commissioner of the CFL, June 1, 1984, it was obvious that while his preference was to be forward looking and expansionary, the reality of the CFL was to address familiar concerns. The new Commissioner had met with the Mayor of London informally "to discuss what it would take for the southern Ontario city to acquire a franchise".[53] Mitchell also floated the idea of "neutral site" games in London and Halifax. The idea was "to test those particular markets as potential franchise areas"[54] by playing pre-season games involving eastern clubs, mainly Hamilton and Ottawa. They would simply shift their home game. The current agreement with the players called for a maximum of 20 games, presently 4 exhibitions plus a 16 game schedule. Any exhibition games in the neutral sites would have to be from the twenty. Immediately, the obstacles were thrown up: the "game would not likely be self-supporting unless there were subsidies from government levels and there are stadium commitments with concessions to be considered".[55]

Television continued to be a factor in a variety of ways. What with the large contract the League had signed with Carling O'Keefe and the networks, there was always the question of how the medium was going to be affected. The year would be a busy one for television, many demands being put on its capabilities. The Olympics, a Royal visit and a Papal mass in Toronto were all occurring during the football season. Each would add to the log jam of programming. Concern was expressed that some games during 1983 required more than three hours to complete. Television networks, not only in Canada, but also ESPN in the United States, had other commitments after the third hour. Thus when a proposal to increase the amount of time a team had to put the ball into play from 20 to 25 seconds was made, it received little support. It was defeated by a 2–7 vote.[56] The League could ill afford to be legislating regulations which would add valuable seconds and minutes. It had to find other ways. The half time intermission which only the previous year had been increased, was cut back to 15 minutes "with the team subject to a yardage penalty if it fails to be ready for the second half kick-off and with the home team subject to a fine if it fails to have the team field cleared in time for the second half kick-off".[57]

The starting time of the Grey Cup game was also a question mark. In 1983, the game was played in Vancouver and began at 3:00p.m.PST allowing the game to be shown in the East in Prime-television time. The 1984 game, to be played in Edmonton, could not be played at that late a time since the weather would turn colder as the sun went down. It was the first time Edmonton was to host the game; city and team officials were anxious to see that arrangements were such that the best face was put forward. There were critics who were publicly chastising the league for playing the Grey Cup game outdoors in Northern Alberta when they had the indoor B.C. Place available. Kimball preferred a 12:30 or 1:00p.m.MST start. The TV people "indicated a preference for 1:30".[58] Gaudaur sought to speak to the television networks about a 1:00p.m. compromise.

Television blackouts were also a concern. On the one hand, there was the effect that the televising of a game could have on the sale of tickets. People would stay home to watch the game on television rather than buy a ticket. On the other hand, television revenue was important too. The more people who watched a game on television, the more the case for a larger television contract could be made. The CFL was still concerned with "pirating" of signals by taverns, hotels and restaurants that were able to bring in a distant telecast by means of their satellite dish. In some ways, this too was a "no win" situation. Carling O'Keefe was not opposed since there was increased viewership and beer sales would increase particularly in those target areas. The League had given Gaudaur the authorization "to use his best judgement whether or not to instruct the CBC to install scrambling equipment as a means of protecting the League's primary blackout".[59] Gaudaur asked CBC "to proceed with the installation of the necessary scrambling equipment.[60] The CBC agreed on the condition "that when it commences the distribution of scrambled signals in Canada the League would take such steps as are necessary to preclude the exhibition of unauthorized signals in Canada which are available as a result of the distribution of them in the U.S.A. by satellite".[61]

As always, the League was concerned about the image it por-trayed to the public. Ever since the mid-seventies with the U.S. expansion controversy, government intervention, the Jamie Bone affair and the failed expansion into other areas of Canada, the League was taking a beating in the media. Prior to Gaudaur's stepping aside as Commissioner, club general managers were in-structed to hold seminars for their coaches and employees with "the purpose of improving the image of the League".[62] There was also a meeting arranged with broadcast crews from CBC and CTV and the CFL General Managers. The meeting which took place at the Westin Hotel in Toronto discussed a variety of issues. In what was described as "constructive", the "League officials requested the announcers to stop referring to the small crowds at some CFL games. For another, the League would like to ban sideline interviews and keep cameras away from the play-ers' bench".[63] The League had previously sought to tighten up its rules in an effort to stem criticism resulting from an incident during the 1983 season. Montreal Concordes' defensive back Phil Jones, a former Argo, was "traded" back to the Argonauts "for a brief period . . . but didn't know it. He never left Montre-al. For that matter, he didn't even miss a Concordes' meeting or practice. The "trade" to Argos was a convenient vehicle that allowed the Concordes to dress another player in place of Jones who was injured but not seriously enough to be placed on the injury list. Jones was 'traded back' to the Concordes a couple of days later".[64] It resulted in a by-law change at the Management Council meetings "that will prevent such phoney trades in the future. A team, now, cannot trade a player back to his former team within two days of acquiring him".[65]

It was the Concordes and Joe Galat specifically who had been critical of the League's approach to the new USFL. Amid news that CFL players who were still under contract were practising with USFL teams, the Montreal coach stated: "'I think we wait-ed too long', moaned Galat also the Montreal General Manager, 'We let in the Trojan Horse last year by allowing Ray Jauch and Hugh Campbell to sign with one league while coaching in an-other. That was ridiculous. We're not competing with the NFL;

we're competing with their minor league. It won't be long before we're signing USFL cuts'".[66] Yet another former coach, Jack Gotta, announced his intention to work as a guest coach at a USFL camp. He was careful to say that he would volunteer his services and work for free, not wanting to jeopardize his contract which called for him to earn "$100,000 this year not to coach in Calgary".[67]

The USFL was a spring league. Its games were held at a time when there was no football being offered to the public. The idea was also to restrict team budgets until attendance increased and a television contract was gained. For that reason, coaches from the CFL were desirable, since they had worked under those constraints. As far as the two "name" coaches attracted to the fledgling league, Ray Jauch was fired after his team, the Washington Federals was defeated 53–14 by the Jacksonville Bulls early in his second season. Jauch's team had a 4–14 won-lost record in 1983 his first year.[68] Meanwhile, Hugh Campbell had moved from the Los Angeles Express to coach the Houston Oilers of the NFL in 1984. The Oilers had also signed Edmonton quarterback Warren Moon who had played out his option in '83. The Express had surprised many when it announced that it had signed quarterback Steve Young to a four year contract for a reported $40 million with $34.5 million in deferred payments over 43 years.[69]

Once again, the issue of the Designated Import emerged and assumed some prominence. This time it revolved around Calgary Dinosaur quarterback Greg Vavra. He had led his team to a come from behind win over Queen's in the Vanier Cup game and was selected as the winner of the Hec Crighton Trophy as the most outstanding collegian in Canada. He had been selected by Calgary as their territorial exemption in the 1983 draft. His rights were picked up by Edmonton who released him. Vavra returned to school, led his team to the title, won his award and waited to hear of his fate. At the eleventh hour, the Stampeders signed him. If they had left it any later, his rights would have reverted to the Eskimos. The Calgary born and raised Vavra was clear about his goals: "I prefer to play in Canada. I'm a Canadian and, naturally, ambitions I've set for myself exist in Canada, not the United States".[70] Again, the publicity surrounding the issue resurfaced: "It is generally said that the designated import rule is to blame. In fact, it means that Vavra would have to replace an import to see any playing time and coaches say a Canadian quarterback must be better than an import to make a team".[71]

There was some conjecture that "the bad publicity (Jamie) Bone caused the CFL"[72] was a cause of the hesitation teams had to sign a Canadian quarterback. Calgary, in fact, found itself with two non-import quarterbacks, Vavra and Gerry Dattilio. It would stick with hometown Vavra and send Dattilio back to his city of Montreal.

The League also decided to do away with the Canadian territorial protection. Beginning with the draft of 1985, there were to be no more protected players. Commissioner Doug Mitchell explained: "The League unanimously agreed to do away with the protected player concept. There will be a legitimate non-import Canadian Football League full scale draft. The protected concept allowed the first place team to protect a player of equal calibre to that of the last place team. The League felt that if its draft was to be effective and proper, the last place team should get the first pick".[73]

Just as in Gaudaur's tenure, the Montreal situation kept surfacing. Some had said that Montreal had already suffered its third strike. Joe Galat recalled: "The first one was Black Saturday. That was the day when the Alouettes cut all those veterans, Dan Yochum, Don Sweet, Gord Judges, Larry Uteck, in 1980 in order to save money. Strike two was Skalbania and having a team with Vince Ferragamo, James Scott, Billy Johnson, which finished 2 and 14. The third strike was George Allen leaving. By then I had to stay and pick up the pieces".[74] There were plenty of pieces to pick up. Prior to Bronfman's purchase of the Club, money from trust accounts was used for other reasons. When the Alouettes withdrew from the League on May 13, 1982, it had already received its share of the 1982 television rights, none was available for the

Concordes "which provided the actual service for which the payment was received".[75] It resulted in a change to the CFL by-laws.
A new article, 507, of the Constitution was passed unanimously
by the CFL: any and all revenue received by the League as an advance payment . . . signed by the League on behalf of the member
clubs, shall be placed in a trust bank account for distribution, including interest therein, to the member clubs within seven days
after the first game of the regular season's schedule of the year
to which such advanced payments apply".[76] There were other
"horror stories". The Concordes, on taking over the Montreal
franchise were informed that George Allen had not paid a two
month hotel bill; he had not returned the footballs from a free
agent camp he conducted in California; the Concordes had their
phone disconnected for failing to pay their bill.

On the field, there were two leftovers from the Skalbania days,
Keith Gary and David Overstreet. "They were two of the big
money players. . . . They didn't really want to play and we wanted
to get rid of them but their contracts were guaranteed. One day
the word came down from Bronfman to pay them off and cut
them. When that happened, I knew we were going to make it"
stated Galat.[77] But the Concordes were not out of the woods yet.
Sam Etcheverry was let go. Season tickets for 1983 were at 6,000.
The Club's ills were diagnosed as due to quarterback problems.
Gerry Dattilio was brought back. Two prominent American collegians, Turner Gill and Steve Smith were signed; season's ticket
sales reached the 12,000 mark.

But the Concordes were still pressing for more. Pre-season
games were a problem in Montreal, said the Concordes' Edmond
Ricard. He proposed moving to a two exhibitions and 18 game
schedule and urged the CFL's Players Relations Committee to
explore the possibility with the Association. While the interlocking schedule would continue, he proposed that the two extra
games be with teams in the same division. Ricard also expressed
a familiar refrain: Since the four players on the Reserve list are
being paid why shouldn't they be allowed to dress? He proposed
that the rosters be increased therefore to 38, nineteen imports,

nineteen non-imports. Ricard was aware that by increasing the roster size and dressing 19 Americans, it would "admittedly . . . reduce the number of non-import players in the starting positions". He was convinced, however, that "it would not diminish the unique Canadian aspects of the game". It was the larger playing field, the more exciting playing rules which made the game Canadian, not the players on the field.[78] Ricard elaborated on his reasons for suggesting the changes. The Concordes seemed to be on the upswing. They finished the 1984 season with a 6–9–1 record, the same as Hamilton, but were relegated to third place on the basis of points between the two teams. In a city where comparisons with the Expos and Canadiens were inevitable, the Concordes were criticized by the media for "charging full price for two pre-season games which the coaches publicly describe as secondary games. In mentioning that the reserve list had served its purpose, Ricard stated that it had become yet another source of criticism in Montreal with "comparison being made to a baseball team which permits all players on the roster to dress for a game.[79]

During the season, CFL attendance was down by about 200,000 for the regular season and by some 17,000 for the play-offs. The latter figure was 156,126 which while it was lower than 1983's 173,842, was still the League's third highest play-off game total excluding the Grey Cup. In Calgary, where local talent Greg Vavra had played much of the quarterbacking, the Stampeders attracted 22,332 on the average, in finishing in last place in the West. The Montreal Concordes who finished in third place in the east and played Dattilio only as a back up to Turner Gill averaged 17,345 spectators. The lowest average crowd for the season was in Hamilton with only 14,738 fans.[80] The Argonauts' average attendance of 32,760 was the Club's lowest in 15 years. Both Hamilton and Toronto experimented with early starting times of 5:00p.m. for their Sunday games in July and August. The experiment was less than successful. The B.C. Lions finished with a sell-out of 59,429 for their last home game against Winnipeg and led the League with an average attendance of 41,859 per game. The Eskimos were second at 40,977, the Argonauts third.[81]

In the east, Ottawa finished in last place with a 4–12 record. As a result, George Brancato was fired from the head coaching position he had held for eleven years. Montreal and Hamilton finished with 6–9–1 records, the latter having been awarded second place on the basis of its two victories over the Concordes in the regular season. In the earlier semi-final, Hamilton continued its mastery over Montreal by scoring a 17–11 victory at Ivor Wynne Stadium before "20,736 soggy onlookers".[82]

In the week prior to the renewed hostility between Hamilton and Toronto, indeed even as the Montreal-Hamilton game was winding down, "it didn't take long for the old rivalry to bob to the surface. A-R-G-O-O-O-S, boomed a bellow from a group of brave, if not necessarily wise, Argo followers".[83] An evening was held to honour Jake Gaudaur. The former Commissioner who had been inducted into the Hall of Fame as a Builder on April 10, 1984, was the object of "a meeting of people gathered to congratulate Jake Gaudaur at the Harbour Castle Hotel one more time on all the marvellous things he had done during the 16 years as Commissioner of the CFL"[84]

Gaudaur had always insisted that the way the Grey Cup game was accepted by the public was the best indicator of the vitality of the League. The 1983 game in Vancouver provided the League with its first $2 million gross gate and "Television coverage on CBC, CTV and Radio-Canada" resulted in the "largest viewing audience in television history for a Canadian sports program as 8,118,000 people watched Toronto edge B.C. 18–17".[85] When it was mentioned by some that the 1984 game would attract 20,000,000, with American viewers, there were the inevitable second guessers. They wondered why the game should be risked being played in northern Alberta when there was a beautiful indoor stadium in Vancouver.

> *That can be a mixed blessing actually.*
> *They're apt to witness on the telecast, a*
> *blizzard in the Alberta capital. Cold tem-*
> *peratures? The highest temperature in Ed-*

monton noted lately was a record low for November 18 which happens to be the date upon which the eastern and western champions are scheduled to square off. In other words, it could be a burlesque instead of Canadian football at its finest. Now that the CFL has at its disposal a beautiful covered stadium in Vancouver, it's summer all the time. The field is perfect and 60,000 spectators can get along without overcoats, galoshes, scarves, mittens and earmuffs. Equally as important, the participating athletes are afforded an opportunity to put all their skills on display. The contest is fair to everyone.[86]

The Toronto Argonauts had finished in first place in the east. Some were calling for them to repeat as Grey Cup Champions but others noted that while they finished with a 9–6–1 record, over the last eight games they were 3–4–1. While the Tiger Cats were a poor second to the Argos, the games between the two teams were close. The Argos had won by 8 points and lost one by 5. Indeed the Tiger Cats were playing so poorly at one time that owner Harold Ballard referred to them as "overpaid bums". His comment was pointed to by some as being the reason why they were "apparently reborn".[87] The Tiger Cats defeated the Argonauts in overtime by a 14–13 score to represent the East in the national final.

In the west where Calgary and Saskatchewan both finished out of the play-offs again, the Edmonton Eskimos finished in third place. Their hopes to play at home in the 1984 Grey Cup game were dashed when second place Winnipeg defeated them handily 55–20. Once again the noise of B.C. Place became an issue. The Lions had defeated the Blue Bombers by a 20–3 score in the last week of the season and home fans were looking for a repeat. It was not to be. The Bombers flew past the Lions by a 31–14 score to become the west's representative.

Ever since 1921 when the first east-west rivalry took place on the Grey Cup field, there has been the opportunity for the country's normal geographical tensions to surface. More so, the 1984 game, allowed for even more comparisons to be made. A Hamilton-Winnipeg Grey Cup game was one of the most hard fought and unpredictable guarantees for the League for over 50 years. It was in 1935 that Winnipeg defeated the Hamilton Tigers in what was the first victory for the west. In 1953, Hamilton won the Grey Cup game over Winnipeg when a controversial tackle by Lou Kusserow on Tom Casey in the end zone prevented the tying touchdown pass from being caught. In the next six meetings between the two clubs, from 1957 to 1965, the unpredictable contests included an ejection of Tiger Cat defensive back Ralph Goldston, an incursion by a fan who tripped a Tiger Cat, Ray "Bibbles" Bawel, on his way to a touchdown, the first overtime Grey Cup Game, the "Fog Bowl" when the game was played over two days and the so-called "Wind Bowl" when high winds led Winnipeg to concede 3 safety touches, the margin of the Tiger Cat victory. That 1965 game was the last appearance of Winnipeg in the Grey Cup game. Their coach Bud Grant had long departed to the NFL. Winnipeg was resting its hopes on Cal Murphy, the Canadian coach who had been part of Grey Cup victories as an assistant in Montreal and Edmonton. Hamilton's legendary coaches, Jim Trimble and Ralph Sazio, had also departed from the scene. Al Bruno had taken over the Tiger Cat coaching. He appeared to be spending much time defending his team's being in the game. The Edmonton Journal commented that a Hamilton win would be a "smear" on the CFL[88] because it would be the "first time a CFL team with a losing regular season record would win the Grey Cup in 73 years".[89] Bruno, a former player with the Argonauts in 1952 and more recently a coach at Harvard University and the Tiger Cats' Director of Player Personnel was incensed:

> *Why don't they build the League up instead of downgrading the League when they talk about a team being a smear on the CFL? Every club is losing money be-*

cause of attendance. The NFL is making
money because they back their game up. If
we start to wise up and back our game up
and protect our game, we'd be a hell of a lot
better off![90]

There was also an intense rivalry that continued to grow since the mid-season trade of 1983 when the two teams exchanged quarterbacks. Tom Clements came to Winnipeg; Dieter Brock was sent to Hamilton. Brock had upset Winnipeggers because he wanted to leave the Manitoba capital to pursue a career in the United States. As part of the Grey Cup "hi-jinks", he had "been taking verbal abuse all week. There are 'Brock Buster' T-shirts, 'Brock Buster' placards, 'Brock Buster' songs. The 'Booze Brothers', a bunch of smart alecks from Vancouver, marched in the parade dragging a dummy with a noose around its head and a number 5 Hamilton sweater on its back. One guy beat it with a whip while Winnipeg fans cheered".[91]

And then there was Harold Ballard, the owner of the Tiger Cats. As an incentive for his "overpaid bums" he promised them a diamond ring should they defeat the Argos in the eastern final. He constantly referred to them as the "censored Argos". during the game he wore a jacket, blue and white on one side for the Leafs and yellow and black on the other for the Tiger Cats "and a double brimmed baseball cap with the Leaf Emblem on one side and the tiger on the reverse. Boy George would have attracted less attention".[92]

Edmonton was agog with "Grey Cup Fever". Events were often and well attended. Canadian astronaut Marc Garneau led the Grey Cup parade. The Schenley Awards were distributed: Willard Reaves of Winnipeg was chosen over Hamilton's Rufus Crawford as the Most Outstanding Player; the Most Outstanding Rookie was Montreal's Dwaine Wilson, selected over Edmonton's Stewart Hill; Another Concordes' player Nick Arakgi was the Most Outstanding Canadian with Winnipeg's Joe Poplawski the runner-up; B.C.'s James Parker was the winner over Montreal's Harry Skipper as the Most Outstanding Defensive Player while Winnipeg centre John Bonk was chosen Most Outstanding offensive lineman over Toronto's Dan Ferrone.

In the game itself, Winnipeg spotted Hamilton a 17–3 second quarter lead but roared back to win 47–17. A record for Commonwealth Stadium, 60,081, watched the game, nicknamed the "Tundra Bowl" by one newspaper.[93] The temperature at game time was -11°C and ended with a reading of -17°C. Winnipeg equipment man, Len Amey gave the Toronto Blue Jays credit for the victory. He noted that "the Winnipeg receivers and defensive backs had little problem with the slippery field conditions because they used a baseball shoe recommended by the Blue Jays. Many of the Bombers used a plastic based shoe with a baseball cleat on the outside and smaller spikes on the interior of the sole which helped cut through the thin layer of ice on the frozen turf of Commonwealth Stadium".[94]

As the year came to a close the CFL continued to make news. Earl Lunsford returned to the CFL as General Manager at Calgary. Jack Gotta was hired as the General Manager and Head Coach at Saskatchewan. George Brancato was brought in as Gotta's assistant. The CFL also announced its plans to move its offices from 11 King Street East in Toronto to 1200 Bay Street where the whole of the twelfth floor would be taken over. The structure was to be renamed The Canadian Football League Building with the "league's logo prominently displayed at the top of the building".[95]

Chapter Two

If ever a League was immersed in introspection it was the CFL in 1985—and with good reason. A whole host of problems had surfaced, problems that threatened the very survival of professional football in Canada. When the CFL met in Edmonton in January of 1985, Commissioner Doug Mitchell wasted little time in driving home the point. The League's television contract with Carling O'Keefe would expire after the 1986 season; it was important that the CFL have a good year in 1985 since the TV rating of 1985 would "have a significant impact on the success of negotiations for a new television agreement starting in the 1986 season".[96] After distributing the A.C. Neilson Company ratings for the 1984 season, "he pointed out that if the League was trying to negotiate a new agreement now, it would be difficult in terms of a bargaining position based on the 1984 Neilson ratings".[97]

Television ratings were an important consideration since the League's contract was due to be renegotiated in the next year.The upcoming TV difficulties were highlighted when ESPN of the United Stated decided to not renew its option for CFL telecast rights in 1985. The B.C. Lions wanted to investigate the possibility of lifting the television blackout when there was a sell-out for the Lions' home game. B.C. had a unique problem in that the entire province was blacked out during Lions' home games. Discussion of the possibility was only agreed to on the understanding that it be deliberated without the public's knowledge. Even Carling O'Keefe, owners of the Argonauts "were somewhat disturbed by a statement in a report from the Commissioner which criticized the company for sponsoring television broadcasts of

United States Football League games".[98] They let it be known that the arrangements had been made before Carling O'Keefe was awarded the rights to sponsor CFL telecasts. Similarly they weren't too thrilled with the numerous side deals teams had throughout the League with competitors Molson's and Labatt's.

The in-fighting continued. When the CFL interested The Sports Network (TSN) "in a weekly program of Hits and Highlights of the Week, Carling O'Keefe asked the League 'not to go with them because of the competitive aspect, i.e., TSN being owned by La-batt's". The Commissioner acceded to their request although he repeated: "I am at a loss to understand how in the same breath, they give money to the USFL, our competition, for TV rights".[99]

The Commissioner identified declining attendance as "the most critical problem facing the League today".[100] The perception by the public that the League was "hanging on" would adverse-ly affect television and marketing revenues. The shortfall was blamed on "competitions from other entertainment and sport attractions, the economy and the perception that the League is less than it should be".[101] The observation triggered more ob-servations. Norm Kimball noted that "suggestions for improve-ments are more often greeted with reluctance than enthusi-asm".[102] Nonetheless, he offered that the League should increase the schedule, improve media relations and marketing. Winni-peg's Paul Robson suggested changing the television broadcast crews "so the visiting team commentators are heard in the club's home area as is the case with radio broadcasts". In support, Kimball voiced his concern over "negative reporters" a charge which Mitchell levelled at the clubs themselves whose officials and coaches were "downgrading pre-season games, repeatedly emphasizing the players who are playing out options and consis-tently finding fault with non-import players."[103]

Kimball was convinced that "the decline in attendance is directly related to the decline in quality of play."[104] In his opinion, players were not performing with the intensity for which they are paid." Coaches had to work harder to get more out of the players and the Clubs had to work harder to sell tickets, promote the league and the game."[105]

Earl Lunsford, now the General Manager in Calgary, saw another area for improvement. With most teams using non-imports on the offensive line, the defence was loaded with imports. Since there were "not enough qualified non-import linemen to make all clubs competitive, he suggested some legislation be introduced to place a limit on the number of import players on defence at any one time."[106] Norm Kimball returned to his theme: "Daily practice should start at 10:00a.m. and the full working day dedicated to football. The onus should be placed on players to produce at all times. The club should insist that the coaches have an organized work plan which strives to develop players to their full potential. If they do not have such a work plan they should be replaced".[107]

As always too, there was the inevitable comparison with the NFL. Some members of the media were critical of CFL play as compared with the NFL. Edmond Ricard, the Chairman of the League's Board of Governors felt so; his solution was that "consideration should be given to increasing the import quota".[108] Once again, the shaper of perceptions, television, came in for scrutiny. NFL telecasts were superior to the CFL's "because its TV commentators stress only the positive aspects of the game". As well, only the best game of the week was telecast, it was suggested. There were complaints that the CFL's TV commentators were "ill prepared for the game and did not perform in a professional manner". The commentators were said to "often by-pass the pre-game press conferences", thus not having the "preparation and dedication" of the NFL commentators.

It was clear that the League was struggling with its declining acceptance among the public. It gave the appearance of flailing away at whatever could be grasped as a contributor to the decline. Ralph Sazio wanted "The League to take an aggressive position in a number of issues which apparently are harmful to the League's image as perceived by the media and fans".[109] He advocated: "elimination of the designated quarterback; elimination of the single point after a missed field goal; limitation of the number of imports on defence; application of pressure on coaching staffs to have players ready for a game; requirement of players to devote full time to football and not regard it as a hobby".[110]

Because of the concern about falling attendance, the League commissioned the Longwoods Research Group Limited to study the problem. A market survey had been conducted during the latter part of the 1984 season; the first phase, dealing with schedule related matters, was presented at the CFL's November meetings that year. The report identified twelve factors which affected game attendance. They were:

1. *Identification with team and players.*
2. *Involvement with sports and football.*
3. *Quality of officiating.*
4. *Excitement of the game.*
5. *Involvement with the crowd.*
6. *Television commentators.*
7. *Stadium facilities.*
8. *Ticket prices and outlets.*
9. *Attitude towards the playing rules.*
10. *The League structure.*
11. *The schedule.*
12. *The overall image of the League.*[111]

In addition, the report suggested that "there was evidence of goodwill towards the League and genuine interest in its continuing survival".[112] The CFL was encouraged to take a more aggressive approach, as a League and individual clubs, to advertising, public relations with improvements in marketing".[113]

In an interesting aside, Ralph Sazio, referring to the "identification with players" point, "noted that as soon as a player reaches superstar status his price tag increases to the point that he leaves the League".[114] The solution according to Commissioner Doug Mitchell was that "identification should be concentrated on Canadian players". It's interesting to speculate as to why he suggested such a course of action. Were Canadian players the real superstars? Because they were Canadians, would they not achieve the status "to leave the League"? Were they the team members who stayed in the community and contributed to it after the season?

In Winnipeg, Scott Taylor of the Free Press listed his own 10 reasons for staying away:

1. *Canadian Football is boring.*

2. *The balanced schedule hasn't worked.*

3. *The price of tickets, $17.00 a pop in Winnipeg.*

4. *Player defections. The big stars have gone to the NFL making the CFL look like a minor league operation.*

5. *The size of the roster.*

6. *Lousy concessions. Warm beer and a cold hot dog on a summer evening.*

7. *Weekend games. For years football fans have refused to drive back from the lake to watch a game.*

8. *Great TV delays. Going to a CFL game is becoming a day's outing.*

9. *Player identification. People can't name anyone including General Manager Joe _____ of the Ottawa Rough Riders.*

10. *Marketing. The CFL just doesn't market itself.*[115]

Taylor was writing after the Grey Cup champion Blue Bombers had played two home games in which they drew 3,279 fewer spectators than at the same point last year.[116] He didn't stop there. The next day he listed 10 more reasons as to why attendance was in decline.

11. Drunken, obnoxious fans.

12. Cheerleaders. Some football purist said yesterday he was tired of "the bimbos. They play their loud jungle music and dance around like hookers. I don't pay 17 bucks to watch that".

13. Earl Lunsford. Trade Lunsford bumper stickers are lying around. In '83 the Winnipeg Football Club dumped Lunsford as General Manager and it hasn't made a difference in attendance.

14. Lousy refereeing.

15. The home team always wins.

16. Too many games on TV.

17. Negative media coverage.

18. Minor League football. Earl Lunsford once said: "It really isn't what you are but how you are perceived what is important.

19. I can watch it in the bar, satellite dishes being the problem.

20. Other things to do. This is the most frightening reason of all facing professional football in Canada. For instance, to attend a Blue Bombers game will cost a husband and wife with one child upwards of $100 for an entire evening out. There indeed may be better things to do with $100.[117]

It was a critical situation for the CFL. Revenue from attendance was falling; revenue from television could not be far behind unless the trend was reversed. Ratings had declined especially during the second half of the 1985 season, compounded by blackout conditions in its largest markets of southern Ontario and British Columbia. Blame was placed on the post-September policy of moving from Thursday prime-time games during July and August and which had high ratings, and the poor season by the Argos.[118]

The consensus was that the League was fortunate to have signed its television contract with Carling O'Keefe when it did. Brewery profits had been high and there were huge sums available for promotions. Molson's was anxious to get some summer identification to compete with Labatt's and the Blue Jays and Carling O'Keefe and the Argos. With the resurgence of the Argonauts, there was a feeling that football interest would peak once again. The bidding for the television contract for CFL games had been artificially boosted. "The CFL won a $33 million three-year contract, twice the previous high but also as one senior executive said yesterday, twice what they are really worth".[119] It was obvious that changes had occurred: "The Jays continue to improve, Argos had plunged competitively, Tiger-Cats stumble early when interest is being generated for a new season, marketing of both teams is atrocious, attendance is at post-1960 lows in both cities and the Eastern Conference has remained mediocre over all".[120] And change had occurred on the sponsor and advertising side. Expansion of a schedule to 18 games would add production costs if any of the extra contests were to be shown on television. Brewery profits were in decline and after years of all companies using one size bottle for all, each brand was designing its own. Interchange ability was no longer in. Costs were increasing. Marketing of beer now included different size and shapes of bottles, cans, anything to accentuate the difference between one brand and another. "The CFL clearly has to come up with something to make its product attractive to at least two breweries or get out and sell some other corporate giant on the advantages of a rights bid. A non-competitive situation would be a disaster".[121]

No one knew it better than the CFL. A planning and marketing committee was appointed. Its mission was "to set short and long-term goals for the League and in particular to set a plan of action to turn around the current trend of attendance decline".[122] Meetings were held with the media in different League cities. Interim findings were that the "hard core" of season ticket supporters, while loyal, were not enough to support the franchise, Edmonton perhaps being the exception. The task was to "get the old fans back and bring out new ones . . . to create a desire to want to see something new or different".[123] A number of recommendations were suggested:

> 1. *Financial viability: Financial success was dependent upon putting people in the seats not only from a "gate" point of view but from television as well. No television rights holder desires to hold the rights to a product which is playing before half empty stadiums or perceived to be declining in interest".*[124]
>
> *The report recommended promotions to increase fan support by "1,000 fans per game each year for each team over a five-year period. There was to be an opening night concentration across the League on the assumption that "first impressions are lasting". One pre-season game would include a "bonus" of one ticket for a regular season game, the cost to be picked up by a sponsor. Opening night promotions could include "junior" fans and "senior" citizens being charged half price, the difference again being picked up by a corporate sponsor.*
>
> *Two other promotional games were proposed along the lines of baseball style giveaways. Calendars and radios were sug-*

gested, a calendar because it was seen as a bonus to be "taken home and hung up in an obvious place and not only highlights the schedule of home games and TV games but also contains many other promotional coupons for use of the purchase of CFL products".[125] The radio was perceived to be costly whereas "in actual fact it is a very inexpensive item".[126] Again, it was suggested that with all of these approaches combined, the cost to the League is very minimal because a sponsor is picking up the majority of the cost for the promotional item the fan is occupying an otherwise unused seat, a new fan or new old fan is introduced to the game and lastly our overall attendance is increased with the perception that we are back on the way up.[127]

2. Player Identity: According to the study fans perceived players as "No Stars" because those who were "stars" left to play in the United States. Not only that, there was the perception shaped by the media in some cities "that changes are made for the sake of saving a team a few thousand dollars by dropping a veteran in favour of a rookie".[128] Indeed, the League office had become so sensitive to this criticism that when a major sponsor wanted to use a player from each team on a poster, the CFL offices "felt it necessary to confirm with the General Manager of each team that the player used will be with the team for the duration of the year".[129] The suggested solution was to "ensure that each team does have as many players as possible under long-term contracts for the next five

year period".[130] It was also proposed that higher visibility be given to the CFL's draft by ranking the top 20 available, again to enhance identification. The whole concept was based on the proven formula used by rock promoters. They showed that "no one buys tickets to a rock concert just to hear Lionel Ritchie music. They go to see Lionel Ritchie, someone they identify with".[131]

3. *Schedule: It was suggested that the full interlocking schedule should be reviewed because of some "considerable conjecture of whether this format has been as successful as originally anticipated".[132] Such a review, it said, should not be perceived as "accepting the failure if a move off such a schedule were to be made but only an attempt to increase attendance.[133]*

4. *With respect to rule changes, there were some blunt suggestions. With respect to the Designated Import rule, the message was simple and direct. "Nothing we could do would have more positive impact on the image of the League than eliminating the rule".[134] It was suggested that "no one understands why we put it into effect nor does anyone care". No rule has given the League more static and negative reaction than this rule . . . the media allege that it works to the detriment of the Canadian College quarterback despite Vavra and Dattilio".[135]*

There was no doubt that the media was playing more of an important role or perhaps more correctly that there was more recognition of the value it had to the League. The CFL hired

Toronto Sun reporter John Iaboni as Director of Media and Public Relations replacing Information Officer Larry Robertson. If Commissioner Doug Mitchell's notion that the CFL's image problem was more one of perception than substance was correct, the hiring of Iaboni was a move to change that perception. Part of the problem was the inevitable comparison with the NFL. Some members of the media were critical of CFL play as compared with that of the NFL. Edmond Ricard, the Chairman of the League's Board of Governors agreed; his solution was that "consideration should be given to increasing the import quota".[136] Once again, the shaper of perceptions, television, came in for scrutiny. NFL telecasts were superior to the CFL's "because its TV commentators stress only the positive aspects of the game". As well, only the best game of the week was telecast, it was suggested. There were complaints that the CFL's TV commentators were "ill prepared for the game and did not perform in a professional manner". The commentators were said to "often by-pass the pre-game press conferences", thus not having the "preparation and dedication" of the NFL commentators. Iaboni's job was a big one: he had to change all of that. He had some raw material available from an interim report to provide a beginning.

Each team was encouraged to have its own marketing person in order to make the League's scheme successful. Teams were also encouraged to not engage in "self destruct public relations". The report was very critical of a coach who was quoted as saying about the Montreal situation: "You have to get yourself motivated when you walk in there because there is no one in there to get your adrenalin flowing. It's like playing in a cave".[137] In an effort to have the clubs control its players' and coaches' comments, the report was recommending that "the League office will fine the team for conduct unbecoming a professional football operation".[138]

Public awareness was considered a problem. The secrecy of the negotiation list was deplored. It was not the way to get more publicity for what was the CFL's answer to "an import draft".[139] The CFL was encouraged to

make the negotiation list public, let the me-
dia review the lists, find out who the people
are, follow the chase to sign the player so
that when the player is signed the public
and the media both know who the play-
er is. If the player isn't signed, who cares,
the team has received free coverage and
the fans have been following the develop-
ment.[140]

Clearly the League was feeling the pinch of reduced coverage in many media outlets, particularly because of increased coverage of Blue Jays, American League baseball teams, Expos and National League stories. Since much scouting and recruiting was done via free agent camps it was suggested that the media be invited "to attend the camps even if a team pays the expenses. Even though it is a nuisance to have media around, let them get familiar with the players being signed from these camps. Maybe they will do a human interest story that will introduce a new player to the public back home".[141]

The final item discussed in the interim report was the matter of TV quality control. TV was considered to be the "greatest marketing tool (if) utilized in the proper manner. If not it becomes the greatest marketing deterrent".[142]

There was no doubt that the media was playing more of an important role or perhaps more correctly that there was more recognition of the value it had to the League. That importance was underlined by Iaboni in his "Media Report" presented to the League September 16, 1985. The veteran reporter made a tour of all CFL cities with a view "to observe the home site in game action". Iaboni spoke with each Media/Public Relations Director and their assistants, senior members of the Football Reporters of Canada and drew upon his own personal experience to detail a comprehensive League approach to attack the perception image problem. He found that many clubs had no one person responsible solely for media matters. Toronto, Hamilton, Winnipeg and

Calgary combined "marketing and other club related matters". While there was an assistant who dealt with the media, the latter took "a dim view of the structure because sometimes a request he (or she) has cannot be met until the information officer clears the demand or becomes better informed with the situation in question by talking to his immediate supervisor". In Toronto, Winnipeg and Calgary, the media information people were around the press box on game day but "the media perception of each is that none is qualified to deal with some of the requests they may make. And in Hamilton, the club's information officer is not available because he is at field level as T.C., The club's mascot". Iaboni reported that when the media perceived the League or Club to be "unfeeling" towards their needs, "the term 'bush' surfaces anytime a problem arises". His recommendation was that each club have a person responsible for marketing separate from another for Media/Public Relations.

He proposed making Press Boxes function better with a Code of Ethics for reporters and a Media/Public Relations person who could develop a good relationship with those covering the game. He looked at "the entire procedure from pre-game meal to post-game working facilities. Pampering of the media was the norm, he said, at professional sporting events. The media "include the food rating as something else to talk about regarding that Club". As an example, he mentioned that all clubs aside from Hamilton and Winnipeg provided pre-game meals for media and hot dogs at half-time. Winnipeg served hot dogs at the beginning of the game; Hamilton at half-time. He commented: "Well, you won't believe the number of times media people refer to the serving of 'only' hot dogs at half-time in Hamilton".

Press box allocations were also important. Visiting media were to be placed in the front row "because to make a visitor feel inferior leads to complaints of poor working conditions". Necessary equipment to be included were telephones, electrical outlets, pre-game notes including "records, streaks, birthdays, on this date in Club history, etc. for the home and visiting sides plus the League's This Week In The CFL and official statistical package".

Again, Iaboni stressed perception. There had to be a unity in the approach. When a press kit includes statistics provided "as compiled by their coaches with a kicker stating: The total (QB) sacks in these stats will differ from the CFL Official (stats) because of interpretation of rules on QB sacks", he asked "if our CFL stats are 'Official' then how can we have a different interpretation". He drew a parallel with baseball: "Does one go with the official scorer or does one at the club level interpret things his own way?" Such approaches "leads one to wonder about the professionalism of the entire League", he said.

Clearly, Iaboni was attempting to educate the clubs' media people to the pragmatic aspects of the CFL operations. He spoke of one of the League's initiatives, This week in the CFL, a telecast which sought to highlight the top stories of the week. Club media directors were asked to "send any information to our office and we would gladly incorporate such. No one has responded, leaving the entire compilation of material for the four games each week, covering 8 teams and in excess of 40 players each week"[143] up to the CFL office. Iaboni wasn't complaining about the workload; more so about the lack of communication with the clubs which might prevent the League from promoting "special nights or highlight player milestones, club milestones, anything that may escape our research".[144]

He also recommended the use of a microphone and sound hook-up in the press box, not to repeat the obvious as in Winnipeg where a report of the public address announcer's words were piped into the area, but to make "key tidbits such as 'Willard Reeves needs 3 more yards rushing to record his 15th 100 yard rushing game' or 'his next point will make Trevor Kennerd the first Blue Bomber to score 1,000 in his career', etc."[145] The reality of the situation, Iaboni said, was that with morning newspapers and on-the-spot radio reports, there was a need for quick reports on injuries "especially to front line players. Details which might not be known until a coach's post-game discussion should be made known to the media at the time the injury occurred. It might only be necessary to say that a player left the game "with an injury to the left leg and we will up-date you once we get further details".[146] Later editions and reports could elaborate. The microphone could also be used in conjunction with the Club's record manual to comment on records as they happen, none being too small to be overlooked. The idea was to deluge the media with "statistical information, records, etc. to create more identity for Clubs and players, stimulate interest among the fans".[147]

As a practitioner for 16 years, He was well aware of the mutual interdependence of the CFL and the media. The latter needed information; they were not that well versed in football per se but had to appear as being so; the League needed to get its message out. Iaboni concluded:

> We have a great game with a wonderful tradition and a bright future so the worst thing we can do is to keep all of this a secret when the media is starving for CFL news. The level of reports on the CFL, be it on radio, on TV or in newspapers, depends on how well we accomplish the task of feeding the news required to assist the media.[148]

The CFL immediately upgraded its record manual for 1985. The 1984 version, entitled "Official Record Manual" since the '60s had cost $30,000 to publish 5,000 copies "of which $20,000 was recovered in sales and grants making the net cost to the League $10,000".[149] Beginning in 1985, the expanded version titled: "Canadian Football League Facts Figures and Records" would be available. Twenty-thousand copies were to be printed at a cost of $75,000. If none were sold, the cost to the League was to be $20,000. At the time of the announcement some $55,000 in advertising revenue had been committed. If all were sold "the League could realize a profit of $100,000".[150] The release was to be kicked off with a news conference in Toronto, complimentary copies for members of the Football Reporters of Canada, three hundred copies for each club; the books would also be on sale at Bookstores and clubs could also sell them from their offices at a lower price.[151] In addition, Maclean's was planning a 16 page supplement for its June 24th issue. Editorial content control was to be under the control of Iaboni.[152]

Media accessibility to teams was also considered important. When the Concordes "proposed that the members of the media be prohibited from entering the team dressing room for post-game interviews and that the home club be required to provide another room adjacent to the dressing room for post-game interviews",[153] there was little support. Joe Galat complained that most visiting team rooms were small and that players were complaining about dressing in cramped quarters and "becoming resentful of media questions when trying to dress".[154]

At the time there was a 15 minute delay after the game before the dressing room doors were opened to the media. In many cases, players lingered on the field either being delayed by post-game television and radio interviews or what one team official called "the College reunion atmosphere where players of opposing teams meet at midfield after the game to renew acquaintances".[155] The League took action, deeming such meetings unprofessional". "At the conclusion of the game, the members of both competing teams shall be required to leave the playing field and proceed directly to their respective dressing rooms".[156]

While the 15 minute period after the game was considered the maximum time that the media would wait, anything more was deemed to be "counter productive" by the Commissioner, a change was made prior to the 1985 season. When it was noted that there were more female reporters across the League, the Commissioner "pointed out the possibility of charges of discrimination and human rights violations if such a reporter was denied access to the dressing rooms".[157] The CFL decided to extend the waiting period to twenty minutes, ostensibly to allow the players more time to shower and dress, and "agreed that women reporters would be permitted equal access to the dressing rooms at all times".[158]

In some ways, there appeared to be some resistance to the changes initiated and proposed by new Commissioner Doug Mitchell. When he took over as head of the CFL, he sought to introduce innovations which he had thought would be beneficial to the game. He wasn't in favour of a single point being awarded after a missed field goal, but "his nine bosses rejected it in favour of the status quo; then it was overtime, the Board of Governors 8–1 in favour in February, that has created problems with the TV networks . . . the League Management Council flatly refused to increase the size of the active roster from 34 to 36".[159] Mitchell had also proposed that the League move from its two divisions and create a third. His object was to "eliminate the possibility of a club qualifying for the play-offs in one division with a lesser record than another club which fails to qualify in another division". Mitchell still wanted to guarantee that there would be an East-West Grey Cup game. His proposal called for an East, Central and West Division as below:

East	Central	West
Montreal	Toronto	Calgary
Ottawa	Winnipeg	Edmonton
Hamilton	Saskatchewan	B.C.

His plan called for the last place team in each division to be eliminated, the two remaining "in the Central Division would revert to their former divisions for play-off purposes". It too was not accepted but Mitchell said that he wasn't disheartened. When he was selected as Commissioner, he had a moustache. He shaved it off just before the CFL's May meetings. "He explained: 'It's symbolic I hope to show I'm flexible enough to accept change'".[160]

The NFL wished to play an exhibition game in Toronto in August. Commissioner Mitchell objected and spoke to the Minister of Sport Otto Jelinek seeking to "support his position". The August 24 game was cancelled.[161] It was an important consideration. What with the success of the Blue Jays and the possibility that they would appear in the 1985 World Series, the CFL was finding itself under attack. It had already decided to adjust its schedule in the event of a Blue Jays' victory as American League Champions. The October 20 Argo game was to be moved to Friday October 18; the October 27 contest to Friday October 25. If the Blue Jays were not in the World Series, the former schedule would prevail.[162] Former Argo owner John Bassett was in the forefront of an NFL movement: "My views won't be popular with the CFL but then they never were. I could only speak for Toronto but my view is that Toronto is a world class city and the time is long past when the CFL will satisfy Toronto fans". Bassett's view was based on the success of the Blue Jays. Toronto's baseball fans had responded well to the team. They looked forward to seeing "Big League" cities such as New York and Chicago and "the legendary teams in baseball". Toronto fans, he said, now wanted to see "the legendary teams of football, the Dallas Cowboys and The Washington Redskins" Bassett gave his forecast:

I think there will always be a CFL but it will always be a secondary league with more and more Canadians playing in it. Such a League, operated at lower costs might allow a city like Halifax to have a team. Toronto could even have a second team, one in the NFL and one in the CFL.[163]

There were other problems. While attendance had risen because of the Lions' on-field performance and B.C. Place —they had made a profit of $354,106. in 1983 and $321,172 in 1984 —they also had a long-term debt of $825,670 due in 1985.[164] The real trouble spots though, were in Calgary and Montreal. The Stampeders had a debt of $783,000 in 1984 making their accumulated total amount owing $1.5 million since 1982.[165] Their attendance fell by 7%, an average of 3,500 per game. Club officials feared a loss of in excess of $1 million in 1985. Cost of operations which were in excess of $6 million for 1985 were being kept alive by a whole host of schemes. Corporate donations contributed $300,000; the sale of 20,000 shares of Stampeders' stock at $10 each provided $200,000; a red and white dinner club earned $90,000. There was a $1,000,000 line of credit from the Bank of Commerce secured by $500,000 collateral.[166] Attendance had not increased. During the first three games of 1985 only 45,000 fans came, fewer than 13,000 to a game which the Stampeders lost to the Concordes. Head Coach Steve Buratto was replaced by elder statesman Bud Riley. The 59 year old was with his fourth CFL team as a Head Coach, having held similar posts with varying tenures at Winnipeg, Toronto and Hamilton.

Turmoil would not be an inappropriate word to describe the situation which had evolved in Calgary. In the space of little more than one year, there were three Head Coaches and two General Managers. A coup of sorts was implemented when shares sold to the public were mobilized and a new board of directors emerged. Trades were plentiful, one wag suggesting that "program sales are at an all-time high as no one can tell who's playing without one".[167] The upshot was that Calgary drew 14,100 on the average for their home games in 1985. The break-even point was 24,000.[168]

By October, it was obvious that the League attendance had fallen, franchises were in trouble, and television ratings had declined especially during the second half of the season. CFL Board of Governors held a special meeting in Halifax, October 7, 1985. "The Chairman explained that the meeting had been called in a non-league city in order that the Governors could engage in a frank discussion on matters of great importance to the League". While Maritime hopes had been raised that perhaps expansion to the east was still alive, the real reason for the meeting was that "there have been disturbing reports about clubs in financial trouble, attendance has been disappointing in most areas and the League's public image has suffered through media perception that the League is less than what it really is".[169]

Montreal seemed to be a microcosm of the League's problems. On the surface, it appeared to have turned the corner during the 1985 season. A positive spin was put on developments. In a report to the league in May of 1985 news was given that its campaign was "largely successful", community involvement was high, large corporations had "come forward to offer assistance and the season's ticket base has been doubled."[170] The franchise's future was said to look "more promising than it has in several years." While three of its original partners had withdrawn, there were indications that others would be admitted. Charles Bronfman and the Imasco Group continued to have controlling interest. Season tickets had rebounded. There were 12,144 in 1985 compared to 5,000 in 1984.

Joe Galat of the Montreal Concordes had another problem. His Club had conducted a "free agent camp" in the United States "at a considerable expense and had permitted observers from other clubs to be in attendance".[171] The Concordes identified one player as being an outstanding prospect. When the session was finished "the Montreal Club called the League office to place the player's name on its negotiation list only to learn that an observer from another Club who had been watching the same practice had already called the League office to place the player's name on the other Club's list.[172]

Agreement was given to the Concorde's request that season's ticket holders be given the opportunity to purchase the same seats for the Grey Cup game with a deadline of April 30 instead of April 1. The League agreed with the understanding that "said information and said extension not become public information".[173]

Such concessions were necessary because by now it was apparent to the League that Montreal was indeed a troubled franchise, its magnitude deflected by the highly publicized events in Calgary. In a confidential report to the Board of Governors, Edmond Ricard of the Concordes brought the rest of the League up-to-date with events in Montreal. He said that when Charles Bronfman and his partners joined the League in 1982 "with a three-year commitment to save football in Montreal" they did so "to rescue it from what appeared to be an unfavourable situation".[174] But the reality was much more serious than first thought. It was compounded by the fact that the Concordes "had no identity in the Montreal market and was living in the shadow of past glories of the Alouettes".[175] The French media was critical of the name Concordes and any attempt to resurrect the name Alouettes was tied up in legal complications. Ricard announced that since 1982, the experiment had cost the partners $13,000,000. Even 1985 with its encouraging beginning and improved attendance brought "a negative impact on its home gate receipts" due in part to five straight loses in September and October.[176] The subsequent loss of $3,000,000 for the 1985 season[177] forced the Concordes' management to take a second look at their commitment. Ricard described

> *the partners as dedicated, responsible people but reluctant owners of a football team. Mr. Bronfman is committed to baseball while Imasco is involved for advertising purposes. There is no intention to embarrass the League but the partners would like to turn the Club over to other parties. He emphasized the importance of keeping football alive in Montreal but he acknowledges that the team's field performance has not made it attractive for a purchaser.[178]*

Ricard proposed a deal to the League. The partners could either "pay the $3,000,000 penalty provided by Article 3.06 of the Constitution and turn the franchise over to the League to find new owners" or continue to operate the Club for one, possibly two years under the following arrangement; a) that the League would "waive the $3,000,000 penalty in lieu of notice, with no further notice required"; b) the entire first year loss would be borne by the partners; c) a commitment for a second year would be given "only if it can be projected that as a result of tax concessions or other government assistance, the combined after tax loss after two years will not be greater than $1,500,000".[179] During this 2-year time period, Ricard stated that he and the partners would endeavour to attract other investors with a view to their "eventually taking over".[180]

All felt the urgency to keep football in Montreal. The Commissioner reported "that he had met with senior officials of the Department of Finance to discuss the possibility of tax concessions similar to those available to petroleum exploration and other high risk taxpayers. Such concessions would be an advantage to the private entrepreneur clubs and be attractive to potential investors".[181] When costs of the Montreal operation were questioned, Ricard stated that he welcomed a review by the Commissioner to see if costs could be reduced. He pointed out that Montreal has a unique situation unlike anywhere else. Taxes were higher as were rental costs, media service was in two languages. In addition, wives of players could not find employment if they were not fluent in French; as a result, players' contracts were higher. In view of all of this, Montreal decided that it would not proceed with a motion to increase the import quota to 19 players.[182] When all was said and done the CFL decided to accept the Montreal offer to carry on for one or two years under the conditions described.[183]

At the meetings in Edmonton, in January, Cal Murphy was, once again, chosen as Coach of the Year. The award was accompanied by a $5,000 cheque from Molson's. It was a banner year for the Blue Bombers. No only had they won their first Grey Cup in twenty-two years, the year also saw the construction of a new addition to their offices at the Stadium. The "Blue-Gold" room was inaugurated. Season ticket holders could "'buy' a table for the season and enjoy a meal and drink before and after each home game. This building (would) also house the Blue Bomber Hall of Fame".[184] Prior to the season, Nick Benjamin of Concordia University became the first player to be chosen with the first completely open CFL non-import draft. The 6'2", 270lb. Benjamin became an impressive starter with Ottawa playing all 16 games at the guard position.

The east showed a remarkable amount of balance. Parity had arrived. The Argonauts missed the play-offs with a 6–10 record but first place Hamilton was at 8–8, the same as Montreal. Ottawa earned third place with a 7–9 record. In the play-offs, Montreal defeated its arch rival Rough Riders by a 30–10 score. The Concordes had made a change with two games to go in the season. Joe Galat continued as General Manager but relinquished his head coaching duties to Gary Durchik. A three game win streak was halted when the Tiger Cats defeated the Concordes by a 50–26 score.

In the west British Columbia and Winnipeg were the class of the division, the Lions ending up in first place with a 12–3–1 record, the Blue Bombers at 11–4–1. Edmonton was again in 3rd place at 9–7 while Saskatchewan at 5–11 and Calgary with a 3–13 record were once more out of the play-offs. Winnipeg defeated Edmonton in a close game by a 22–15 score only to fall to B.C. 42–22.

With the Grey Cup game being played in Montreal on Sunday November 24, it was an interesting week leading up to the game. The CFL was not being well received in the city; Grey Cup hoopla seemed a bit strained. Football fever didn't seem to be there. The Concordes had drawn only 11,372 fans to their play-off game with Ottawa.[185] Even out west, the Winnipeg-Edmonton play-off game at times seemed like the Blue Bombers were trying to give the game away. The score was close only because Winnipeg fumbled six times and was intercepted twice.[186] Attendances at Hamilton and Vancouver were good. Twenty-four thousand, four hundred and twenty-three at Ivor Wynne Stadium, the largest of the season and 59,478 at B.C. Place. But the Grey Cup game, the League's showcase, and Montreal didn't seem to blend together.

There were attempts to generate excitement. In the Schenley Awards, British Columbia's Mervyn Fernandez was selected over Hamilton quarterback Ken Hobart as the Outstanding Player; another B.C. stalwart Michael Gray was chosen Outstanding Rookie over Ottawa's Nick Benjamin; Outstanding Canadian Player was Hamilton's Paul Bennett. Winnipeg's Joe Poplawski was runner-up. Bennett was second to Winnipeg's Tyrone Jones as Defensive Player. Another Winnipeg player, Nick Bastaja was Offensive Lineman; Dan Ferrone of Toronto was runner-up.

League meetings discussed items such as 4 down football and a proposed 18 game schedule with 2 exhibition games for 1986. The four downs were dismissed, Mitchell stating: "We have a unique game and I don't want to make it another USFL".[187] The 18 game schedule would have to be approved by the Players' Association who would naturally want to be paid more money for the two extra League games. "Mitchell said he feels it is illogical for teams to voluntarily compensate players for two extra League games. . . . It would be a poor business decision for running business is not a voluntary payment centre".[188] The lawyer argued that the total number of games, pre season and scheduled, would still be 20. Players were obliged to play twenty no mater how they were split between exhibition and regularly scheduled.[189]

Although there were 56,723 officially in attendance for the Grey Cup game, generating receipts of $2,041,230, it was obvious that all was not well in Montreal. Some called it "the last tango for the Canadian Football League in Montreal . . . The usual dancing in the streets seems subdued . . . one of the quietest Grey Cup festivals in years, despite the fact that thousands of football fans have been arriving from across the country".[190] In the game itself, the Lions prevailed over the Tiger Cats 37–24. Lui Passaglia scored 19 points and was chosen as Best Canadian in the game. He also provided a key play. With B.C. one point behind and 3rd down and nine on their own 38 and two minutes to go to half time, Passaglia lined up to punt. Hamilton's Mitchell Price broke through and appeared ready to block it. Passaglia sidestepped him and picked up a first down at the 51 from where B.C. quarterback Roy Dewalt connected with a 59 yard touchdown pass to Ned Armour, after which the game never appeared to be in doubt.

As part of its quest to restore goodwill and a sense of its roots and role in the community at large, the League made a number of initiatives. Among these was the naming of Bill Davis, as chairman of the Board of Governors. The former Ontario Premier had been serving as the President of the CFL Football Foundation, having been asked to do so by Mitchell in 1985. The Foundation had been an initiative of the Commissioner who had hoped to assist minor football. Davis would assume his new position in 1987.

After years of festering, the CFL decided to do away with the Designated Import rule in 1986 and treat the quarterback position as a category separate from "players". Ever since its inception, the rule had been pilloried by press and public alike for its effect on discouraging non-imports at the quarterback position. The 1970 regulation came about when Edmonton's Norm Kimball "proposed that quarterbacks be placed in a separate roster category from imports and non-imports".[191] The Designated Import legislation arose from that. In 1986, it was Winnipeg's Paul Robson who proposed that a "Club be permitted to dress for a game a maximum of 36 players of whom not more than 16 may be imports of whom three may be designated as quarterbacks".[192] Robson's rationale was that each club was presently carrying a third quarterback on its reserve list and such a change would allow a team to give him playing time. There was always a need to develop quarterbacks. Discussion resulted in some modifications to the proposal. Some were concerned with the increase in rosters; others with whether one of the three quarterbacks could partake of other roles and duties. After the motion was approved with a total roster of 35, the League issued a directive.[193] Team rosters were fixed at 35—thirty-two players including not more than 13 imports and a "maximum of three players who shall be permitted alternate for each other during the game at the quarterback position exclusively". The quarterbacking position was defined to include "holding the ball for a kicker on a convert or field goal attempt". There were other conditions: the player named as a quarterback could not enter the game at any other offensive or defensive position, be on the field for a kick-off or when the opposition was scrimmaging the ball. The quarterback could not replace any player, other than a quarterback in case of injury or whatever reason.

While each Club was allowed 35 players, fewer could dress. If 35 were dressed, 3 quarterbacks could be so categorized but only one could be in the game at any one time. If 34 were dressed, 2 would be named as quarterback with the same restrictions. If 33 were dressed, one would be a quarterback with the same restrictions. If the club chose for whatever reason to dress 32, there were to "be no restrictions on the quarterback position".

Violations would be subject to a fine and be considered "valid grounds for protest". A later clarification allowed "a quarterback to be a kicker but not permit a kicker to be identified as a quarterback".[194] The League was clearly hoping that by developing a quarterback category consisting of players who could be import or non-import, it could recoup some of the Canadian public's confidence that it wanted to tear down any perceived roadblocks for non-import quarterbacks.

The only non-import quarterback in the CFL at the end of the 1985 season was Greg Vavra of Calgary. After a season of reduced playing time, he was picked up by B.C. Lions with whom he played two games in 1986.

For the first time in its history, the CFL College Draft was to be telecast live by TSN from the Toronto Convention Centre. Since a number of players had attracted NFL attention, there was a fear "that a Club might be faced with a dilemma of possibly wasting a choice or missing a chance on a star player".[195]

The fear was that Canadian players such as Reuben Mayes, Marcus Koch and Michael Schad, all first round draft prospects, would choose to play in the NFL. The League struck a Committee of three "to review the list of candidates and select a maximum of 12 to be invited to the draft meeting at League expense".[196] In the end the CFL put its best face on when the three, in spite of being 1st round choices in the CFL, cast their lot with the NFL's New Orleans, Washington and Los Angeles respectively.

One ongoing area was in the matter of players' relations. From time to time there were grievances and differences in interpretation of the Collective Agreement between the League and its players. Ralph Sazio noted that the players "were invariably represented by Ed Molstad who is fully familiar with the procedures and understands the thought processes of various arbiters".[197]

Sazio was referring to the former Edmonton Eskimo defensive lineman who had been legal counsel for the Association since the early 1970s. Not only that, having played with the Eskimos and negotiated his contract with Norm Kimball, those factors and his continuity were

perceived to give the Association an advantage. On management side, Sazio stated, "the Club is usually represented by an outside lawyer who has to be thoroughly briefed on the machinations of football disputes. Then, quite possibly, the Club is placed at an immediate disadvantage".[198] Sazio recommended that the League appoint one person to represent it in these negotiations. His suggestion was Richard Rendek "a practising lawyer in Regina and a member of the League's Player Relations Committee".[199] The League concurred. Richard Rendek was asked to become and accepted the position of Counsellor-at-large for the League.

The CFL was able to effect its 18 game schedule as part of the new collective agreement signed with the players in 1986 and it was able to do so at no extra cost. In effect, revenue from two extra games was a bonus for each Club. The players had been hopeful for an increase in pay since they were moving from a 16 to 18 game schedule but the CFL argued "that the players were paid on a per season basis, an annual payment basis . . . a player's contract never stated how many games you play in". The new contract was to specify 18 League games.[200]

The agreement, announced in Vancouver on April 28, 1986 called for training camps to be shortened to five from six weeks. Players with two years' experience were to receive $100 more than 1985's $400 with 3 year veterans to be paid $600 per week. There were also new salary minimums: first year players were to receive $26,000 for '86 and '87 and $28,000 in 1988. In the preceding contract veterans of one year received $26,000 and rookies $22,000. The contract also called for two year veterans to have a minimum of $32,000 for '86 and '87 and $36,000 in '88. The minimum annual compensation for a three year veteran was to be $38,000 in 1986, '87 and $40,000 in 1988. There was also some protection for a veteran of 6 years or more. He would receive full payment of his contract if released after September 1; five year players would be similarly treated after September 15. All others would relate to October 1, the "previous across the board date for all players".[201]

Grey Cup compensation was increased: a minimum $11,000 for the winners, $6,000 for players on the losing team. Divisional semi-finalists were to receive $1,800; finalists $2,200. Players on the first place teams were to receive $1,200. The contract also dealt with the issue of practice times. Clubs could start at 1:30p.m. "subject to the agreement of a majority of veteran players".[202]

While Greg Vavra faded from the scene, his former team, the Stampeders, was the focus of public attention for much of the year. Their financial woes were the subject of much debate. There was concern as to whether the franchise would survive. It was unable to pay its assessments to the CFL during December of 1985 and January 1986. The League agreed to waive them so as not to hinder the search for new operators who would not want to take over past debts.[203] Mixed signals seemed to be emanating from Calgary. In the midst of a campaign to keep the Stampeders in the foothills city, Council was asked to subsidize the football team's rent of $500,000 for McMahon Stadium. The proposal to do so for a three year period was turned down by a 7–6 vote.[204] The Club was distraught. An earlier plan to provide a group led by business man Doug Hunter with a loan of two million dollars and a $4 million line of credit "prompted hundreds of letters and phone calls from people opposed to taxpayers' money being used to prop up the sports team".[205] Some six million dollars was needed over the next five years. The Alberta government was offering a $1 million loan guarantee; the club, after first considering a $6 million loan and a break on the rent had begun a fund-raising campaign with the purpose of raising

$4 million. After five days it "had raised only $202,000 in donations and $61,000 in pledges".[206]

Mayor Ralph Klein "who spear-headed the efforts to grab the rent subsidy, said the Council left him sick and disappointed".[207] Linebacker Bernie Morrison, an eight year CFL veteran was especially bitter: "I'm thinking just how gutless the City Council is. I put eight years in the city on and off the field and its not the type of place I want to raise my family in".[208]

The Calgary team was officially listed as community owned, as were all the western teams. There were some who felt there was private money involved, a reason given by dissenting politicians and the public as to why public money should not be spent. Surely, these critics said, the League had an emergency fund with which to deal with such concerns. By mid-February, the Stampeders seemed to be assured enough of their resources that they announced they would operate for 1986. A group of businessmen agreed to form an interim Board of Directors. Personal contributions of $10,000 to $20,000 would give a much needed injection of money. A season ticket campaign with a target of 25,000 was initiated for the new community-owned operation. The provincial government agreed to give a loan guarantee of $1,000,000 "if the city offers some financial assistance also".[209] The local media got involved to the extent that the public was bombarded with the message. Eventually 20,413 season tickets were sold in the month, the result of "an all-out sales blitz which resembled a charity drive . . . to preserve a tradition. The blitz included everything from charity style dinners to a stripathon organized by exotic dancers".[210]

There were strong indications that the change taking place in the public's attitude towards the CFL was continuing; that the competition for the entertainment dollar was intensifying; that perhaps new approaches to the marketing of the League were needed. The years of criticism directed at the League seemed to be peaking. One reporter likened the situation to the "feminists' favourite 'only joke': 'How's your husband, Ruth? Better than nothing, Irma'. He continued:

> So are the Stampeders Irma. So is the CFL. It's become fashionable to fire darts at Commissioner Doug Mitchell's rag-tag band of recent years, mostly because it offers such a large inviting target. The League takes so many polls, becomes defensive about so many contradictory policies, and lives so far beyond its means, it sounds like our government. If the Stamps had folded, it didn't take a rocket scientist to figure out the whole League would be in trouble. A future with no professional football in six CFL cities, an NFL franchise in the domed or soon-to-be domed playpens of Vancouver, Montreal and Toronto was not difficult to picture ... The Calgary crisis may finally have convinced the Governors it's time to bring in the old bus for a check-up.

The feeding frenzy continued. Another reporter with the Toronto Sun reported that the League did have an emergency fund. It quoted "confidential sources" that the money was "spent on new office space and salaries for enlarged staff". The Sun continued: The fund has disappeared and no one seems to know much where the money, as much as $753,000 in June 1984, was spent".[211] Commissioner Doug Mitchell denied the story. There was no emergency fund, he said, the money had been "used to bail out the Montreal franchise in 1982 when the Alouettes became the Concordes".[212] General Managers canvassed were unaware as to whether the fund still existed. Bob Ackles of B.C. said he knew it once existed. Paul Robson described the Sun story as "ludicrous" while Joe Galat of Montreal seemed to come down on both sides: The CFL has a new high profile office you know but I really don't know if that's where the money went".[213] A beleaguered Doug Mitchell was angry in denying the story and "reportedly retained the services of a lawyer to investigate whether the story carried by the Sun was libellous".[214]

The play-off format came under-fire. Some blamed the western woes on the fact that some of their teams had better records than clubs which qualified for play-offs in the east. The fact that three of four teams in the East qualified for play-offs while 3 of five did in the west, meant that the two western teams could be eliminated from contention early resulting from a drop in attendance and "substantial cash flow reductions". In a report prepared for the League, Commissioner Mitchell met the problem head on but his solution antagonized traditionalists. He recommended that the top finisher in each division be given a bye. The next four top finishers in the CFL regardless of division were to be given "wild card" berths. The net effect was that the two surviving teams would compete for the Grey Cup game, which would not necessarily be an East-West match-up.

It was radical, perhaps too radical for some. Scenarios such as a Saskatchewan vs. Calgary game in "a yawning Montreal or it could be Ottawa versus Hamilton in an equally indifferent Vancouver"[215] were debated. Milt Dunnell, an observer of the Canadian football scene for years continued:

> the true aficionado with team ribbons fly-
> ing from the lapel and a concoction of rum
> and coke in the side pocket is able to disre-
> gard such trivia as having a League with
> the same club name as Rough Riders and
> Roughriders as long as the Tiger Cats get
> the traditional win over Argonauts and the
> Saskatchewan stubblebenders score occa-
> sionally over the Winnipeg Blue Bombers.
> At least that's the way it has always been.
> But there is evidence that the love fest could
> be cooling. Two teams had a death rattle in
> their throats at the end of the past season.
> Grey Cup tickets are no longer something

you have to obtain in the last will and testament of a rich relative. There has been an alarming dip in Grey Cup television ratings.[216]

Dunnell's comments about the ratings were confirmed in Mitchell's report to the League. He called the drop "frightening". In 1983, the total rating was 8,118,000; 1984, 6,897,000; and in 1985, 5,283,000.[217]

Former Commissioner, Jake Gaudaur, entered the fray. He too was wary that a Grey Cup game could be played without the traditional East-West rivalry: "the East-West confrontation is essential to the Grey Cup. If we ever get around to a situation where it's east versus east or west vs. west, the Grey Cup game will lose its identity. Under a wild card play-off format, that's exactly what could happen".[218]

In the end, there was a compromise. The League accepted a Winnipeg proposal. The play-off structure would remain as it was in 1985 unless the fourth place team in one division had a better record than the third place finisher in the other. In that event, the two top teams in the one division would play a two game total point series to determine a winner; the other four teams would play-off with each other, 1 vs. 4 and 2 vs. 3, to determine its champion. The two division winners would meet for the Grey Cup; East vs. West would be preserved.

An increasing number of complaints had been received about the League's official ball, the Spalding J5V. The major ones had to do with the size. They didn't seem to hold their shape and often new balls were of different sizes. By the end of the year, complaints had increased to the point where the Commissioner was left with the decision as to whether to pursue an American machine-made ball from Wilson or Rawlings or stay with the Canadian, hand made, Spalding product. It was an important consideration. After all, the vast majority of quarterbacks in the CFL were still American; they were used to throwing the machine made balls which were manufactured at lower tolerances and held their shape. Indeed, the imports' proficiency at throwing was what made them attractive to the CFL coaches. There was some thought that they were being handicapped by using the "oversized" J5V Spalding ball.

The League invited and "received proposals from Spalding, Rawlings and Wilson to provide official footballs for the League".[219] Perhaps because Spalding balls were the only ones made in Canada, the material used was from the same source as the other two, it was given a chance "to match or improve on the Wilson offer . . . the most attractive of the three".[220] The result was a new three year contract with Spalding which called for the manufacturer to supply each club with 125 J5V balls per year at no charge. A further 175 balls per year were to be available at special prices of $41; $43 and $46.25 over the life of the agreement. Twenty-four Grey Cup balls were to be supplied to the League each year at no charge.

As a further means of sweetening the deal, Spalding was to give to each club at no charge, "96 dozen golf balls or 80 autographed footballs or a combination of the two".[221] Spalding also paid a royalty fee of $12,500, $15,000 and $17,500 in each of the three years. The League also gave Spalding something more tangible in addition to "official football of the CFL" status. It was to receive a full page ad in the League's Records Manual plus a full page in each Club's program. For its part the CFL would ask that the ball conform to NFL dimensions and "have input into the quality control" with the officiating director inspecting the first production "to ensure that the standards are being met".[222] Commissioner Doug Mitchell estimated that the total package would "save the Clubs collectively nearly two hundred thousand dollars over the three years".[223]

A similar type of arrangement was entered into with Ravensknit, the Canadian subsidiary of Champion Products of the USA. In the three year agreement, each Club in the CFL would be provided, in the first year and at no cost, 120 pairs of game pants, 200 Jerseys and 200 name plates, all conforming to Club standards.

Additional supplies could be purchased at $64 per pant and $45 for each sweater with an increase of 10% annually for inflation. As an added benefit, "each Club would be provided with a hundred and fifty sets of T-shirts and shorts".[224] The total value to the League was estimated to be $164,000 over three years. The deal with Champion meant that the League would not allow any authorized person in the bench area wearing a uniform to wear any headgear or other article of clothing with a commercial identification "unless approved by the League".[225]The arrangements were good for each party. The suppliers' products were given "official" status; the League received sponsorship and other contra items in return.

Rule changes in the CFL for the 1986 season were few. [226] The football was made to conform to the NFL size. The CFL had always allowed the manufacturer to work within the same size tolerance of the American ball but whereas the NFL insisted on the lower end of the tolerances, the CFL had accepted the higher. Since many of the quarterbacks had difficulty throwing the "fatter" CFL ball; the League decided to insist on the lower tolerance limit since all of its quarterbacks were more comfortable with it.

In an effort to provide leadership and to be seen doing so. Commissioner Mitchell left for an eleven day trip having been invited by the European Football League to visit Italy, England and the Netherlands. The CFL became a founding partner of the International Football Federation. Visions of an expanded world where the CFL could play a "big time" role were contemplated. There were 375 teams playing in eight countries of Europe, the largest group in England with 80 teams. The League received a request from the Italian Football League to allow two coaches and eight players "to come to Canada at their own expense and spend a week or ten days at a club training camp in the role of observers".[227] As far as the CFL was concerned while the European calibre of play was not up to CFL standards, there was the "great potential for television exposure and the playing of pre-season games".[228] A group from France had previously attended the Montreal training camp in 1984. By the end of the 1986 season, a group from England, London Gridiron Football U.K. Ltd., actually made a preliminary presentation to the League to inquire about a franchise.[229]

Expansion was still a major consideration based on the information that "our market research and general assumptions are consistent and that is the East-West concept of Grey Cup must continue".[230] As a result, the thinking was that expansion should occur in the East in order "to equalize the play-off structure".[231] CFL market research showed that 73% of fans felt the League should expand; the Maritimes and London seemed to be the most viable areas. A five year target time was recommended to be pursued.

The League decided to play an exhibition game in the Maritimes at Saint John, New Brunswick. There was a dual purpose: to increase the viability of the League beyond the franchise areas; to demonstrate to the Federal government the League's interest in the Maritimes by testing the interest for a potential franchise there.[232] There had been hints from the Federal government of support for a stadium. Interest in the game was such that two breweries, Labatt's and Moosehead, wanted to be involved but exclusively.[233] Among the details of the game between Montreal and Winnipeg, the first $50,000 was designated for the CFL players' pension fund; the next $25,000 was for League expenses with the rest being split between Saint John and the Football Foundation. The players were not to be paid for participating in the game.[234] The game, won by Winnipeg 35–10, attracted 11,463 spectators in the stadium normally holding 8,000. It was described by Mitchell as an "outstanding success".[235]

The game also served as the re-introduction of the Montreal Alouettes. The team officially known as the Montreal Football Club and Company Limited dispensed with the Concordes name, and re-introduced the Alouettes with a new part owner. Norm Kimball of the Edmonton Eskimos joined the team in March as part owner and Chief Operating officer. It was in keeping with the plan that Bronfman and Imasco would phase themselves out. The hope was that Kimball, long recognized by many, as one of the most astute General Managers in the CFL, could turn around the Montreal situation.But returning with the name was a problem. The Superior Court of the Province "ruled in favour of five former Montreal players in a suit against the League".[236] The players had been part of the Alouettes when owned by Sam Berger and later Nelson Scalbania. When the latter turned the team over to the CFL, the five were left off the 65 player roster. The court ruled that when the League acquired the title to the contracts of the 65 players on the Montreal active roster, it also accepted 'all liabilities under the player contracts'".[237] The judge ruled that "when the League later assigned the contracts to the new Montreal Club (Concordes) there was a specific exclusion of contracts with other players who were not presently active but who may be entitled to compensation for services previously rendered".[238] The five and their judgements rendered by Mr. Justice Denis Derocher were: Junior Ah You, $118,587; Ron Singleton, $15,002; Richard Harris, $17,465; Sonny Wade, $18,514.94; Dan Yochum, $15,000. The League's Montreal solicitor, Alan Hilton recommended an appeal but the news was yet another opportunity for critics to sound off against the CFL.

Leo Cahill returned, again, as General Manager of the Toronto Argonauts; Don Mathews, coach of the victorious B.C. Lions' Grey Cup team of 1985 was selected Coach of the Year, winner of the Annis Stukus Trophy. He immediately "donated his $5,000 award to wheelchair athlete Rick Hanson's Man in Motion tour.[239] The Saskatchewan Roughriders kicked off a nationwide appeal for support selling memberships to the Rider Pride National Booster Club at B.C. Place Stadium the site of the Saskatchewan Expo '86 reunion".[240]

Among the CFL rules approved for the 1985 season, the League sanctioned a proposal for regular season overtime. There had been the possibility of overtime in play-off games, two 10-minute halves with a kick-off between them. In 1985, the League decided to change the format to two 5-minute halves with a 90 second intermission and a kick-off to start each half. Each tied game during the regular season would see the two five minute halves in an attempt to resolve the tie. If at the end of the overtime, the teams were still tied, the game would end that way. The play-offs would continue with "a further 10 minute overtime session until a winner is declared".[241] Not all were happy with the decision. The Players' Association declared its opposition since the decision by-passed the collective agreement. As well, the television networks were not enthralled. They preferred a definite starting and finishing time for their telecasts. It made it easier to attract sponsors and also to schedule programming. Overtime could mean a decision to cancel a program which followed football or the overtime. It meant for complaints from one constituency or another and the possibility of increased costs without reimbursement. The League "decided not to pursue the idea of overtime because of the resistance by television networks".[242]The concept was introduced into League play for the first time in 1986. Two games needed overtime, neither one producing a winner. Saskatchewan and Hamilton tied in Regina at 21 on September 14 while in Ottawa November 1, Edmonton and Ottawa played to a 16–16 draw. The new play-off rule change was also put into practice that year. Montreal as the third place team in the East had a 4–14 record while in the west, Winnipeg and Calgary ended in third and fourth places with identical 11–7 records. It meant that under the new formula, 1st place Toronto and second place Hamilton with 10–8 and 9–8–1 records respectively would play a two game, total points to count series to determine the Eastern representative in the Grey Cup. In the West, Edmonton, as first place finisher at 13–4, would play Calgary while 2nd place B.C., at 12–6, would meet Winnipeg in semi-final sudden death action. Mitchell's original proposal would have seen the same 6 teams involved but since all 4 Western Clubs had better records than the two eastern, it was conceivable that the Grey Cup game might not have had an eastern representative in B.C. Place Stadium.

In the first play-off weekend, all went according to form. The Argonauts took a 14 point lead over Hamilton winning in the Tiger Cats' lair 31–17. B.C. defeated Winnipeg 21–14; Edmonton beat

Calgary 27–18. During play-off weekend #2 Edmonton rolled over B.C. by a 41–5 score. In Toronto, Hamilton mounted one of its traditional play-off comebacks and won by a 42–25 score to win the round.

To some extent the debate about the League intruded on what should have been a joyful week for the CFL. James Murphy of Winnipeg won the Outstanding Player award and the $5,000 which went with it. Calgary's Harold Hallman was chosen as the most outstanding rookie worth $2,500. The top Canadian was Winnipeg's Joe Poplawski. He had been runner-up the previous two years. His award was worth $3,500. The Defensive Player award went to B.C.'s James "Quick" Parker. It was accompanied by $3,500. Saskatchewan's Roger Aldag won the Offensive Line-man Award and $3,500. It was the first time since 1974 that a division swept all the awards and further testimony to the feeling that the West was best and the East still played "dumb football".

Some 59,621 spectators made their way into B.C. Place Stadium. Expectations among most of them were that the Jackie Parker coached Eskimos were prohibitive favourites over Al Bruno's Ti-ger Cats. When it was all over, the Tiger Cats were Grey Cup champions. Led by itinerant place kicker Paul Osbaldiston and quarterback Mike Kerrigan, who had replaced '85 Outstanding Player runner-up Ken Hobart, the eastern representative won a decisive 39–15 victory. It was a glorious culmination to a check-erboard year for Osbaldiston. He started with B.C., moved to Winnipeg and found a home in Hamilton. He kicked 6 field goals to tie a CFL Grey Cup record. In Hamilton, there was a huge outpouring of emotion. Fans took to the streets after the game to celebrate, some too exuberantly. At least one car was turned over, buses rocked, phone booths ripped out of their moorings and fires set. Police arrested 13.[243] The majority of the fans who entered the downtown area were noisy but well behaved. Po-lice closed off the area around Gore Park to let fans dance in the streets, chant "We're number one" and Oskie Wee Wee the night away." One fan tried to snatch the steel football from the statue outside the CFL Hall of Fame and gave up when the big metal titan wouldn't budge. A two kilometre stretch of King Street from Wellington to Bay, which was closed from 8:30p.m. to 11:30p.m., was wall-to-wall people".[244]

For owner Harold Ballard it was "one of the nicest things that's ever happened to me in life. I've waited a long time and there's been a lot of grief and misery and now I want the Stanley Cup. We'll get that too, you'll see".[245] On Tuesday, December 2, an estimated 10,000 gathered along the slushy streets to celebrate the Tiger Cats at City Hall. The noon hour crowd saw Harold Ballard present the city with the Grey Cup flag, the first one since 1972. A civic reception was followed by a private party for the players many of whom would leave afterwards for their homes.

To some "the Grey Cup game is like one of those scratch and win lottery tickets. When you erase the layers of show biz parades, breakfasts, luncheons, dinners, speeches, beauty pageants and obligatory bets between Mayors, you are left with a message that begins "sorry".[246] The lament was based on the fact that for the fifth time in seven years, the West was a heavy favourite; that according to the interlocking schedule, it was the best against the sixth. "It isn't even a good excuse of a grand national drunk any more"[247] whined one reporter.

The introspection and darts hurled at the eastern teams continued to question how the CFL could survive. After all, where Edmonton once drew crowds of 50,000 for any game, only 24,000 and 32,000 attended the play-off contests. The Argonauts and Rough Riders were for sale, the latter without a price tag, the owners ready "to donate them to a responsible group with the good of the community at heart".[248] Could the Alouettes survive with their small crowds? Who would pick up the bills in Hamilton after 83 year old Harold Ballard died?

There was more of a new dimension to it than the product on the field. The Hamilton-Toronto final game was riveted with emotion. As one reporter put it "Anyone who didn't like the Argos - Tiger Cats thriller has got no ear for music".[249] It was perception that was the reality:

> *The CFL suffers in comparison with the*
> *NFL and with major League baseball*
> *which has cut into allegiances in Ontario*
> *and Quebec for Toronto and Montreal fans.*
> *Playing Ottawa and Hamilton isn't nearly*
> *as socially stimulating as playing New York*
> *and Chicago. In Toronto, eyes turn long-*
> *ingly towards Buffalo where quarterback*
> *Jim Kelly has instilled fresh hopes. Across*
> *the country, NFL office pools keep stats not*
> *to find out who won but who beat the point*
> *spread.*[250]

To many the Grey Cup game had seemed a foregone conclusion. After all, it was the best place team in the country versus the sixth best. As if to underline that conviction an Angus Reid poll was released. The survey showed that "only 40% of Canadians feel the survival of the CFL is very or quite important. The survey also shows that only 28% of Canadian adults bothered to keep track of the CFL this year but 49% plan to watch the Grey Cup game . . . 70% said they would be against any form of government funding to keep the League alive".[251] As if to underline the severity of the results, a spokesman for the polling firm was quoted as saying: "When I look at these stats, I figure the League is living on borrowed time".[252] As if to underscore that sentiment an announcement was made in Ottawa on the same day that if "area businessmen could show the financial stability to maintain it", President of the Rough Riders, Terry Kielty, would recommend "the franchise be transferred to the community group as a gift from owner Allan Waters".[253] The Club had been bought in 1977 for $1.5 million and "had lost an estimated $5 million"[254] since then.

Chapter Three

A commemorative stamp was issued by Canada Post in what should have been a year of constant celebration for the CFL. It was the 75th playing of the Grey Cup Game. But in 1987 the very existence of the League was continually called into question. Crisis followed crisis as Clubs scrambled to come to grips with new realities; the public pressing for more information, the League reluctant to make too much public.

The first new awakening was the expiry of the CFL's television contract. The three year $33 million bonanza worth more than $1 million per year to each Club expired after the 1986 season. When negotiations began on a new contract, the scope of the reality became more evident. Rights holder Carling O'Keefe was given thirty days to submit a proposal. After two delays and extensions, it finally "offered a two year proposal at $4,700,000 per year".[255] The league informed Carling O'Keefe that the bid was not acceptable and pursued other avenues. It turned to CBC, CTV, Labatt's and Molson's for bids. In October of '86 Molson decided against purchase of the rights but did offer to be an advertiser. Labatt was interested only if "there was a total lift of television blackouts in the Toronto area." CBC and CTV responded with $3,300,000 and $3,100,000 for 1987.[256] All parties seemed aware that the League was in a poor bargaining position. The networks and Carling O'Keefe were offering to telecast only 54 of the 81 games but still wanted the "exclusive rights to the other 27".[257] The networks were asked for "certain promotional rights which they refused to consider."[258]

With the blackouts particularly in the southern Ontario area perceived to be the stumbling block, the League sought to remove it. They requested new "tenders" on the basis that there would be some relief from blackouts. The League was clearly in a quandary. Figures showed that lifting a blackout in Calgary would increase the potential television audience by 4% but lifting it in the Toronto/Hamilton area "could amount to a potential average increase of at least 24%"[259] The finding, presented in the League's report on TV Blackouts and Start Times was significant. The same report catalogued the fall in numbers of viewers suffered by the CFL: 1983, 952,600; 1984, 736,800; 1985, 837,000; 1986, 735,000.[260]

The effects of lifting blackouts and catering to the Ontario TV market would eventually have its effect. There was the Canadian tendency to "cottage" during the summer. The League had long refrained from playing weekend games during the summer for this reason. On the other hand, television was attracted to weekend games. After all, even at the cottage people could watch the game on their TV sets. Some even felt that there were too many games in the summer, not a traditional time to play football. It was a double-edged sword for the CFL. It wanted high viewer numbers for its television sales but not necessarily at the expense of fewer "bums in the seats."

Television was both a saviour and an irritant. There was no question that the League needed it as a source of revenue to sustain it in the style to which it had become accustomed. Yet the developing policy of lifting blackouts and catering to the large markets was annoying westerners who saw 5:00 p.m. and 6:00 p.m. starts to their games as just more evidence of the West catering to the East. And the Argonauts didn't seem to be benefiting from it. Its operating costs for the 1988 season were expected to be $2,000,000 with "radio revenue lower by $100,000 because of the cancellation by CFRB of the existing contract."[261] The radio station's contract with the Club giving it exclusiveness to Argo broadcasts was ineffective because of the League's attempt to generate more sponsorship money with blackout restrictions be-ing lifted.

While the League was lifting its blackouts in the Toronto/Hamil-ton area on an experimental basis in order to attract more reve-nue from television advertisers, satellite dishes continued to pose a threat in the smaller League centres. In Winnipeg with the bars lobbying to stay open Sunday afternoons, their "pirating" of the game's signals "would seriously impair the team's home gate."[262] It was an old problem but there had been changes in government. Prior to 1984, there had been an interventionist approach but latterly it was one of allowing "market forces" to work. The Commissioner recalled that "the former Liberal gov-ernment had laid several charges of satellite piracy against bars which were stealing signals. When the government changed in 1984, all such charges were dropped."[263] Cal Murphy, General Manager of the Blue Bombers, "advised that a former Winnipeg player, Steve Patrick, is a member of the CRTC and has promised his co-operation if the League acts quickly."[264]

Having identified a problem and finding a solution, however, were two different matters. Everybody seemed certain that the lifting of the blackout particularly in the Toronto/Hamilton area, was the key. The Argonauts again seemed to be central. They also were the stumbling block. Their owner was Carling O'Keefe, which was vying with Molson and Labatt for the beer market. Would they be willing to give assent to the lifting of the black-out, should a rival win the TV rights? The Argonauts also had a written agreement with CNE Stadium whereby they would have to pay additional rent should the blackout be lifted. The football Club had also signed a contract with radio station CFRB giving them exclusive control over the broadcasting of Toronto games.

When the League offered to make some concessions, Carling O'Keefe replied that it could not improve on its offer. Labatt withdrew from discussions on January 20 1987.[265] The networks were clearly in the driver's seat. The League decided to "break the schedule into packages and sell them independently, hopefully to encourage competitive bidding from the networks." [266] They didn't bite. On a package of 21 games CTV offered $1,500,000 and wanted the blackout lifted for all Friday night games; CBC's offer was $1,100,000 for 22 games. Both said the games were too hard to sell. When the League sought to purchase air time to produce its own games, the networks refused.[267]

In the end, the League, with few options remaining, decided to develop its own production, utilizing a variety of independent television stations. CFL Productions a League subsidiary was to be responsible for 42 games, selecting the play-by-play announcers as well as selling the advertising. Global Television, CHCH in Hamilton and independent stations serving the whole League were attracted and formed the CFL Productions' on air marketing arm, the Canadian Football Network (CFN). CBC "eventually offered to participate if it could produce its own games and use its air crews. The League agreed to this but retained the right of independent appraisal of CBC's on-air performances".[268] The League's network was to show the Friday night games, as well as late Sunday ones after Labour Day; CBC had Saturday and Sunday games. The remaining games mostly on Thursday nights and not carried by the League or CBC "would be assigned to TSN for $20,000 per game".[269]

With the realization that it was "a mammoth undertaking with great risk involved," the League also knew that there was "a potential to realize nearly $12,000,000 in revenue which could be enhanced by lifting the blackouts in each of Toronto and Hamilton and a commitment to lift a blackout anywhere if a stadium has achieved 90% sell-out 48 hours prior to game time".[270] It was Toronto's Ralph Sazio who injected some financial reality into the situation. He noted that in order to reach 1986 levels of revenue from television, the $4,000,000 rights fee added to the hoped for $12,000,000 from advertising would be reduced by the anticipated $5,000,000 cost to the League in producing the games. The alternative expressed by Norm Kimball was to accept the television networks' offers "in the total amount of $4,700,000, each team to receive only $500,000".[271] Kimball summarized:

The League position was either to accept the networks' offer and be at their mercy with limited prospects for the future or to accept the challenge of becoming master of its own destiny where its future depends largely on its own efforts. Without a formal resolution, it was unanimously agreed to proceed on this latter basis.[272]

The CFN had only one goal: to resurrect the value of the television rights by a three pronged approach:

1. *Demonstrate that the capability existed in Canada to produce NFL calibre programming.*

2. *Re-establish the premium value to advertiser participation in CFL telecasts.*

3. *Demonstrate that properly produced and marketed programming will generate substantially increased revenue.*[273]

What the League considered to be the beginning to a list of responses to the financial problems began in October of 1986 with the submission of a report by Leo Cahill and Paul Robson. Titled Report on Roster Considerations for 1987, it had its genesis in a discussion about Club rosters. It centred around the continual question of import and non-import players. There was a conviction as expressed by Earl Lunsford of Calgary that the product on the field was damaged because of the use of "inadequate personnel in key positions . . . a club will generally use non-import players in the leftover positions where they may not be best suited to play there." His solution was to increase the number of imports to 16 which combined with the quarterback position meant only seven non-import starting spots rather than the current ten. Hugh Campbell questioned the wisdom of the proposal. Would this lessen the incentive for aspiring Canadian players? Would it jeopardize the League's relationship with the CAFA and CIAU and more realistically would it result in the same sort of media criticism which the Designated Import rule had generated? Campbell mentioned "that there is more stability in a Club roster among its non-imports, while the regular turnover of import talent is a subject of complaint."[274]

Other general managers had different views. Ottawa reported that high schools were dropping football programs because of insurance costs. Toronto reported similarly, citing equipment, coaching and insurance as expenses. Cahill also expressed a reality which had been developing for some time: "The better quality non-imports are in a highly favourable bargaining position . . . they have reached salary parity with imports."[275] Hamilton's Joe Zuger continued along that line. Present non-imports were "somewhat complacent" because of the lack of competition for their jobs. "The large turnover in import personnel is due to greater competition for positions," he said.[276]Earl Lunsford agreed: "When Calgary recently added an import offensive lineman, the play of the non-imports suddenly improved."[277] Zuger expressed the opinion that "an increase in the number of imports would not necessarily increase overall salary costs. Some imports will play for less than what some non-imports are receiving." As for the fans, Lunsford, speaking from many years in the League as a player and General Manager, "pointed out that he . . . has gained the impressions that fans do not really care where the players came from. The game itself is exciting and could be more so with improved talent".[278]

Cahill and Robson's report, based on information shared at meetings September 28 and October 4, was thorough and clear. It highlighted some concerns. Some non-imports, specifically offensive linemen were being demanding and being paid "salaries far in excess of their ability to perform and the reluctance of coaches to play import players at line positions has enabled non-import linemen to demand higher salaries. . . . Compounding the entire problem is an abundance of import players willing to sign contracts at salaries well within the League's ability to pay."[279] The Report however stressed the wider context. Television revenues were uncertain; gates had fallen; prices of tickets even for strong franchises had increased in order to generate needed operating revenue. "In plain and simple language," they stated, "We have been operating beyond our means for some time. . . . We require $1.2 Million in television revenue annually just to exist".[280] Western teams were having problems with fund raising because of the perception that monies were going to salaries "rather than building a reserve fund for the long term stability of the franchise".[281] Privately owned teams were being forced to "depend on the enthusiasm of their ownership to continue to absorb losses".[282] Clearly, in Robson and Cahill's minds the League had "reached the 'Catch 22' point, where to field a competitive team, we face bankruptcy or to live within our means and be non-competitive".[283]

Figures were provided to show the concerns graphically. Players' salaries as a percent of gross gates had increased dramatically. In 1981 they stood at 58.4%. By 1985, they represented almost 75%. In the same period, salaries had increased by 50%, $14,688,700 in 1981 and $21,280,000 in 85. In the same time period the average import had moved from $52,600 to $72,259 while the average non-import was at $34,300 in 1981 and $53,189 in 1985. The Report laid out three strategies for dealing with the problem:

1. *Determine a roster size and ratio which is viable economically and competitively;*

2. *Accept a formula which will distribute talent to non-competitive teams;*

3. *Affect salary cost controls.*[284]

At the same time that revenues to the Clubs and League were shrinking, the CFL also instituted a "Stabilization Fund." Effective January 1, 1987 each Club was to remit a lump sum payment of $52,000 each year until $260,000 had been contributed. Concurrently, $4,000 was to be sent to the League office monthly until a further $200,000 had been collected. The total amount of $4,500,000 (500,000 × 9 Clubs) was to be used in the event a Club withdrew from the League Constitution. "The chief concern was that community-owned and operated frontlines were not in a position to pay such a sum in the event they become insolvent".[285] The idea was that the Stabilization Fund could "be used as an interior source of financing for the League to operate a franchise until a new franchise owner(s) could be put into place".[286] It would also contribute to the League since the Fund's annual earnings were to be "paid to the League and become part of the League's operating funds which at the end of 1986, was $2,524,000".[287] At the same time, it was made clear that it was "not a source of financing for a member Club which may be encountering financial difficulties. . . . Unanimous approval of members voting at a duly constituted meeting of the Board of Governors"[288] was required.

Curiously enough however, it wasn't the community-owned Clubs which were suffering the most. League gate equalization figures for the year ending December 31, 1986 showed that the four eastern Clubs, all privately owned had withdrawn funds from the League's gate equalization fund. Montreal received $281,342; Hamilton $208,851; Ottawa $171,676; and Toronto, $82,230. Only Saskatchewan in the West received funds in the amount of $67,281. The two largest contributors were Edmonton at $221,547 and B.C. at $362,612. Each put in the limit which was determined by taking a maximum of $20% of the difference between the Club's gross gate minus the League average.

Clearly the League needed to regroup. In what was called "a clandestine meeting in San Diego", [289]the CFL met to lay the foundations for the new approach. In a report prepared by Norm Kimball and Paul Robson, the following proposals were made:[290] Each Club was to "target its gross gate revenue at a minimum of $3.6 million." In addition "a maximum amount of $2.8 million" was to be set aside for salaries including players on the Reserve List, Injured List and Non-Active List." As part of the means of equalizing talent and lowering salary costs, an equalization draft was proposed. If such a draft did not work, Clubs would have to make decisions whether "to renegotiate or terminate through the waiver process." In any event, "Kimball cautioned that this discussion should be treated in a confidential manner . . . no reason for this information to become public . . . strictly an internal matter of cost control." Further, he stated: "There could be damaging consequences in media reaction, fan perception, and player morale if this subject reaches the public forum."

There were some dissenters. Saskatchewan's newly appointed General Manager, Bill Baker, complained that he had inherited a number of "long-term bonus commitments to high priced players." He doubted that he could meet the $2.8 million salary target and suggested he should not be penalized as a result. For Edmonton's Hugh Campbell, he had a variation of Yogi Berra's conundrum: "If people don't want to come to the game, how are you going to stop them?" In other words, Campbell asked, perhaps with one eye on the 1986 figures that showed losses in Montreal ($1,145,250) Ottawa ($1,985,573) Toronto ($2,670,954) Hamilton ($1,700,714) and Saskatchewan ($2,785,495), "How can a Club be forced to attain the gate revenue target of $3.6 million?"

Injuries could have an undesirable and unanticipated effect on the salary structure; all Clubs knew that. The League decided that while all teams would be bound by the salary cap of $2.8 million, Clubs whose injury costs were over the allowable $200,000 limit would not be penalized. If a Club did otherwise exceed the cap, twenty percent, originally proposed as 33%, would be required to be contributed to the Stabilization Fund.[291] Another area of concern was the player who was in his option year. The Players' Agreement called for him to receive 105% of his contract in his option year. Larry Shaw of Calgary asked how

> the salary limit will respond if a veteran player elects to play out his option with a mandatory 5% increase in his salary. Mr. Kimball replied that the solution to that problem is not to permit a player to play out his option if it is not possible to

negotiate with the player, the Club should release him.[292]

The League's response was to limit each Club, commencing in 1988 to $3,000,000 in expenditures "to cover all competitive aspects including salaries and allowances for players, coaches, personnel directors, scouts and trainers and the cost of training camps and tryouts." Each Club would be restricted to one head coach, four assistants and one personnel director. A sliding scale of penalties was put into effect:

(a) *20% on the first $100,000 in excess of $3,000,000.*

(b) *40% on the second $100,000 excess*

(c) *80% on the third $100,000 excess*

(d) *100% on any amount greater than $300,000 in excess plus loss of draft choices at the discretion of the Commissioner.*[293]

When the "special draft" was discussed, there was a fear that too much knowledge by the players and public would harm the League. Mitchell asked directly: "Can a draft of sorts now be held without it becoming public information that a certain player was available for the draft and another was not, and only this player and not that player?"[294] The result was an indication of some of the methods of misinformation: "it could be done discretely with subsequent announcements about being traded"; (Robson). "The head coach should be able to control his staff . . . no reason why a player should know whether he was or was not made available for the draft; (Faragalli) the waiver process be used by each Club to expose to the market those players whose costs now exceed their value." (Galat)

Almost immediately, the report was leaked and the League was again putting out fires. Some had blamed Leo Cahill for the information which "appeared in an Ottawa paper of January 9th which prompted adverse reactions from the Players' Association, the media and general public".²⁹⁵ At the Management Council meeting in Edmonton, January 21/87 "on a point of order" Cahill stated emphatically that he was not in any way responsible for a lapse in security following the meeting of January 7th.²⁹⁶ The League was still sensitive to stinging criticism it received, again from an Ottawa source, for meeting "in the United States when the value of the Canadian dollar was low as well".²⁹⁷

The owners denied that there was to be any such process. George Reid, President of the Players' Association, took their word at face value: "There will be no equalization draft and no 24-man protective list in the CFL." He said that's what the owners have told him and he is taking them at their word.²⁹⁸ Clearly, however it was the adverse publicity surrounding decisions which bothered the League. Mitchell's plan was "to turn the adverse publicity around to make it a positive message. The Clubs are acting collectively to improve the League's product and to help the non play-off Clubs to be more competitive without damage to the quality of the Clubs already in a competitive position".²⁹⁹

What the League termed its Competitive Balance Plan took place during the week of February 15, 1987. The three teams with the worst records — Montreal, Ottawa and Saskatchewan-, were able to select four players each from the non-protected list from each of the remaining six teams. No team could lose more than two players. The "secret equalization draft" was "intended to be strictly hush-hush."³⁰⁰ The Hamilton Tiger-Cats were reported to have been "howling because they had two players pilfered".³⁰¹ Eastern All-Star centre Marv Allemang was chosen by Ottawa and running-back Walter Bender by Saskatchewan. The fact that the word "pilfered" was used illustrates that some of the Clubs were attempting to deflect the criticism of the secret draft from themselves to elsewhere. Saskatchewan probably benefited mostly from the plan in terms of quality, picking up quarterback John Hufnagel from Winnipeg. The CFL plan to have Clubs lower their salary costs continued in other areas. Argos announced that centre Willie Thomas, reportedly earning $85,000, would have to take a pay cut or be released.³⁰² Thomas signed later with the Alouettes as a free agent. Winnipeg's running back Willard Reeves was asked "to take a hefty pay cut in his $160,000 a year contract, which he had signed with Paul Robson".[303] The League's Outstanding Player of 1986, the Blue Bombers' James Murphy, was reported to be having difficulty negotiating a raise from his $90,000 salary.[304]

Throughout the League, the reality of the lost television revenue was everywhere. While an optimistic Doug Mitchell informed Clubs to budget for television revenue of $400,000, a shortfall of $800,000 from the previous year, Saskatchewan's Bill Baker estimated that his Club was "starting the season $1.5 Million worse off than last year".[305] Edmonton and Calgary were counting on a "$450,000 rent abatement." In addition, "the two clubs approached the Alberta Gaming Commission for the rights to jointly stage a lottery with $100 tickets offering opportunities to win new houses, new cars and vacations",[306] something Saskatchewan did in 1986 to earn close to one million dollars. The cost cutting moved into the organizations. Edmonton froze the salaries of "all employees including secretaries, coaches, players and support staff with three or more years tenure with the team".[307] B.C. did similarly with General Manager Joe Galat and Head Coach Don Mathews taking salary freezes. While most teams invited some 90 players to training camp, Winnipeg sought to lower expenses by bringing in only seventy as a further cost-cutting scheme. The day before training camp began the Blue Bombers released seven-year veteran lineman Mark Moors who was also the Player Rep. The somewhat bitter Moors "had some advice for younger players. I wouldn't recommend Players' Association involvement to anyone who wants a nice secure career in the CFL".[308]

Province-wide lotteries, $1 Million lines of credit, government assistance, less expensive hotels and seeking cheaper fares from airlines were all becoming standard practices for CFL teams in 1987.

Compounding all of the League's problems was the Montreal Alouette franchise. They "reduced ticket prices by $2.00 in an attempt to lure more fans into cavernous Olympic Stadium".[309] The club also divested themselves of the "hefty pacts of quarterback Brian Ransom ($100,000) and offensive lineman Glen Keeble ($75,000) while negotiating salary cuts with defensive end Doug Scott and tight end Nick Arakgi. The latter was returning to action after suffering two broken vertebrae in his neck early in the 1986 season.

Both Charles Bronfman and Imasco Limited had informed the CFL that they wished to withdraw from ownership. They would continue their involvement until an additional $3,000,000 was lost. "The loss in 1986 was close to $4,000,000 making their cumulative losses since 1982 close to $20,000,000.[310]Kimball, who had joined the Club in March of 1986, suggested that it "was not in their best interests to withdraw quickly but that they should first explore other alternatives". [311]

A poll confirmed what was long felt: If the team's performance improved, fan interest would "increase from 3% to 41%. The major challenge was to appeal to the Francophone community which is 73% of Montreal, and change its perception of the Club as an Anglophone operation which reluctantly condones the Francophone." [312]

Kimball proposed to Bronfman and Imasco, "in return for their undertaking to assume responsibility for all liabilities of the Club to date plus the posting of a $2,000,000 line of credit",[313] he would assume control of the Alouettes and seek other investors. The League was also to "guarantee that the 1987 season will be completed. . . . The League will somehow to be responsible for costs beyond "the $2,000,000 line of credit if further partners could not be found."[314] This last point was not well received by the CFL; it chose to strike a committee of Ottawa's Dave Gavsie and Toronto's Ralph Sazio to meet with Kimball "to develop the details of an accommodation package that will be acceptable to all parties.[315]

By April, Kimball was able to announce to the League that he had attracted Edmonton businessman Jim Hole as a partner with the Alouettes. [316] By June it became obvious to all that the franchise was in deep trouble. Only 4,000 seasons' tickets had been sold; "a substantial number of cancellations particularly in block purchases from the business community" [317] were made. Norm Kimball had "reached the conclusion albeit reluctantly, that Montreal was no longer a viable market for a football franchise."[318]

A special meeting was called at the Airport Marriott Hotel in Mississauga, Ontario. The CFL was presented with five alternatives. It could continue the present operation in the hopes that improvement would occur. It could use the League's new Stabilization Fund to provide financial support. It could have a three game trial period to buy some time to revise the 1987 schedule. The team could be moved to another city, London was mentioned, but there was no large stadium and time was too short. The operation could be terminated immediately, the schedule reconstructed, Montreal's home games eliminated, its away games taken by teams in the bye position for the most part.

In the end, the League chose the latter option. A formal resolution was passed. The Alouette ownership was to be responsible for all debts incurred to that date; the League would pick up the salaries of the players on the roster for one game. All contracts of the players were to be terminated after that and the waiver process would disperse them throughout the League.[319]

Winnipeg moved to the Eastern Division.

There were other decisions.Bill Baker flew to Calgary to meet with George Reed to inform him personally. Norm Kimball was given a vote of thanks "for his contributions to the League as a Club executive for 22 seasons and in particular his most recent efforts to direct the Montreal Club into a viable franchise operation."[320]Kimball's two committee roles were filled by Winnipeg's Ken Matchett on the Television Committee and Saskatchewan's Bill Baker on the Player Relations Committee.

One month later, while the Alouettes and Norm Kimball had faded from the public's mind to a great extent, they were still uppermost at CFL meetings. Grey Cup ticket prices, which had previously been set at $45, were readjusted to $60 along the sideline and $50 in the east end zone of B.C. Place. At a previous meeting, the League had awarded the 1990 Grey Cup game to Montreal but had not publicized it. It was moved to Vancouver. Similarly a meeting scheduled in September for Montreal was also transferred to Mississauga. There were second thoughts from some about the League's hasty rush to rescue Norm Kimball. B.C. felt that the League was "entitled to more specific information about the disposition of the final payment by the major partners in the amount of two million dollars."[321] Ottawa stated that while they weren't looking for a detailed and itemized report on disbursements, nonetheless, Dave Gavsie said he "would feel more comfortable if he could see a letter from Mr. Kimball to the Commissioner confirming that neither he nor Mr. Jim Hole had received any personal benefit from the two million dollar payment by the major partners."[322] There was also a fear that the League, in agreeing to pay for the one game salaries, opened itself to possible suit for monies due to creditors by the Alouettes.

The Montreal demise presented even more problems just when it appeared that the League had its television concerns under control, The CBC dropped two games from its telecast schedule and renegotiated its financial commitments. The League's CFN was also forced to drop two games of the revised schedule while TSN was forced to drop seven in reducing its telecasts to 12 games. CTV had been a lukewarm participant and had even intervened against the CFN when it applied to the CRTC for a licence application. The most dramatic effect, of course, was with Radio Canada, the French language of the CBC. Two major sponsors, Carling O'Keefe and Petro-Canada, cancelled their contracts. The League pumped some funds into the operation because "it was deemed important that the League continue to enjoy French language exposure not only in Quebec," [323] but wherever the League's message was lacking.

There was some backtracking on advertising contracts. They had to be revised. Where alternative dates were not acceptable, the League issued credits. Carling O'Keefe was given $160,000 in credits. [324] The "net effect of Montreal folding (was) estimated at between three-quarters to a million dollars."[325] There was also the loss of potential advertisers. "Those who were considering a CFL buy preferred to invest discretionary television budgets in other properties (i.e.,) Blue Jays, Canada Cup, Olympics."[326]

In mid-season, the teams were asked to assess their season's financial state and their prospects for 1988. B.C. had budgeted for revenue of $9.2 million and a profit of $140,000. After the first four home games, attendance had declined by 40,000 "reducing projected revenue by $1.1 million and a resulting operating loss of $660,000." Part of the blame was attributed to Saturday night games starting at 5:00 p.m. for 8:00 p.m. prime time viewing in the East. B.C. with its season ticket base of 27,000 was projecting total expenses of $7.7 million and salary reduction of $300,000 for 1988.[327]

In Edmonton, the Eskimos had budgeted for a loss of $500,000 on football operations. In spite of the adverse League publicity which had "damaged the game's image in Edmonton," [328] the Club was not in financial trouble. It had 28,000 season tickets, a player budget of $2.8 million and an overall expense budget of $7 Million.[329]

Calgary was having cash flow problems. A loss of $1 Million was indicated based on the average attendance of 21,000 and 19,000 season tickets. The original budget had been based on a break-even attendance of 27,000.

In Regina, the effects of "increased ticket sales, rent concessions, forgiveness of 1986 rent and a lottery"[330] had trimmed the projected loss from $1 million reported at the May 11 meeting to $100,000. It had a season ticket base of 17,000, expected revenue of $5.2 million from all sources and expenses of $5.3 million. Its total gate forecast was $3.5 million. Winnipeg was anticipating gate revenue of $4.3 million plus other sources amounting to $625,000. Total expenses, including "roster costs of $2.9 million" was forecast at $5.6 million. The loss of $740,000 in football operations would be offset by "off field producing revenues of $530,000. The net loss for 1987 was estimated at $200,000 bringing the Club's total deficit to $400,000.[331] Winnipeg had 19,000 season ticket subscribers and was planning to raise prices in 1988.

In Hamilton, the costs of the operation were $7 Million and included players' salaries of $2.9 million. Hamilton had 8,000 season tickets; the 1987 loss was predicted to be as it was in 1986, $2.7 million. Joe Zuger, Hamilton General Manager, described the Club owner, Maple Leaf Gardens Limited, as "very positive and helpful." Indeed, in spite of his ongoing losses, Harold Ballard "sprung for about $100,000 to have rings made for his Grey Cup Champion Tiger Cats".[332]

In Toronto, where Carling O'Keefe had been taken over by another company, the Argonauts expected to lose $1.5 million as a result of $4.8 million revenue and expenses of over $6 million. Player costs were $2.6 million and, according to Sazio, exceeded net gate receipts. The Argonauts had 18,527 season tickets and its "walk in crowd (had) been below expectations" [333] Ottawa was anticipating total revenues of $4 million and total costs of $5.8 million which included $2.8 million player salary costs. Off field revenues were expected to reduce the loss to $500,000 for 1987. Ottawa's season ticket sales were 10,000.

Almost all were in agreement that the on field product of the game was excellent. It was in the area of marketing and public perception where improvement was needed. It was the media who had "downgraded the League unjustly. Somehow it had to be convinced that a quality product is being provided and is definitely worth another look."[334]Mitchell confirmed what some had been saying all along, that the games were exciting and TV ratings on the increase. Indeed, one report suggested that CFL telecasts "have never been better particularly those produced by the CFN. They're not home grown cheer leaders. Analyst Neil

Lumsden is the best thing that's happened to CFL telecasts in years. Knuckles Irving and Dave Hodge can't make the games any better but they certainly made them sound better. Together, they've made the CFL action so entertaining, some viewers may be tempted to rush out and buy tickets."[335]

The League had taken a calculated risk in operating its own television productions, some said it had no real option: advertiser confidence had been low because of the Montreal collapse and "other organizational difficulties"; the breweries had no competitive incentive to bid on the rights; previous to the League's takeover of production "the calibre of CFL television programming had been steadily declining" with the networks unable or unwilling to correct the situation or indeed, acknowledge it; the decline in viewership was blamed on the games and the League with the networks unwilling to shoulder any of the blame. The bottom line was that advertising revenue had declined dramatically. Attendance was down close to 300,000 less than 1986 at stadiums throughout the League.[336]

Team	Avg. Attendance	Stadium
B.C.	36,474	59,476
Calgary	23,837	38,190
Edmonton	33,581	60,081
Saskatchewan	23,161	27,637
Winnipeg	26,841	32,946
Toronto	27,355	54,545
Hamilton	16,999	29,355
Ottawa	18,354	34,838

With the plethora of problems ready to surface at any time, the League decided it needed an Executive Committee "to form accessory plans and with authority to act on behalf of the Board of Governors when necessary".[337] Committee members were the Commissioner, Ken Matchett of Winnipeg, Sazio of Toronto and Chuck Walker of B.C. There was a feeling that perhaps the time had come to eliminate the cap on what wealthier clubs could contribute to the gate equalization plan, or perhaps that it was time to do away with the equalization plan altogether and replace it with some sort of gate sharing practice as was the case in the NFL. Later, it was recommended that the gate equalization plan be replaced with "gate sharing arrangements . . . (and) visiting teams would receive 40% of the gate. The home Club would receive 60% minus appropriate taxes. The money accrued by visiting Clubs would be pooled and divided eight ways at season's end."[338] As forward looking as it appeared to be, the plan was turned down, not accepted at the Governors' level.

There had been some rumblings from various sources about the import/non-import quota usually ending with the suggestion that the quota be abolished. Mitchell was adamant: "There's no movement afoot to change the existing Canadian-American ratio. . . . We've operated as the Canadian Football League and are very committed to Canadians. I'd have to be dragged across the parking lot, kicking and screaming if we ever reduced the number of Canadians"[339] It was not entirely evident that the Commissioner had the complete respect of his members. A request that notice of motion be waived for a telephone conference meeting on October 30/86 "to deal with the Commissioner's contract" had been defeated by a 6-3 vote. Not until November 26 was it discussed and then it was renewed until May 1989 but with a 40% pay cut to a reported $165,000.[340]To what extent the cut was voluntary is unknown. There was a fear that the Commissioner's power was being eroded. He had suspended Saskatchewan's James Curry for a hit on Argonaut quarterback John Congemi. The one game suspension was not being served since the player, with his Association's backing, had appealed. "If I told you I like the process, I'd be less than candid. We're working towards putting the Commissioner's authority back into these matters, he said bluntly."[341]

In early January, the affairs of the CFL attracted a wider interest because of the ownership situation. Allan Waters had offered to turn the Ottawa Club over to the community for the token fee of $1. On January 2/87 Paul Robson resigned as General Manager of the Blue Bombers to take a similar position with the Rough

Riders. He signed a three-year contract. In Winnipeg the successful Cal Murphy moved into the General Manager's position, his replacement as coach, the youthful Mike Riley, son of the former Winnipeg coach Bud Riley. In Ottawa, the new owners were identified as "The Ottawa Rough Rider Limited Partnership and a general partner 685367 Ontario Limited"[342] They would begin operations with a clean financial slate.

As the 1987 season was coming to a close, Ottawa, the city where the Grey Cup game of 1988 was to be held, was in danger of folding its franchise after the 1987 season. Some of the limited partners of the Community operated Club were reluctant to make further contributions to its operation. A further $450,000 was necessary. The outlook was "not promising".[343] Ottawa Mayor Jim Durrell, invited to ensure the League that the Grey Cup plans were well under way, offered some unsolicited advice to the CFL. He stated that the League's overall image was at fault. "What is needed," he continued, "is for the League to address the problem by making changes to improve its image. . . . advocated expansion to the U.S.A., modification in playing rules, revision of the import quota, and elimination of the television blackout."[344] The Mayor said that the media criticism across the country was "a well orchestrated campaign to destroy the League. . . . The public perception of Canadian football is that it is inferior to the American game in its presentation and entertainment value."

Some major reforms were announced for the 1988 season. It was to begin one month later than in 1987, July 20 being the target date with training camps opening around June 15. The League would still play an 18 game schedule but squeeze them into 16 weeks, the "double headers" being played prior to Labour Day on the understanding that a Club would not have to play within 3 days of its prior game.[345]

In the East, Winnipeg finished with a 12-6 record, Toronto at 11-7, Hamilton, 7-11 and Ottawa won three and lost 15 to end up in last place. In the Western Division B.C. was 12-6, Edmonton 11-7 and Calgary in third place with a 10-8 record. Saskatchewan at 5-12-1 missed the play-offs. Toronto defeated Hamilton in the East semi-final 29-13 and Winnipeg in Winnipeg by a 19-3 score. Its opponent in the Grey Cup Game was to be Edmonton. The Eskimos had defeated arch-rival Calgary 30-16 and first place finisher BC 31-7. Criticisms of the CFL and its Canadian quota system came under renewed attack. Just one week prior to the Grey Cup game, Harold Ballard launched a salvo:

> *The salvation of the Canadian Football League lies in ditching the sport for the version played south of the border. We should play on their field and have four downs and break down the resident rule: Everyone seems to like American football so who are we to sit and buck it? . . . It's a shame to deny thousands of boys in the United States a chance to play in Canada and if we can get some of those hillbillies out West to think that way, we'll be alright.*[346]

It sounded as a typical Ballard grab for the headlines, but there was enough of an echo to what was being said that John Robertson, a reporter with the Star, rushed to challenge Ballard. Pointing out quality Argo players who happened to be Canadians, Robertson asked: "How long can we perpetrate the myth that Canadians can't sell tickets if we keep letting these guys go out there and play so great?" Challenging Ballard's belief that the CFL should go to unlimited imports, Robertson wrote:[347]

> *That would not only get rid of those Canadians but would also destroy the native belief that CFL football is a different game and a more exciting game. If we used only Americans who can't make the NFL, they could turn out to be as marketable as the now defunct World Football League or the equally defunct US Football League. Oh yes, one more thing Harold, when you do*

your Tepperman number for the benefit of the gullible Canadian media, make sure you alienate the Western owners. We've all been getting too chummy lately. Disunity is where it's at. Go for it Harold. We desperately need a CFL downer this week, anything to take the fans' attention from Sunday's Grey Cup game. It could be a classic.

In the lead up to the game, the week's festivities in Vancouver included the presentation of the CFL's outstanding player awards. Winnipeg players won the majority of them: Quarterback Tom Clements, the Most Outstanding; Defensive back Scott Flagel as the Outstanding Canadian; Chris Walby as the Outstanding Offensive Lineman. Other awards were presented to Toronto's Gill Fenerty as the Rookie of the Year and B.C.'s Gregg Stumon as the Outstanding Defensive Player of the Year.

In the 75th playing of the Grey Cup Game, 59,478 spectators and a nation-wide audience watched John Robertson's prediction come true. It was a "Classic" contest, settled as the game was ending by Gerry Kauric's 49 yard field goal with only 45 seconds remaining. The Joe Faragalli coached Edmonton Eskimos defeated the Argonauts 38-36 to claim the newly renewed cup which had been rebuilt at a cost of $15,000; It now contained the name of every player who had been on a winning Grey Cup team.

There were highlights which would keep fans talking for a long time: Henry "Gizmo" Williams ran a missed field goal back 115 yards for Edmonton's first touchdown; Danny Barrett, on a quarterback draw, sprinted 25 yards into the end zone to give Argos a 36-35 lead with less than three minutes to play; the strong performance in relief by Edmonton quarterback Damon Allen who took over from Matt Dunigan with his team trailing 24-10 and led them on two 80-yard drives; the running of Milson Jones "whose clutch carries down the stretch enabled the Eskimos to keep their . . . drive alive."[348] Some reporters saw the game as a chance to counter the prevailing negative publicity about the CFL and the Canadians in it. Milt Dunnell, paraphrasing Mark Twain wrote: "The reports of Canadian Professional Football's demise are greatly exaggerated."[349] Others pointed out that Edmonton started only 11 imports among the 24 and played nine Canadians on offense in the greatest game in CFL history . . . some corpse, eh?"[350]

Once again it was decided to hold a draft to aid the two last place teams in each division. Whereas in 1987 it was called the Competitive Balance Plan, in 1988 it was more appropriately named the Equalization Draft. Held in March, the rules were streamlined. Only Ottawa and Saskatchewan, the two last place teams in their divisions were eligible to choose up to three players from the other six teams. Ottawa was to have first selection. Edmonton, Toronto, B.C. and Winnipeg were allowed to protect 26 players, Hamilton and Calgary, 27. No team could lose more than one player from its roster with the selecting team responsible for the existing contractual obligations.

It was contracts and money which attracted most of the headlines. Once again the CFL was attempting to stay below a $3 Million expense cap. Throughout the League, higher paid players were either waived, traded or re-signed to a lower contract. Edmonton's Matt Dunigan was sent to B.C. Roy Dewalt, signed as a free agent by Winnipeg in June, was traded to Ottawa in October. Tom Clements, it was rumoured, was asked "to take a whopping $100,000 cut in his $280,000 contract."[351] Clements chose to retire, forcing the Blue Bombers to go with two first-year quarterbacks, Sean Salisbury and Lee Saltz. Slot back John Pankratz was able to receive money he felt owed to him by B.C., $12,500, only after he threatened a law suit. Outstanding Player Lui Passaglia was placed on waivers by the Lions in order to re-negotiate his contract. Passaglia was later re-signed but that was not the case with defensive lineman Rick Klassen "who was to make $125,000 this year and has been asked to take a 40% pay cut"[352] Klassen, who was later signed to a contract by Saskatchewan, had flippantly announced that "he'd do it if General Manager Joe Galat revealed how much he made and then took a similar cut."[353]

Managers and coaches were not immune, the League seemed anxious to leak information that all were doing their part. Argonaut coach Bob O'Billovich was awarded the Annis Stukus Trophy as CFL Coach of the Year for 1987 and the $5,000 that went with it. He was seeking a three-year contract renewal "or at least a two-year deal with a raise in the second year. For all his worth, the Argos wanted him to sign a new contract for two years without a contract increase in either season. He settled for a one year deal with the same pay level."[354] Winning Grey Cup coach, Joe Faragalli, "took a reported 20% cut in pay when signing a long term contract."[355] Among the General Managers, Joe Galat revealed that he had "agreed to a substantial cut in pay" as had Winnipeg's Cal Murphy and head coach Mike Riley. In Ottawa, General Manager Paul Robson took a "$40,000 cut from his reported $110,000 contract".[356]

The CFL seemed to be convulsing. The widespread reports about its woes spawned all sorts of 'solutions'. Some wanted to go back to a 16 or 14 game schedule; to start practices later in order to allow players to have a career outside football to encourage them to settle in the community and thereby develop more identification with it. There were calls for expansion into the United States, four downs and 10 metres football, removal of the yard between the opposing lines, moving the goal posts to the end of the goal area to make for more difficult points after touchdowns. Some even wanted to remove the extra point attempt altogether, substituting the running or passing of the ball for the after-touchdown score. And of course there were still those who advocated the removal of awarding a point for a missed field goal attempt. The League seemed to be more interested in fine tuning its rules rather than tampering. Winnipeg even proposed playing an exhibition game in Ottawa on June 29 and experimenting with four downs and the elimination of the one yard restraining zone on the line of scrimmage"; [357]it was defeated 3-2 with two abstentions.

Rule changes approved by the League included the elimination of blocking below the waist on interception and fumble returns, the shortening of half time from 15 to 14 minutes and the speeding up of kick-off procedures following a touchdown or field goal.[358]

There was a change in rosters for the 1988 season. The League decided to allow each team to dress 36 players, 20 of whom were non-imports, 14 imports and two quarterbacks. In 1986, it had been 35 players (13 imports, 19 non-imports, 3 QBs. There had been a downward adjustment in 1987 to 34 players (13 imports, 19 Non-imports, 2 QBs). The "Designated Import" returned with a bit of a twist. He was to be a "special team" player and originally able "to enter the game at another position only upon the understanding that another import player is required to leave the game for that play".[359] At a later meeting "special team" was defined to include those related to the kicking game rather than a "short yardage" unit. The same meeting clarified that the "designated special teams player," if he had replaced an import of another position, "could remain in the game provided there was no increase in the number of imports on the field."[360]

The League was also attempting to restrict those who wanted to play out their option. Any such player who signed a contract with another League could not return to the CFL in the same year. If he did so in some other season, his status as a veteran was to be forfeited.[361]

The NFL wished to play an exhibition game in Toronto. Promoters scheduled it. The League objected and it was cancelled.A similar game was scheduled for Montreal which now was a non-CFL city. When Mitchell complained to NFL Commissioner Pete Rozelle, he was told that "The clubs arranged their own pre-season game." The CFL decided "to inform the Federal Government of the League's displeasure".[362]The NFL's promoters in Toronto were persistent. They asked the CFL to withdraw its objections, specifically the Argonauts' control over which football teams could play at CNE Stadium. They cited a statement from Hugh Campbell saying he had "no objections" to such a game being played. Campbell for his part declared to the League that his statement had been taken out of context and "emphasized that he is and always has been totally opposed to such a game and urged that the League do everything to prevent it."[363] The promoters attempted to appeal to the CFL's need for cash from a game which would probably attract over 50,000 spectators. They offered to play an "NFL-CFL double header." The League wasn't buying. They voted to continue "to oppose the playing of an NFL game in Canada".[364]

In spite of its consolidation approach the League was attracting interest from afar. Expansion outside the country was becoming an option. There was a proposal from a group in London, England seeking to hold a pre or post-season game. In addition it wanted to discuss televising games throughout Europe "and eventually to have a franchise in the League."[365] An American, Russell Moon of Norcross, Georgia, had also sent a certified cheque for $25,000 while "making application for new membership based in the Province of Quebec."[366] A third application was received from Sentry National Sports Production Limited. The firm invited the CFL "to hold a pre-season game in Los Angeles in July, 1988. Sentry would fund and promote the game and pay the expenses of the teams involved and in return, would expect to receive exclusive rights for expansion into the USA for a period of three years. It would guarantee at least two new teams during that time."[367]

The feeling was that Sentry in part was attracted by the League's efforts to control its costs but that the proposal raised more questions than not. Did the League want to play a pre-season game in NFL territory when it was objecting to that League's proposed exhibition games in Montreal and Toronto? Did the League want to expand into the USA? If it did, should the League give that right "exclusively to other persons?"[368]

The League was constantly seeking to address the concern about its image in an effort to upgrade it. Player cards were one way of addressing the situation. They had been part of the CFL since the fifties but had fallen out of favour in the seventies. The entrance of baseball onto the Canadian scene had revealed the huge latent interest in sport cards. The Players' Association was "dealing with the producer of player cards who was creating a collection series such as done in hockey, baseball and the National Football League."[369]If the League chose to get involved, it would cost "less than two thousand dollars a Club," the remaining 50% to be borne by the players. O Pee Chee bubble gum was making a similar proposal which Cal Murphy was to flush out for a late meeting.

In a more specific way, however, the League addressed the "Image" problem by hiring a public relations firm from Toronto. Fraser Kelly Corpworld Inc. was comprised of Fraser Kelly, "well known as a former journalist in the print, radio and television media . . . Bill Wilkerson . . . background in government industry and banking . . . Larry Stout, a former CBC news commentator."[370] Kelly and Wilkerson had approached the Commissioner and "offered to help develop a coherent communications strategy which combines the flexibility and imagination of each franchise with the collective clout of the League as a whole and at the same time being aware of fiscal responsibility.[371]

It was exactly the message that the League wanted to hear when the trio appeared at a January Management Council Meeting. The "great interest in the League across Canada" had to be "translated into attendance." Tradition was an asset. Cities could be twinned, east with west, to develop new rivalries. There needed to be a co-ordination of "the kinds of messages being sent out by working with the League Office to accentuate the positive so that the same message is treated the same way in each city."[372] The firm foresaw "sessions with head coaches or media directors as well as general managers . . . at a cost of $800 per Club per month for three months or a grand total of $21,600."[373] The proposal was unanimously endorsed by the Management Council.[374]

Edmonton, the self-styled "city of champions" because of its hockey and football successes continued to be the model for a CFL operation. Its season ticket base in 1987 was 27,000, still a far cry from its high of 52,000 in 1982, but the highest in the League and the envy of the other Clubs. It was for that reason primarily that the League and the Players' Association decided, once again, to resurrect the All Star game with yet again a different format. The Grey Cup Champion Eskimos met the League All-Stars on June 23 at Commonwealth Stadium. A record turnout of 27,573 saw the All-Stars prevail by a 15-4 score. The All-Stars' quarterbacking duties were shared by former Eskimo now B.C. Lion Matt Dunigan along with erstwhile B.C. player Roy Dewalt, now a member of the Winnipeg Blue Bombers.

Money woes continued to be the dominant news about the CFL prior to the opening of camps. It was obvious that "the Clubs missed the opportunity to build up reserve funds during the halcyon days of high television revenue."[375] Not only that, according to Doug Mitchell "a good rule of thumb for a Club is to keep its player salary cost at less than 50% of its overall revenue".[376] That was not happening. As a result the Clubs' financial reports read like a litany of woes prior to the opening of training camps in 1988. Almost every Club was counting on a high "walk-in" count to augment their season's ticket sales. Ottawa had sold 12,700 was hoping for another 1,000. If it averaged 21,000 for each home game, it would still incur a loss of $1,200,000. Even with attendance of 25,000 and a break in taxes and rent the loss would still be in the neighbourhood of $100,000. Toronto had sold only 9,571 season's tickets but it was "in a more fortunate position with its generous ownership." Leo Cahill, in a subtle reference to President Ralph Sazio's approach declared that Argos would not have "any problem in meeting the expense cap since costs are strictly controlled." Hamilton's season's tickets were at 6900 with a hoped for goal of 8,600. A new stadium rental plan was being pursued in order to reduce costs. Winnipeg's report was encouraging. Eighteen thousand season tickets were sold. Over 20,000 were anticipated. Expenses were high, making the $3 Million expense target doubtful. In Saskatchewan, there was a "large deficit." Response to the ticket campaign was disappointing with only 12,000 sold. While average attendance in '87 was 23,699, severe drought conditions prevailed in the south where the Club's main support was. The City of Regina had agreed to replace the turf at Taylor Field and the Club was opening a CFL merchandise shop at the stadium. In Calgary where the glow of the Winter Olympics was still in the air, the Club was hoping to "capture the local enthusiasm." Fifteen thousand seats had been sold toward the Club's target of 22,000 and a profit of $100,000. There was an accumulated debt of $1,600,000 which still had to be paid. In B.C., the Club had a "substantial debt on its Surrey training facility, high rental at B.C. Place Stadium and the legacy of bad publicity arising from its financial position and its relations with players Dewalt, Pankratz and Passaglia." It had sold 12,000 season tickets and paid $300,000 to the Club's creditors.[377]

At a subsequent meeting in September, the Clubs agreed that they should give a monthly outlook update to each other in order "to provide an early warning system to isolate trouble spots in the League."[378] The reports revealed some of the areas which affected the teams' profit and loss. There were debts to service. Saskatchewan, for example, began the season with a deficit of $1,000,000, "financed by three bank lines of credit in the aggregate of $800,000 and a stabilization fund loan of $200,000."[379] One of the major unknowns was the number of injuries a team would suffer. Contracts would continue to be paid and replacements would be brought in. An uncontrollable rise in expenses was the result chiefly because of the nature of the game. It was therefore in the best financial interests of the League to legislate as much safety, through the rules and equipment, as possible. Examples of equipment were multi-cleated shoes and knee braces; examples of rules were prohibition of blocking below the waist on returns and interceptions and the rule banning "spearing" or making primary contact with the helmet.

On the field a young rookie running sensation from Simon Fraser, Orville Lee burst onto the scene but not even he was able to propel Ottawa past another dismal season. Lee was the League's

Outstanding Rookie for 1988 but the Rough Riders finished with a 2-16 record costing Head Coach Fred Glick and General Manager Paul Robson their jobs. Hamilton at 9-9 with Al Bruno back at the helm, returning after suffering a heart attack in 1987, finished in third place in the east. Winnipeg with an identical 9-9 finish was awarded second place and hosted the eastern semi-finals defeating the Tiger Cats by a 35-28 score. Hamilton's Grover Covington was selected as the CFL's Most Outstanding Defensive Player. Toronto Argonauts, at 14-4 were the class of the Eastern Division during the season but it was Winnipeg which prevailed in the final, defeating the Argos 27-11 in Toronto. The Argonauts not only lost the chance to appear in the 1988 Grey Cup game, they also lost General Manager Leo Cahill, who was relieved of his duties, again.

In the West the Stampeders under Normie Kwong as General Manager and Lary Kuharich's first full year as head coach, finished with a 6-12 record and in last place. The Western semi-final was played between B.C. Lions, 3rd place finishers under head coach Larry Donovan, 10-8 in his first full season, and Saskatchewan which under General Manager Bill Baker and coach John Gregory, finished second with an 11-7 record. B.C. won a surprisingly easy 42-18 victory led by Matt Dunigan and David Williams, selected as the Outstanding Player in the CFL. Saskatchewan's Roger Aldag was chosen the Most Outstanding Offensive Lineman and receiver Ray Elgaard as The Most Outstanding Canadian. B.C. travelled to Edmonton to play the first place finishers also with an 11-7 record. Again, the Lions provided the upset, defeating Edmonton by a 37-19 score winning the right to travel to Ottawa to contest the 1988 Grey Cup.

It was the smallest crowd for a Grey Cup game since 1975 but that was because of design rather than poor fortune. The League had decided where possible to move the game around to various cities in the League, the chief stipulation being seating capacity of over 50,000. There were all sorts of dire predictions about the foolhardiness of playing the game outdoors on November 27 when the domed B.C. Place was available. None of the fears about frozen turf or blizzards or freezing weather materialized. A capacity crowd of 50,604 at Lansdowne Park watched in 57°F (14°C) temperature. The field was dry, the wind somewhat gusty and the sky overcast. While the stadium capacity accounted for a difference in attendance of close to 9,000 from the previous year, it was obvious that a decline in attendance at all levels of the CFL was in progress. It was down for the season games, the regular season and play-offs by a total of more than 170,000 spectators from 1988 figures.

The 76th Grey Cup game made headlines for a number of reasons. It was the fifth Grey Cup game to be played in Ottawa, the first since 1967 when national unity, the Grey Cup and the CFL were all enmeshed in Confederation year. As mentioned previously, the weather in Ottawa at the end of November was a constant source of speculation. It was also the first time that two teams from the geographical west of the country met. Commentators were having a field day with the fact that the traditional East-West confrontation translated into Winnipeg vs. British Columbia. But it was the money woes of the League and B.C. which were the subject of scrutiny by commentators. There were rumours that the B.C. Club couldn't pay its hotel bills earlier during their season's visit to Ottawa. "During Grey Cup week, the players checking into their Ottawa hotel were asked for their personal credit cards"[380] as a precaution. The team itself was expected to lose $2 million on the season and "had to get a line of credit for that much from the B.C. government."[381] Only last minute fundraising by private business allowed the Lions' Cheerleaders to attend. Larry Donovan referred to his Club as "a crisis a day organization and if we don't have our crisis, we've not had a day."[382]

The old complaint about the CFL's "revolving door syndrome being a curse to the League" was made. There was the constant turnover of players and the resultant lack of fan recognition — barriers to the League in its attempt "to lure back the big crowds.[383] B.C., it was pointed out had used "eleven different combinations on the offensive line; its "offensive triumvirate" were first year with the Lions Matt Dunigan, Anthony Cherry and Dave Williams. The Bombers had made changes seemingly out "of desperation." Top quarterback Tom Clements retired, running back Willard Reeves went to the NFL, receiver Jeff Boyd was traded to the Argonauts. Gone also were linebacker Tyrone Jones, cornerback Roy Bennett and defensive back Scott Flagel. Even so, youthful Winnipeg Coach Mike Riley rejected the suggestion that it had been a rebuilding year.[384]

There were two key plays in the Grey Cup game of 1988 won by the East (Winnipeg) by a 22-21 score. One occurred in the third quarter. B.C. was ahead by 4 points and chose to gamble on its own 20 yard line. It was third down and a "long yard" to go. The Winnipeg team stopped Dunigan's quarterback sneak and Trevor Kennerd kicked a field goal to bring The Bombers to within one point of B.C. The second instance occurred when Dunigan spotted a receiver in the end zone and threw for what he thought was going to be the winning touchdown. Instead, as Dunigan recalled later, a Winnipeg player who had been blocked out of the play, Mike Gray, had the ball hit his hand, deflect off Winnipeg safety Barry Thompson and back into the arms of Gray who by this time was lying flat on his back.[385]

For Gray, the hero of the moment, it was a curious turn of events which brought him to that point. The import from Baltimore and the University of Oregon had signed with B.C. in November 1984, was left unprotected by the Lions and was taken by Ottawa in the Equalization Draft of 1987 in February. He was released by Ottawa in June of 87 and signed by Winnipeg as a Free Agent later that month. Trevor Kennerd provided the winning margin by kicking a field goal with less than three minutes to play, his 14th point of the game. The Blue Bombers also won all of the individual awards presented. Wide Receiver James Murphy was chosen as the Offensive star of the game; Punter Bob Cameron received the Dick Suderman Trophy as the Canadian Star and Defensive Tackle Michael Gray was the Defensive Star.

Minutes after The Bombers won, a wild street party started in Winnipeg and downtown traffic ground to a halt. Hundreds of fans in cars and on foot streamed into the streets honking horns and screaming their joy. About 130 city bars, hotels and restaurants held Grey Cup parties. Sidewalks quickly became littered with discarded beer bottles and cans.[386]

Chapter Four

The 12th of December of 1988 was a significant date for the CFL: The Toronto Argonauts were sold and the CFL replaced its Commissioner. The Argonauts had been owned by Carling O'Keefe Limited which had been part of Rothman Enterprise Limited until sold to an Australian company where it came under the control of IXL Canada Inc.[387] The new owners were seeking to sell the team during the 1988 season; by December, it wished to retain only a 5% share in the Club. The remaining 95% was sold to Harry Ornest and his family who owned, "OFE Inc., a Missouri corporation",[388] thus winding up the Argonaut Football Club Inc. and forming The Toronto Football Club "as a limited partnership with OFE Inc. as the general partner and Carling O'Keefe's interest held as a limited partner".[389]

OFE Inc. formerly owned the St. Louis Blues of the NHL and had been inactive since selling that franchise. Ornest was from Edmonton and lived in California while retaining his Canadian citizenship. His plans were to live in Toronto for nine months of the year.[390]

Carling O'Keefe's decision to sell the Argonauts "resulted from a new corporate policy of not being directly involved in the operation of sports franchises".[391] Under its new arrangement as a minority shareholder, it would "retain the marketing rights of the Toronto Football Club for a period of 21 years and would also retain the rights to operate a football team in the SkyDome on the happening of certain events".[392] Both were of concern to the CFL. The exclusive rights to market the Argonauts could be in conflict with a League Marketing plan while the new SkyDome, due to open in 1989, was being touted as "world class" and as such some were calling for world class, i.e. NFL, football for it. While media coverage indicated a $5 million sale[393] the only reference to money in the League minutes was number three of five undertakings Ornest had to give the CFL—he was to provide "$1,500,000 working capital to the Toronto Club for at least one year".[394] To some, Ornest was really interested in bringing in an NFL team; the purchase of the Argos and their exclusive lease with SkyDome would allow him to do that. "Terms of the Argonaut lease with the Dome allow the owner of the Club 18 months under the same lease to bring in another football team if the Argos ceased to play in the CFL, or the Eastern Division of the League folds or the CFL folds".[395]

The League was adamant that corporate ownership was not one of its priorities. Carling O'Keefe was a culprit as far as the CFL was concerned. The "ambitions of corporate ownership" were considered to be "sometimes at odds with the ambitions of the League".[396] CFL officials were concerned that Carling O'Keefe, which retained a 5% ownership of the Argos, was involved with a "Toronto group that is pursuing an NFL franchise".[397] The rumours appeared to have been well founded. Argo President Ralph Sazio was rumoured to be a member of the group. He denied it but former Argos General Manager Leo Cahill, who blamed Sazio for his release from that position, threw some oil on the fire. He "implicated Sazio in the affair by revealing a letter from a high powered Washington law firm that provided hints on obtaining an NFL franchise. Cahill said that he had obtained the letter from Sazio".[398] A further source of irritation to the League occurred when one of Carling O'Keefe's officers "was photographed wearing an NFL jacket".[399] The brewery was taking the position that it was not promoting an NFL franchise; that it was concerned "about public reaction and was attempting to undo the harm which may have been caused".[400] "Ornest added that negotiations are proceeding behind the scenes to resolve the matter".[401]

When Carling O'Keefe President John Barnett was reported to have said that his firm had not been paid T.V. money owning to it from the 1988 season as owner of the Argonauts, the by now sensitive CFL sprang to defend its fiscal integrity.

> Shown Barnett's statement, (CFL President Bill) Baker said it was true but that Carling O'Keefe negotiated away the money as part of the new television deal. Carling signed a two year $15 million television and promotional deal with the CFL last month. 'There's no confusion' said Baker, 'as part of our negotiations we kept Carling's T.V. money, which was Toronto's money last year'.[402]

The same meeting of the CFL also dealt with the replacement of Douglas Mitchell as Commissioner. Toronto representative Ralph Sazio asked to have the Argonaut sale moved up on the agenda so that prospective owner Ornest "would have some input into the question of league leadership".[403] Mitchell's tenure as Commissioner was tempestuous and fraught with problems. He was decidedly pro-Canadian in his approach and at times seemed to be the recipient of much bad publicity aimed his way particularly from eastern clubs. During his tenure, the Alouettes had folded, the League lost its huge television contract, initiated the CFN. While it was an artistic success, it was not bringing in the necessary revenue. His initiative in moving the CFL offices to a higher profile location and the corresponding increase in League expenses was a source of speculation by the media. Indeed even after he had stepped aside as Commissioner there was conjecture about an approach made by Mitchell in 1986 to the Federal government. Mitchell had submitted a brief "on his own initiative to federal Finance Minister Michael Wilson in November, 1986, asking for a $10 million grant, a $20 million interest free loan, another $9 million grant to match team contributions to the stabilization fund and tax concessions for Club owners that suffered losses".[404]

Former Commissioner "Jake" Gaudaur was critical of the approach saying: "In recent years that league has suffered from a perception that it is not major league. If that had happened, it would have been perceived as a Canadian charity".[405] He also criticized his successor by saying that "two large financial mistakes were made": the turning down of "between 9.4 million and 12 million over two years in a new television contract"- Instead Mitchell created the CFN which "brought in only $5 million over two years"- and the turning down of the Alouettes' offer of $3 million to fold the team. Instead the CFL kept the team alive only to see it succumb prior to the 1987 season. Gaudaur continued to be critical of Mitchell, terming his assertion to Ottawa in August 1987 "about a lack of advertising support . . . 'incredible'".[406]

When Mitchell was appointed Commissioner, it was widely reported that "the Argos and the Ti-Cats were advocating (former Argo and lawyer) Mike Wadsworth. The Ottawa Rough Riders supported them and maybe that was the problem. The western Clubs sensed another eastern plot was taking shape. They unified behind Mitchell, the Calgarian, and the Montreal Alouettes joined them to produce a 6–3 margin".[407] In Calgary, Mitchell had turned down the presidency of the Winter Olympics for 1988. "The CFL offer was simply a diversion that found him in a moment of weakness".[408] Mitchell's whole tenure seemed to be "a never-ending exercise in crisis management" as he "agreed to try to keep the CFL from being a sporting obituary".[409]

In a radical move, the CFL decided to eliminate to position of Commissioner much as had been discussed in the seventies. Mitchell was replaced by a two-man team. Roy McMurtry, a former Ontario Attorney General in Bill Davis' Cabinet combined some of Davis' and Mitchell's duties as Chairman and Chief Executive Officer. Bill Baker of Saskatchewan was President and Chief Operating Officer. The move was controversial.

The appointment of the twin positions was not without question. James Hogan of B.C. was concerned that the Board of Governors, who were making the decision, had to vote for both or none rather than deal separately with each one. There was also some discomfort "with the fact that one of the appointments would be a part-time position".[410] That was McMurtry's. He was taking over from Bill Davis, the former Ontario Premier who had been appointed first Chairman of the League's Football Foundation in October of 1985. Effective 1987, he was named Chairman of The Board of Governors, the League taking the position that it wanted someone of stature in that position who was independent from the clubs. His too was a part-time position bearing a stipend of "not more than $12,000". The League continued its approach with McMurtry's appointment, it being "clearly understood by the Board that the senior position of the two would be Chairman and Chief Executive Officer. . . (who would assume the) duties of Commissioner until the duties were formally divided".[411] It was not all unanimous however. Ralph Sazio, Joe Zuger and Winnipeg's Ross Brown "without intending any disrespect for the two individuals named . . . opposed the principle of currently appointing two people . . . would prefer that the Board appoint one party and give him the authority to hire the second person".[412]

Baker, whose nickname while he was playing with Saskatchewan and B.C. was "the undertaker", had excelled as a player for eleven years. He left a position as vice president of IPSCO to become General Manager of the Roughriders after the 1986 season. Some credited him with the resurgence of that franchise; others particularly in Calgary were upset with him. The Stampeders charged that while they were trying to abide by the salary cap, Baker's team was not. Calgary "traded veterans Richie Hall and Vince Goldsmith to Saskatchewan for next to nothing in order to get down to the limit. Both turned in sound seasons for the Roughriders as did defensive tackle Rick Klassen who was pried loose in the salary dispute with B.C. Lion".[413] Saskatchewan under Baker's leadership was reported to "have overspent the cap by $400,000".[414] However, the bottom line was that with "bingos, telethons and other fund raisers appealing to a community spirit, the work paid off this season (1988) as Saskatchewan made a small $29,000 profit, thanks to a hefty increase in attendance as fans packed Taylor Field to at last see a winning team".[415] Both appointments were effective Sunday January 1, 1989.

The political benefits of Roy McMurtry's appointment as Chairman and CEO became apparent prior to the 1989 season. One of the concerns of the League had always been the loss of identification of the player with the community. Players did not stay after the season and one of the major reasons was that they were not allowed to pursue a career if they did not have landed immigrant status. McMurtry had asked that each Club "report directly to him with specific problems concerning immigration and work permits for players, coaches and their families . . . (so as to allow him) to intercede with the proper government authority".[416] The invitation was repeated once again at the Management Council meeting two weeks later. By June, McMurtry was able to advise the League's Board of Governors that "he had met with senior officials of the Department of Immigration and Employment, including the Minister, and has been informed that effective immediately, all U.S.A. resident players, coaches and their wives will be entitled to obtain employment authorization and work permits without going through the regular validation procedure and which will be effective during the terms of the players' and coaches' contracts".[417]

It was a double barrelled bit of good news for the Club. Not only would they be able to develop better community relations but, as was noted by Dr. Ross Brown of Winnipeg, it "would make such persons eligible for provincial Medicare after three months".[418] Clubs were asked to temper their enthusiasm by Chairman McMurtry. He "cautioned that any public announcement on this matter should come from the Ministry".[419]

McMurtry was also busy lobbying for the CFL on other matters. He had met with Jean Charest, the Ministry of State for Sport to discuss the formation of the new World League of American Football and the possible inclusion of a team in Montreal. His lobbying in this matter proved unsuccessful. The NFL had staged an exhibition game in the summer of 1990 in Montreal. A report to the CFL declared it to be "neither an artistic nor financial success with the attendance below expectations".[420] In addition, there was the new World League of American Football which was to be funded by the NFL and would include a franchise in Montreal. Each Club was urged to lobby the Ministers in their respective areas but political workhorse McMurtry "reminded the members that Government officials are under constant pressure to provide assistance for various causes, so it is often difficult to obtain a commitment on a specific issue in such politically sensitive situations".[421] The League was also being hit with the loss of revenue because of the imposition of the new Goods and Services Tax (GST). Across the League the total impact was expected to be $2.5 million in one season . . . no exemption will be permitted".[422] It was noted that horse racing was granted an exemption because it was "deemed to be an agricultural activity";[423]In Hamilton, Harold Ballard, served notice through Maple Leaf Gardens Limited, that he was intending "to withdraw from the League as of January 31, 1992"[424] a notice which was in keeping with the CFL constitution and "the requirements of the Ontario Securities Commission to disclose any significant events concerning a public company".[425]

Ballard was not planning to operate the Club in 1989; it was necessary to find a buyer if the League were to continue to operate in Hamilton. Ballard had "lost an estimated $3.3 million last season and a reported $20 million in the last 11 years".[426] His battle with the City of Hamilton over Ivor Wynne Stadium was like a soap opera. The City wanted $300,000, it said, owed in Stadium Rental. Ballard refused to pay it. "On the morning of the Grey Cup, November 27, 1988, Ballard had a truck cart away all the team's equipment from Ivor Wynne Stadium".[427]

When all the smoke and dust settled, the Tiger Cats were sold to David Braley, a Hamilton businessman, hand-picked by Mayor Bob Morrow. Even then, the saga continued. Braley's deal with Ballard called for him to take over the Club debt-free, effective March 1, 1989. Any accrued revenues and debts to that point would be looked after by Maple Leaf Gardens Limited.[428] The City of Hamilton, led by Bob Morrow made "a number of undertakings to assist the Club in its re-organization".[429] Braley was "prepared to commit up to $1,500,000 in excess of Club revenues. . . through a wholly owned company 815562 Ontario Limited"[430] and attract other investors from the community. On the City's part, a first effort to consummate the deal was declared illegal by the acting City Solicitor. There was objection to the agreement which would see Braley pay only $1 a year rent whereas Ballard was charged $300,000 which was still less than the $500,000 actual cost, according to Morrow.[431] In the end Braley was "to pay $100,000 a year rent plus $25,000 for play-off games. But the City is to pay the team $300,000 a year for the promotional use of the Ti-Cats' logo and trademark and 10 new stadium billboards worth up to $125,000. Beyond that the City would shell out up to $67,500 for security and $6,700 for clean-up costs previously paid by Ballard".[432]

In a poll taken for the Hamilton Spectator by Decima Research on March 29, 456 interviews were conducted in order to discover the feelings of the fans. Summarized, it found that: 90% were aware of the sale; 49.5% called themselves football fans; 66% felt that the city should make concessions and support the team financially; more women were in favour of the support than men; 65% of all felt that the demise of the team would hurt the city, 85% of them fans and 46% non supporters. Thirty five per cent of Hamiltonians said that they attended a Tiger Cat game in 1988; ten per cent attended more than five games. The survey also found that 29% attended a Blue Jays' game, 19% a Maple Leafs' game and 5% saw the Buffalo Bills in action.

On questions surveying attitudes about the CFL, the following statements elicited the indicated responses. "Hamilton Tiger Cat games aren't as entertaining as they used to be"— 38% agreed; 31% disagreed; 31% didn't know. "The CFL is not as popular as it used to be" — 67% agreed; 17% disagreed; 16% didn't know. "People are more interested in other professional sports such as baseball and hockey" — 56% agreed; 25% disagreed; 14% didn't know. "People don't know very much about last year's team" — 58% agreed; 22% disagreed and 20 % didn't know.[433]

While Harold Ballard might have been looked upon as a maverick and loose cannon by the public and media, he was held in high esteem by his players and by the CFL. He had always paid his bills. The League passed a motion thanking him for being "unfailing in his personal commitment and financial support of the Club" from 1974 to 1988 inclusive.[434]

Meanwhile in Ottawa, the Rough Riders were undergoing a similar trauma. After two unsuccessful seasons as a community owned Club, Paul Robson was replaced as General Manager by the first female to hold that position with a CFL Club, Jo-Anne Polack. Head Coach Fred Glick was let go; Steve Goldman was the new field man in charge. The Club had lost $2.5 million during its last two years of operation and was on course to lose a further $1.1 million in 1989.[435] The Rough Riders were asking the League to extend the time by which the Club had to pay the CFL its debt. The amount was $750,000. It was made up of a loan of $500,000 plus Stabilization Fund loans of $400,000 less Ottawa's share of the 1988 T.V. revenue amounting to $333,000 and other smaller loans.[436] In addition, the team was asking the city "to return to the Club, revenues generated from football games. . . profits from stadium rentals, concession income and parking revenues".[437] That included: rent owed from '87 and '88 seasons of $161,337, parking revenue for '89 (estimate) of $50,000, food concession revenues (estimate) of $72,000, beer revenues of $117,300 ('89 estimate), private box ('89 estimate) revenue of $43,250 and the city write-off costs of game-day parking of $170,000 for a total of $614,687.[438] It was also seeking a grant from the Regional Municipality of Ottawa-Carleton "for $500,000 in recognition of the Club's economic contribution to the area".[439] A fourth creditor was the Province. The Club was asking the Ontario government to forgive an outstanding debt of $260,000 "the team owed in amusement tax, which was levied on all tickets of more than $4.[440] City Council agreed in a 9–7 vote on August 2, 1989 to the Rough Riders' request. Regional government also acceded. The CFL froze the debt owed to it by Ottawa and released the Club's share of television revenues for the months of June, July and August so as to inject some much needed working capital into the Club. Only the provincial government refused to bend over its amusement taxes owed.

Controversy swirled within the Ottawa region. One alderman, Lynn Smith, who voted against city assistance, declared: "the message I got from residents of my ward is that 99% don't want to further subsidize the Rough Riders and the League".[441] Jo-Anne Polack was blunt: "It's no secret the CFL cannot absorb the negative repercussions of another team folding".[442] Mayor Jim Durrell, a supporter of the plan was delighted: "Obviously we think the football Club performs a valuable function in our city. We want to be a strong, well balanced, healthy city and the football club. . . is one of those ingredients".[443]

Calgary too was having serious "cash flow" problems. It needed an immediate two payments of $150,000 each from the League for the last two weeks in July to make up for "a delay in the receipts of moneys from promotions".[444] There was an understanding that the Club would "repay the League forthwith upon receipt of other revenues".[445] But this was not always the case as funds were needed elsewhere. By mid-July, the observation was made by League President Bill Baker that "it would appear that at the end of the 1989 season, the member clubs collectively will be in debt to the extent of $17.5 million with no plans in place to retire the debts in 1990".[446]

Foremost among the debtor clubs was the B.C. Lions. The community owned operation was looking for a buyer. Prior to the beginning of the 1989 season, it had "a deficit of $8.8 million which could reach $10 million by the end of the season".[447] It owed $3 million to the League, much of it from the Stabilization Fund. After five possible buyers withdrew from purchasing the Lions, largely because of the debt, the Club underwent a form of bankruptcy, the "heavy debts were absorbed by the Province".

Bill Baker's approach to the huge B.C. Lions' debt was simple: "Creditors will 'have to take some big swallows and accept write downs on debt or the CFL will fold, leaving creditors with nothing".[448] His style was there for all to see: "We're going to white knuckle it to get things done. I'm not going to be involved in an organization that keeps dragging on like this. So hang on. We're either going to land this SOB or else we're going to crash it. We're not going to keep flying around and wait until we run out of gas".[449]

Mining promoter Murray Pezim "bought the B.C. Lions as a favour to Premier William Vander Zalm".[450] Pezim, an 80% owner of the Club along with 6 minority owners who "kicked in $100,000 towards the purchase price of $1.7 million",[451] was given an extended deadline "to November 15 . . . to file a letter of credit in the amount of $2,000,000 to guarantee the operation of the B.C. Club in the 1990 season together with a conditional letter of withdrawal".[452]

Injuries were causing clubs problems. It was an expense that would fluctuate. A rash of injuries and subsequent signing of re placements could wreak havoc with a club's budget. According to the Collective Agreement, injured players were not to be released; their contract was in effect until they were healthy enough to play. Only then could a club release the player on the basis that he was not good enough to make the team. That was the theory. In practice, said the Players' Association, it was "amazing how often the same scenario's (sic) repeat themselves from each Club. The names may change, but the events continue to repeat themselves, i.e. releasing players while they are injured".[453]

Typical of the situation was the case presented as "grievance #9" to the Association membership.[454] A player was injured during training camp, placed on the injury list temporarily and given his release approximately 5 weeks after the injury. The next day, August 4, the player, as was his right under the Agreement, "served written notice on the club and submitted to an examination by a neutral physician". Once his report was received, August 31,

1988, the Club was advised that the player would make himself available for a "further examination by a neurologist". A subsequent examination in October with a report from the neurologist in mid-November was received and by January the Association served a "Notice to Arbitrate" to the Club. By this time, January 13, the Club responded in a letter "indicating that they acknowledged their responsibility but were not in a position" to pay the player. On March 29, 1989 the Association sent a formal letter to the Arbitrator "requesting that he render his decision in favour of the player". That decision was made on June 14, 1989, in favour of the player, almost one full year after the original injury. The player was awarded his full contract "in the sum of $41,667.67 plus interest in the sum of $6,875.00". The Club was to also make the "contribution to the pension plan, deduct dues from the player's monies and remit them to the CFLPA . . . costs to the CFLPA in the sum of $1,250.00". The Arbitrator gave the Club terms: by June 23, 1989, $18,541.67; July 23, August 23 and September 23, $10,000 each. When the Club failed to make the August and September $10,000 payments, the CFLPA sent a formal demand on October 10, 1989. "On November 2nd, 1989 the balance of the payments and costs were received from the CFL".[455]

Largely due to continuity and the long-term experience of George Reed, President of the CFLPA and Ed Molstad, Legal Counsel, the Association was gaining strength. As former players, both were aware of the operations of the League. Molstad, who had an outstanding career with the University of Alberta and the Edmonton Eskimos, had been Legal Counsel since the seventies succeeding John Argo who was still active in a capacity as Senior Advisor. He represented the Players' interests in legal matters and brought continuity to the interpretation of the contract. More and more the League was being forced to recognize that the CFL was a partnership rather than a fiefdom run by owners. When CFL Commissioner Doug Mitchell had suspended James Curry of Winnipeg for his hit on John Congemi, the Argonaut quarterback, and fined him $2,000 despite there not having been a penalty on the play, the Players' Association sprang into action.

The player had received written notice but not the CFLPA as the Agreement called for. The Association grieved; its view was upheld and "the matter was settled on the basis that the player was repaid the sum of $2,000.00".[456]

When the League passed a stipulation that players who played out their option and sought to try out with another League's team would not be able to return to the CFL in the same year of their failed NFL try-out, the Association once again challenged. They had only become aware of the regulation by virtue of a press release dated March 29, 1988. On the same day it served notice that the proposed League policy was "contrary to the terms and conditions of the Collective Agreement".[457] The League disputed this contention. Rather than back down, the Association pursued the matter with a test case. An interim injunction was granted for the Province of Alberta in favour of the Association on August 10. With the publicity surrounding the case, the Federal Government got involved because of the Competition Act. Subsequent meetings with the CFL caused them to rescind the regulation, pay the player in question $5,000 and $3,000 to the Association for costs.[458]

The Players' Association continued to flex its muscles. During the next year, the League directed its member clubs to refrain from holding back a portion of players' salaries. Some clubs held back as much as twenty-five per cent of a player's paycheque paying it all back less income tax at the end of the season. It was a handy source of cash flow for the various clubs during the season. Some clubs depended on that source to keep them going. Cal Murphy "estimated that withholding would provide additional cash flow of $28,000 per week while it would cost $11,000 in interest to borrow the equivalent amount from the bank". The Players' Association would only allow it if the other clubs or the League would guarantee that the holdback would be paid in case of a Club's inability to do so. The League refused. Any holdbacks in the Clubs' possession were to be given to the players "forthwith".[459]

The Collective Agreement between the CFL and its Players Association was due to expire June 14. The League's position was overseen in its negotiations by Edmonton General Manager, Hugh Campbell. In his summary to the League he "reported that the Player's Association negotiating team is fully aware that the Clubs cannot afford to increase monetary benefits at this time" so the discussions were concentrating on non-monetary issues.[460]

In money matters, the CFL and the players decided to bury the concept of the All-Star game. In its stead, each Club was to pay a grant of $1,200 to the CFLPA and "require its head coach to participate in the Association Awards Dinner". There were other compensation deals struck: Pre season payments would be $200, $225 and $300 for one year veterans, an extra $100 added to each category for each of the next two years. Playoff byes were worth $1800 in 1989 and $2000 in '90 and '91. Finals were worth $2400 for each year while Grey Cup Winners received $12,000 and losers $6,000, the players not to "participate in any further income from the Grey Cup Game in 1989 and 1990 but will in 1991".[461]

The League also received a report done by Angus Reid Associates. The polling organization conducted a survey of 1,506 adult Canadians in 1988 of whom 3/4 were classified as sports fans and 2/3 of those or 753 representing 50% of the adult Canadian population comprised the "CFL audience". The findings were interesting: major changes to the rules were not supported, neither four down football, eliminating the point on a missed field goal nor "reducing import restrictions would enhance the appeal of the CFL".[462] Perhaps it was with this survey in mind that the CFL rules committee proposed only minor changes to the game. Bill Baker, attending his tenth rules meeting, his first as Chief Operating Officer stated: "Everybody in the room wanted to play Canadian football rather than something else".[463]

In the east, the Winnipeg Blue Bombers and Toronto Argonauts, each with a 7–11 record met in Toronto's SkyDome in the playoff game with the Blue Bombers victorious by a 30–7 score. Probably, it was the main reason for the decision to fire Bob

O'Billovich as Argo Head Coach. In the division final, Winnipeg was edged out by first place finisher (12–6) Hamilton by a 14–10 score putting the revitalized Tiger-Cats into the Grey Cup game once again. Ralph Sazio retired from the Argos, his last meeting the February 23 one in Hamilton where his career started in 1950. A vote of thanks was given by the League to Sazio who was described as an "influential force on the League's governing body since February 1968 and previously had distinguished himself as a player and coach since the 1950 season".[464] Sazio's replacement with the Argos was Mike McCarthy whom the Club hired from Hamilton in November of 1989.

In the west, the Edmonton Eskimos were led by the outstanding quarterbacking of Tracy Ham and finished in first place with an impressive 16–2 record. Third place Saskatchewan (9–9) met and defeated the Stampeders in Calgary 33–26. The Roughriders continued their march by humbling the mighty Eskimos in Edmonton by a 32–21 margin to represent the west.

It was Saskatchewan and Hamilton to meet for the Grey Cup. The Roughriders always seemed to be "getting by"; always looking to "next year", always perilously close to folding as had Hamilton lately. Both teams were a "long standing cultural obsession"[465] in their community, their only professional sports franchise. There was a strong bond, historically, between the citizens and their football team. "The fortunes of both franchises have fluctuated; at times fan support has wavered. But there is too much baggage, too much personal history tied up in their lore for a sport-watching citizen of either place to completely let them go".[466]

While Hamilton had won more than its share of Grey Cups, Saskatchewan, since its first appearance in 1923 had only won once, in 1966. Nineteen eighty nine was only the second time since 1977 that the team had even made the play-offs. Its Western Division win against Edmonton brought 1,000 delirious fans to the airport to welcome home the team. "Rider Pride" was alive and well not only in Regina but in all of Saskatchewan. Ever since 1948, they were a provincial team forging links to a province-wide community through dinners, bingos, memberships and with as many Saskatchewan natives among their non-import contingent as possible. Fans drove from miles around to Regina to watch their team play, streamers and pom-poms of green and white waving.

There was a resignation of sorts. The Schenley Distillery Company had decided that it no longer would sponsor the CFL's Outstanding Player Awards. Ever since the first presentation was made to Billy Vessels in 1953, the Schenley Awards had been synonymous with outstanding achievement in the CFL. By 1989, however, the firm decided that the "considerable moneys" spent each year "did not increase sales and therefore could no longer be justified".[467]

Yet another tradition was being questioned. The Miss Grey Cup competition was coming under closer scrutiny. Ottawa Rough Rider General Manager Jo-Anne Polak and the CFL's Director of Marketing Morrey Rae Hutnick both of whom were in their first year with the League questioned the contest. President Bill Baker asked "Whether there would be any objections from the Clubs if the Miss Grey Cup pageant were discontinued".[468] Dr. Ross Brown of Winnipeg seemed to speak for the majority when he stated that such a decision should be made by the League rather than the local Grey Cup Organizing Committee. Hand-written notes in the margin of Winnipeg's minutes expressed the thought that "Jo-Anne and Morrey Rae aren't running the league yet".[469]

Nonetheless, there was some concern in Toronto that the days for such beauty contests were long past, that people in that city would not support such a concept. As late as October, "Miss Hutnick advised that it was not planned to hold the Grey Cup Pageant as had been done in previous years".[470] It was not a universally accepted position. A compromise was put into effect after much behind the scenes discussion. "Each Club could send its Grey Cup Ambassador who would make appearances at various functions without any contest between them . . . one of the ladies should be named Miss Grey Cup since the League has not made any decision to discontinue the event".[471]

Both teams had held their pep-rallies prior to the game but it was Saskatchewan which was making the greater impression. The team had been shut out of the week's awards doled out by the CFL. Edmonton and Hamilton representatives won those. Tracy Ham, Rod Connop and Danny Bass were chosen Outstanding Player, Offensive Lineman and Defensive Player. Hamilton's Rocky DiPietro and Stephen Jordan garnered the Canadian and Rookie Awards. After all, they were the two top teams in the country, according to the season's standings. Saskatchewan almost seemed like an aberration. Ms Saskatchewan, Pheona Wright, "won" the Ms Grey Cup Pageant; a woman of the nineties, a Fine Arts student, raised on a hog farm who worked summers for the Department of Highways driving oil trucks and spreading gravel".[472]

The site of the Grey Cup Game, Toronto's SkyDome provided a stark contrast to the perception of the Roughriders: "I'd hate to try to sell it (the game) if it weren't for the dome"[473] said Peter Labbett, Chairman of the festival Committee. The up-to-date technical marvel with its retractable roof ensured that the "game is a far greater draw because it will be played under perfect conditions . . . spectators won't have to bundle up. They can dress for a dinner out, drive to the dome and then enjoy the game in comfort".[474] Ticket prices were scaled at $100 for Skyboxes, $70 for between the goal lines, $60 for most end zone seats and $50 for the worst, where one could not see the Jumbotron viewing screen. Some would also be able to see the game from Windows, the restaurant overlooking the field, an item which had not escaped the Argos or the league who were negotiating for a fee per person from Windows, the restaurant, of up to $60 for the Grey Cup game. It all seemed so efficient, so "taking care of business". To some, Toronto seemed unaware of the game. "All this national festival east versus west stuff is just too hokey for the urban sophisticate to fathom . . . the hub of western civilization remained unaltered by a football game between the teams of two hick towns".[475]

Prior to the Grey Cup game, expatriates and those in Toronto for the game gathered at Maple Leaf Gardens for a pep-rally. Harold Ballard had made it available at their request for $15,000, considerably less than he would normally charge. It was a three hour display of enthusiasm. There was the Pride of the Lions Marching Band waving green toques and playing stirring music, Premier Grant Devine, Gainer the Gopher, Toronto Maple Leafs' Wendel Clark and the Flame, Sandy Monteith, who jetted a stream of fire from his appropriately coloured helmet. The most popular welcome was saved for two Saskatchewan legends, Ron Lancaster and George Reed, imports who stayed. There was a party atmosphere: youths in long green underwear, grandmotherly types with bouquets of white and green balloons, cheerleaders, a mock arrest and booing of someone dressed up as a Hamilton fan. Once again, the west was demonstrating how to turn the Grey Cup into a national celebration.

The game was climactic in every sense. It "was the Canadian Football League at its finest—a dizzying series of offensive strikes sprinkled with bone-rattling defence that brought the most remarkable franchise in professional sport its first Grey Cup in 23 years".[476]

A record SkyDome attendance of 54,088 fans saw Dave Ridgeway kick the winning 35 yard field goal on the second last play of the game edging the equally magnificent Tiger Cats 43–40. It was described as "Blue Collar Football" by Hamilton's coach Al Bruno, "the best Grey Cup Game ever" by many others. It was a tonic for all. "In a province still battered by poor harvests and a weak agricultural economy, the success of the Roughriders has been the biggest news in every region of Saskatchewan in the past week".[477] Typical of the reactions was the report: "For the third successive year, the CFL produced a stunning Grey Cup game. The financially troubled League is consistently written off, yet has produced three wonderful endings to three of its darkest seasons".[478]

The game produced 15 Grey Cup records including most points scored in a game. There were some electrifying moments: a magnificent catch by Tony Champion to pull the Tiger Cats into the lead with 44 seconds to go, superb quarterbacking by Saskatchewan's Kent Austin who was selected as the game's most valuable player and of course Dave Ridgeway's winning field goal with time running out. He was selected the winner of the Dick Suderman Trophy as the Outstanding Canadian in the game. Meanwhile, back in Regina:

> Within an hour of the game's conclusion, traffic on Regina's main arteries (was at) a standstill as Roughrider fans whooped and waved banners and flags from the backs of their pick-up trucks.
>
> Albert Street, the city's main north-south thoroughfare, was shut down for several kilometres by ecstatic fans who soon abandoned their vehicles and wandered through the streets. The drivers of huge semi-trailers joined in the celebration blowing their foghorns.[479]

When the Roughriders returned home, 18,000 fans went to Taylor Field in 10°C weather to welcome the Club. "They drank free hot chocolate, waved green, white and red signs saying 'I love the 'Riders' and sent up cheer after cheer for the Roughriders and everyone associated with the Club from the coaches to the ball boys and the office staff".[480]

It was a sober outgoing President, Tom Shepherd, and first year General Manager and former player, Al Ford, who addressed the Club's Annual Meeting less than three weeks later. "Winning the Grey Cup cost the Saskatchewan Roughriders more than a quarter of a million dollars and pushed the team's debt to an almost unmanageable $1.6 million".[481] Ford said that the Club would have made a "profit of $85,000 a season but lost $195,000 because of the cost of the three play-off games".[482] The Club's "post-season expenses were $280,000"[483] he said.

The League itself generated $3,944,430 from the game versus $2,211,115 in 1988. Its expenses were higher too—$2,016,598 in '89, $1,574,789 in '88 but its net income was tripled: $1,927,831 against $637,326.   Combined with net income from play-off games of $57,053 ($46,985 in '88) the League distributed the money according to finish.

Table of Net Income Distribution*[484]
1989 Grey Cup and Playoff games

Distribution	%	1989	%	1988
Saskatchewan	15.0	$297,732	12.0	$82,117
Hamilton	14.0	277,884	12.0	82,117
Winnipeg	12.5	248,111	15.0	102,647
Edmonton	12.5	248,111	12.5	85,539
Calgary	12.0	238,186	11.0	75,274
Toronto	12.0	238,186	12.5	85,539
B.C.	11.0	218,337	14.0	95,804
Ottawa	11.0	218,337	11.0	75,274
	100.0	$1,984,884	100.0	$684,311

Perception and economic reality were two serious concerns facing the CFL as it entered the nineties. As far as Ron Lancaster, former outstanding quarterback with Saskatchewan and at the time a commentator with the CBC, was concerned, perception was the "League's main problem . . . we are not perceived as a first class operation". The League had gone "downhill" in the area. It had to work "like heck to get that perception back". The point was driven home to Lancaster during a post Grey Cup luncheon. During that game Tiger Cat receiver Tony Champion, playing with a severe rib injury, made an outstanding twisting catch in the end zone to tie the game at 40 points apiece. The superlative play was described to Lancaster as "a Superbowl Catch: . . . He didn't say it was a great catch, he compared it to an NFL feat". That perception, "that the CFL is somehow second class even when the League puts on one of its greatest shows, that bothers Lancaster. The League needs someone at the top that people know. The person has to have a deep concern for the League, be willing to commit himself for the long term and have credibility with football people".[485] Just as much of a concern to Lancaster was the view that the league was living "too much in the past". In a reference to the condition that the public had lost identification with the present day CFL, he was of the opinion that "the fans know who played in the past. They know about Jackie Parker's famous touchdown run in '54, but they don't know about today's stars".[486]It became obvious as the year progressed that the CFL's two man leadership team was in trouble. The League seemed to understand how the twin Commissioners it appointed last January were supposed to function but did anyone else? You could never tell exactly who was in charge at any given moment, possibly because no one really was. Sometimes Bill Baker, the President and Chief Operating Officer appeared to be the boss but then statements from Roy McMurtry, the Chairman and Chief Executive Officer, sounded equally authoritative. Were these fellows interchangeable, overlapping or redundant to the same degree? Who could tell? Another worse possibility arose. In the confusion the fans might cease to care. Two heads are better than one, the old saying goes, but that didn't apply to the CFL. The set-up had only one virtue, a highly dubious one. When things go wrong, you couldn't tell whose fault it was and in professional sport, that can never work. The buck cannot stop at two desks. Someone's got to be in command.[487]

By the first week in October, Bill Baker had resigned effective December 31. Family and personal concerns were cited as reasons as well as the frustrations presented by the twin arrangement. Baker was said to have had a "pass rusher's mentality", with a clear goal of reaching the quarterback, "cognizant that a single hesitant stride is a step towards failure".[488] He was said to have maintained his "lineman's mindset", his term as CFL President characterized by "setting objectives and chasing them down . . .

believes in meeting confrontation head on, forcing issues and figuratively speaking, butting heads".[489]

The CFL formed a search committee of three men to find a successor. It was chaired by Roy McMurtry and included Ti-Cat owner David Braley and Eskimo President Bill Gardiner. Ralph Sazio for one was calling for a return to a single Commissioner.[490] The experiment was over. The public seemed to be confused by the titles President, Chief Operating Officer, Chairman and Chief Executive Officer. That or the numerous stories during 1989 which hinted at friction between the two men in charge of CFL operations. In any event, the resignation of Bill Baker paved the way for the return of the title "Commissioner" and the discontinuation of "President" and "Chief Operating Officer".[491]

In the end, it appeared that financial reality won out over perception. The CFL announced that its new Commissioner was Donald "The name is Crump not Trump" Crump,[492] a chartered accountant who in his position with Maple Leaf Gardens and the Tiger Cats, both Harold Ballard operations, had "a great deal of experience in how to tie down loose cannons".[493]

Crump's background as a Chartered Accountant with Peat, Marwick, Muthed and Company, Revenue Canada, Famous Players Canada, Canadian Tire Corp. Ltd., Bushnell Television, in addition to his work as Treasurer of Maple Leaf Gardens and the alternate governor of the CFL's Tiger Cats was greeted with mixed enthusiasm by League personnel. There were those who suggested that "Crump's strong financial background (was what) the CFL needed these days. We have to get our financial situation in shape so we can function in an efficient manner within our fiscal restraints".[494]

Not all were convinced. The President of the Edmonton Eskimos, Bill Gardiner, and Calgary's General Manager, Norm Kwong, "questioned whether the CFL needs Crump's financial brains at this time. Someone more personable and able to sell tickets might have been a better choice".[495]

At times the CFL appeared to be fractured; clubs seemed to carry on their competitive stance off the field. So much so that Crump was photographed bringing a 5 metre long bull whip into his office.[496]

If there was one issue that typified the growing sniping among the clubs, it was the area of "free agency". It surfaced between British Columbia and Winnipeg. Lary Khuharich left Calgary after the 1989 season and became B.C.'s Head Coach and Director of Football Personnel. Noted for his volatile personality, he had first raised the ire of Winnipeg's Cal Murphy in 1988 when he signed free agent Scott Flagel, a six year Bomber veteran. Now, in 1990, Khuharich was saying that "he thought some of the Stampeders 'will matriculate to the B.C. Lions'".[497] Murphy had his staff phone newspapers in Vancouver "looking for stories in which Khuharich talked about the possibility of some Stampeders following him to B.C."[498] In 1989, there were three free agents who changed teams. It was the most in any year. Notable among them was Damon Allen who signed with Ottawa "two days after his contract expired . . . (and) provoked angry cries from the Eskimos of tampering".[499]

While it was always professed publicly that there were no "under the table" deals between clubs to ensure compensation for free agents, it soon became obvious that some clubs were operating with such an understanding. Edmonton's Joe Faragalli threatened a bidding war: "Obviously we've got more money to spend than most people and players want to come here. But is that any good for the League? We've got to have some sanity here. I think either there has to be some compensation when free agents are signed, which is our personal philosophy with the Eskimos, or maybe we should just not have it in our league".[500]

Despite the concerns expressed by the clubs about their very real financial difficulties, there appeared to be an inability to live within their means. Every club had exceeded the $3,000,000 "competitive expenditures" limit for the 1988 season.[501] As an example, Winnipeg's Mike Riley was selected as the CFL Coach of the Year. He stunned the Blue Bombers and their supporters when it was announced that he was leaving the Grey Cup Champions to take an assistant coaching job with Stanford University.[502] The announcement seemed to serve its purpose. Riley was re-signed to a contract to coach the Blue Bombers for the '89 season.

Some wondered just how serious the problem was; others saw action by Calgary and Ottawa as being a sign that they were interested in fielding the best teams that they could, regardless of financial worries. When Toronto Argonauts left their top offensive lineman, Dan Ferrone, unprotected during the League's Equalization Draft, they believed he would be unclaimed. After all, they reasoned, Ferrone was 30 years old, was earning in the range of $85,000 as the Argos "highest paid Canadian" and with the combination of his age and salary "he might slip by".[503] Calgary Stampeders, financially strapped or not, acted otherwise. They claimed the respected lineman with no hesitation much to the chagrin of the Argos. In Edmonton where heir apparent Damon Allen played out his option, the Eskimos were shocked when the Ottawa Rough Riders signed the "free agent" to a contract for the 1989 season. They were stunned for three reasons. Allen was being counted on as the long-term quarterback since Matt Dunigan had been traded to B.C. for the 1988 season. There was also, in the past, a gentleman's agreement that players playing out their option would not be pursued by member CFL teams. Perhaps the overall cause of chagrin in Edmonton was that the Rough Riders whose financial problems were well publicized and who were in a sense being supported by the very solvent Eskimos, would spend the money for a high salary when Edmonton was not prepared to do so. In the end, however, it was new coach Steve Goldman, who had been the offensive co-ordinator with Edmonton and who knew Allen well, who would prevail. The move propelled Tracy Ham into Edmonton's starting quarterback position.

The Eskimos were able to exact a high price from B.C. Lions for the 1988 trade of Dunigan. At the time of the deal the Eskimos were sent receiver Jim Sandusky and "future considerations". The "future" arrived in January of 1989. Sent to the Esks to complete the deal were linebackers Gregg Stumon and Jeff Braswell, running-back Reggie Taylor, defensive back Andre Francis and B.C.'s first round draft choice who turned out to be linebacker Leroy Blugh. According to Edmonton coach Joe Faragalli: "The B.C. Lions got the huge diamond; Edmonton Eskimos get the six rubies".[504] B.C. General Manager Joe Galat described the deal as an attempt to "not let them have any of our untouchables and we bought them off basically with more players".[505] His reference was to the original terms of the deal. B.C. was to "protect two players on their roster; Edmonton would select one of the unprotected players. B.C. would protect another player and the Esks would choose again".[506]

The revised deal not only protected B.C.'s "untouchables", it also helped it to trim its already high players' budget.

The whole matter festered and became a consideration in the League's fourth Equalization Draft. The two teams in each Division, Ottawa in the East with a 4–14 record and B.C. in the West with a 7–11 performance were to be recipients of the Draft. Some general managers balked at allowing B.C. to take part. Toronto and Winnipeg both had the same record in the East. Whereas B.C. finished fourth in the West, the Argos and Blue Bombers made the play-offs in the east. Winnipeg's Cal Murphy, perhaps still incensed that B.C.'s Lary Khuharich had suggested that "maybe Cal needs to get a dictionary to look up the term 'matriculation'",[507] and explained: "If we're going to let B.C. take people, why shouldn't we? We had the same record".[508]

British Columbia did not endear themselves to its League partners when they announced that free agents Chris Major and Larry Willis were signed away from Calgary's roster and followed later with Ray Alexander. But the biggest collective shock was registered in what was described as "one of the most memorable press conferences held in Ottawa—outside Parliament Hill—",[509]the Ottawa Rough Riders announced the signing of five free agents and the acquisition of two players by trades. The "free agents" were Glenn Kulka, Toronto; David Williams and Anthony Cherry, B.C. Lions; John Mandarich of the Edmonton Eskimos; Bryon Illerbrun of Saskatchewan. Those traded to the Riders were Terry Baker from Saskatchewan and Rob Smith from B.C. Later, in June, the team some had dubbed the "Rough Raiders", acquired their sixth free agent: Gregg Stumon from the Eskimos.

Reactions were "swift and for the most part, bitter".[510] "(The Riders) took money out of our pockets and now they're buying our players"[511] said Joe Faragalli. He was referring to the fact that the League agreed to freeze Ottawa's $750,000 debt to 1993. Faragalli, among others, agitated "to force the Riders to pay back that sum immediately".[512] Calgary's Normie Kwong was "deeply disappointed". The Stampeders were also deep in debt. He criticized the Rough Riders for their "total disregard for their seven partners . . . others besides them have to win too".[513] Toronto Argonauts' General Manager Mike McCarthy was concerned "that the Riders actions would disrupt the league's salary scale and financial position".[514] Joe Zuger in Hamilton commented that it was "wrong to have other teams doing their work for them . . . an admission that the Riders don't have the ability to go out and find players within the financial structure".[515] The Argos cancelled a proposed planned scrimmage with Ottawa in Kingston on June 23, the profits of which were to go to amateur football in Kingston. Ottawa reacted to charges that the team was ignoring the salary structure and cap. Jo-Anne Polack countered that her team was $140,000 under the $3,000,000 salary cap in 1989 and "besides, how we spend the $3,000,000 is up to us".[516]

There was open questioning as to how a team like Ottawa, so mired in debt, could sign David Williams from B.C. for a reported $125,000 compared to the average for wide receivers of $54,000; Mandarich and Kulka were said to have signed for $100,000 and $80,000, the average for defensive linemen being $56,000 in 1989. Offensive lineman Illerbrun was to receive $80,000, compared to the average of $53,000. Cherry had turned down $55,000 from B.C. and joined the Rough Riders for $75,000.

Perhaps seeing the writing on the wall, Ottawa announced that they would not participate in the Equalization Draft. In the meantime, Argos, Stampeders, Bombers and Eskimos announced they would not contribute any players to it. B.C. was undaunted; they wanted it to continue. CFL Commissioner Don Crump put the best face on the situation: "I can understand the other teams' being annoyed. But if as a result of these moves, the league becomes more exciting and Ottawa ends up with a winning team and contributes to the gate equalization plan, then maybe something good will come out of all of this".[517]

It was later in the day when the CFL commissioner announced the cancellation of the CFL equalization draft trying in the process to put a positive spin on the whole matter.

> *The exciting events of the past several days seem to demonstrate that there is a definite effort being made by the teams to create parity among the member clubs of the CFL! Because of that, it seems unnecessary to hold the draft so it's hereby cancelled.*[518]

It was, indeed, hard to tell that teams were cash-starved judging from the way quarterbacks were being wooed to come to the CFL. Saskatchewan courted and won over Notre Dame quarterback Tony Rice. B.C. Lions had both West Virginia's Major Harris and Boston College-New England Patriot, Doug Flutie on its negotiation list. The mixed messages being sent to the public about finances and the perceptions thereof, continued. Calgary Stampeders announced a $1.4 million loss for the 1989 season, almost double the $764,000 loss in 1988. Calgary's shortage for the previous three years was $2.9 million. "That figure combined with a $1.3 million debt carried into 1987 season brings the deficit to $4.2 million.[519] Interest rates were such that it was anticipated that in excess of $400,000 would be needed just to service the debt during 1990. It meant that even if the Stampeders drew 11,000 more fans in 1990, it would be no further ahead financially.[520]Ottawa was reportedly asking the CFL to "turn a blind eye" to the $750,000 it owed to the League, much as was done with the B.C. Lions' $800,000 debt when Murray Pezim bought the Club.[521] Edmonton Eskimos, the League's most stable franchise, reported that it had a profit of $13,000 for the 1989 season "the second year in a row the Eskimos have made a profit, a feat that unfortunately has not been matched by any other CFL Club".[522]

Cancelled though the draft was, the "raiding war" on free agents continued. Edmonton Eskimos signed Keith Gooch as a free agent from B.C. They made no mention of reimbursement whereas when they signed Hamilton free agent Mike Walker, Hugh Campbell proposed to compensate the Tiger Cats saying that "he believes in compensation for signing a free agent because it tends to keep a team competitive".[523] Even Winnipeg ventured into the fray by signing free agent receiver Eric Streater from B.C. Lions. He was the 12th player to switch teams under free agency. Calgary was once again struck when the Argonauts re-claimed Dan Ferrone. The popular lineman had been taken by Calgary in the 1989 Equalization draft and had played out his option. Calgary's Normie Kwong pressed Toronto for compensation, something which Mike McCarthy seemed to lean towards. The whole situation prompted the Players' Association Counsel Ed Molstad to issue a statement against collusion. He aimed straight at Hugh Campbell describing his "admission that he'll compensate Hamilton as an overt breach of the Collective Agreement and that the Association will act on it if Campbell doesn't back off".[524] Reports were that the Commissioner, Don Crump, "shrugged it off as a normal course of business".[525]

It did appear that money was a problem in the League. If not, why all the players declaring themselves "free agent"? Some left to find greener pastures over the border to the United States, Gill Fenerty, Tony Champion, Gerald Alphin and Romel Andrews among the 10 who did so. Yet there were others, some 12 in all, who were unsigned by their clubs because they said they couldn't afford them. Yet they were coveted and given contracts with other CFL Clubs.

Even a "blockbuster" trade involving Toronto and B.C. added to the controversy and at the same time seemed to be considered part of the solution. The Argos sent quarterback Rick Johnson, linebackers Willie Pless and Tony Visco, slot back Emmanuel Tolbert, defensive back Todd Wiseman and defensive tackle Jerald Baylis to B.C. in return for disgruntled quarterback Matt Dunigan. A further trade saw the Argos receive James "Quick" Parker and a 1991 fifth draft choice from B.C. in return for the rights to quarterback Major Harris, the highly touted player from West Virginia.

In May, Dunigan was traded in March, the quarterback's agent announced that B.C. did not honour a verbal commitment to reimburse Dunigan for bonuses and appearances. "The lapsed payments ($50,000–$100,000) were critical in Dunigan's demand for a trade after two seasons with the Lions".[526] Therefore, said the Agent, B.C. lawyer Peter Perrick, Dunigan was declaring himself a free agent. When the quarterback left the Lions, he was under contract for $205,000. It was said that his goal was to sign a contract with Toronto for $300,000, topping the previously highest CFL contract of Tom Clements, quarterback with Winnipeg in 1987. Argos had offered a $240,000 contract which was turned down before Dunigan signed with the Club. General Manager Mike McCarthy would only confirm that the agreement was for "more than $1 and less than $1 million".[527]

League relations appeared to be even more strained when Argonaut owner Harry Ornest criticized publicly the League's decision to play the '91 Grey Cup game in Winnipeg. At the heart of the issue was money. The Grey Cup game and television revenues were considered primary assets in generating profits. Weather in the west during late November play-off games had reached folkloric proportions. Visions of blizzards, gales, frozen fields, and numbing temperatures were conjured up. The NFL, it was said, would never allow its Super Bowl to be played in an open arena in the north, not even in Chicago and New York if ideal playing conditions couldn't be guaranteed. Indeed, western teams in the CFL (most would argue that Winnipeg was in the west even though the Blue Bombers played in the eastern division of the CFL) had generally been in favour of finishing the season earlier. They wanted to avoid the type of late November weather often striking the west "so that a play-off game can be played under the kind of conditions that allow the athletes to put on their best show".[528]

Critics of the CFL's decision to award Winnipeg the 1991 Grey Cup game were more in favour of alternating the game between domed stadiums in Toronto and B.C. "The concept of moving the league's showcase game around the country is a noble one . . . it isn't likely to be a profitable one. And without profit, there will be no league and noble motives won't matter".[529] An incensed Cal Murphy took dead aim at Ornest, asking that the question be put on the League's agenda in order "to squelch speculation"[530] that Winnipeg was about to lose the game. Murphy, citing recent Grey Cup games in Edmonton and Calgary, complained that Winnipeg was being singled out unfairly. It's a (Toronto Argonaut owner) Harry Ornest issue". The Argos boss' rebuttal was blunt:

> *What I'm trying to do is insure that Cal has a football job for a long time even if he doesn't realize it. With some of the recent neanderthal thinking by guys who haven't got a dime invested in the league, one would think that we were as successful as the National Football League and I'm including Cal Murphy.*[531]

Winnipeg was confirmed as host of the '91 game; the League "agreed to establish a 'business plan' that would cover all future Grey Cups".[532]

When the CFL agreed to a new television contract with Carling O'Keefe Breweries, the two year agreement was to begin in 1990 and called for $12 million plus "promotional support" of an additional $3 million. Within those figures, the League had to address two Toronto concerns because of its change in its blackout policy. The CFL was experimenting with the lifting of the black-out in its large southern Ontario market. In the process however, it meant that contracts the Argos had were being, if not broken, bent. Radio station CFRB, the "exclusive voice of the Argos" cancelled its contract. The Argos made a hurried agreement with CJCL but the decision cost the Argos $100,000 in lost revenue for the 1988 season. In addition, the Exhibition Stadium Corporation was also suing "for a share of the revenue received for lifting the blackout . . . approximately $180,000".[533] The television revenues were to cover those expenses.

The CFL announced that for the first time since 1984, its games would be shown on American television. There was to be little financial return to the League since the American Rights holder Molson's Brewery sold the package to Sports Channel America. The latter also carried NHL and would telecast 23 live CFL games including the Grey Cup from Vancouver. League officials were happy. More than 10 million cable households were served in the U.S. in the country's top six markets—New York, Chicago, New England, Philadelphia and San Francisco.[534] Commissioner Don Crump tied the two circumstances together: "With the League back on TV in the United States, having players of this calibre (Harris, Flutie and Rice) playing in the CFL will entice even more good players to come up here. I think signing all three would be a big deal".[535] Echoing that line was Winnipeg's Cal Murphy. "When players aren't able to see the games on TV, Canada is a real foreign country to players".[536] Short term gain was not a consideration as far as Crump was concerned: "I think by showing there is interest in the United States it will help us attract investors for next year".[537]

There had always been the feeling that the CFL's rules were sound. Only minor changes were made at the CFL's meetings in Edmonton where Saskatchewan's John Gregory was selected as Coach of the Year and winner of the Annis Stukus Trophy. In return for Saskatchewan's first Grey Cup win since 1966, Gregory was rewarded by General Manager Alan Ford even before the end of the regular season ended. His contract was extended "through the 1990 season with the proviso that they would discuss a further extension" prior to the start of the schedule.[538] Gregory showed up at the Awards Dinner wearing "a set of suspenders only a coach could love. Little men in striped shirts ran up either side, their eyes covered by their hands."[539] He also presented his Hamilton counterpart Al Bruno "with a referee doll, complete with arms, legs and a head that could be pulled off".[540]

It was a reference to Bruno's "'heat of the moment' shots at the officiating"[541] in the 1989 Grey Cup game. Gregory had expressed the thought that "hopefully we'll never be in the ditch again. It's nice to be on the highway rather than in the ditch".[542] It was also recognition that "no matter how good a coach you are, you might be only a missed call, a missed block or a missed player away from the unemployment line. In the here today gone tomorrow world of coaching you get your kicks when you can".[543]

The reality of that statement hit home, east and west, midway through the 1990 season. In Hamilton, popular Al Bruno, the longest serving head coach in the CFL was released. He had begun the season in some controversy when owner David Braley offered him a one year contract with "a 5% pay cut from his estimated $100,000 salary".[544] Bruno accepted, grudgingly, only after the owner's "assurance that his assistants got a raise".[545] By late September, Bruno was replaced by director of player personnel David Beckman. The 'Cats had lost 5 games in a row. Forgotten were his accomplishments of four Grey Cup appearances and a 1986 win over Edmonton and his "knack for inspiring his charges to great heights in post-season play".[546]

In British Columbia, what seemed to be at first glance a promising relationship was becoming a "circus". When owner Murray Pezim, the self-styled "world's greatest promoter", bought the Lions, one of his first acts was to hire former star quarterback Joe Kapp, the former Lions' quarterback from the sixties to return as Club President and General Manager. Pezim was quick to seek to influence the CFL. He advocated expansion into the United States saying without it the League was going 'nowhere' . . . You'll just get duller and duller. You can't keep giving them (fans) what you've been giving them".[547] In turn, former Calgary Coach Lary Khuharich was signed on as Head Coach. The team was constantly in the news, not all of it of the type to connote stability. Free agent losses and gains were recorded, each one having a domino effect. Matt Dunigan's trade set off a search for quarterback replacements and the eventual signing of Major Harris and Doug Flutie. Harris' agent accused Joe Kapp of lacking integrity.[548] He charged the Lions' President with preparing a "lower priced contract" than one discussed and agreed to the previous evening in negotiations. Kapp replied that figures "discussed the night before were only proposals, not an actual offer".[549] Harris eventually signed after coach Lary Khuharich was sent to Pittsburgh to talk with the quarterback. The former West Virginia standout became disenchanted, however, as Flutie and Paopao became the Lions' choices to play.

B.C. was attempting to forge new ties with the community, to heighten its visibility in the Province. Kapp began a Team-Up program "designed to integrate the Club and its players into the community through a series of tie-ins with service, charity, community groups and corporate sponsors".[550] Premier Bill Vander Zalm agreed to be the team's honourary head coach, "a signing that gives a whole new meaning to the term political football",[551] suggested one wag. It was part of Kapp's community bonding, to show "support from our leader, making a statement to the public that the Lions are important".[552]

Murray Pezim was seen on Vancouver's Howe Street, complete with the B.C. Lions Cheerleaders, trying to convince his stock market friends to buy season tickets and proving that he was "the world's greatest promoter".[553] Promotion was the name of the game. The Lions were back in the public eye. Former NFL player Mark Gastineau was brought in to generate more publicity, sell season tickets and encourage speculation that he might suit up to play defensive end for the Lions. He actually did suit up and played in the Lions first game a 38–38 overtime thriller with Calgary. Gastineau blocked a field goal attempt; B.C. scored a touchdown following it. However, he did not live up to the pre-season hype surrounding him and did not finish the season.

At times it was like a 3-ring circus, the spotlight shifting from Khuharich to Kapp to "the Pez". Then the beam faded as it moved from one to the other finally resting on "the Pez". Defensive co-ordinator and linebacker coach Charlie West was first to go. He "quit because he couldn't get along with Khuharich"[554] even though the two had known each other and had worked on the same coaching staff with Kapp at the University of California in 1982–83. Former Lions' player Jim Young described as a "marketing gopher for Kapp and Khuharich"[555] and who had been an assistant coach in 1989 replaced him. Next to leave was Larry Cauterize who was in charge of quarterbacks, receivers and running backs. He originally came to the Lions with the hope of working with his former college quarterback Matt Dunigan. His replacement was Jim Young who was given the additional duties of receiving and running back coach.

Meanwhile, as the Lions moved into their season, it became obvious that there were trouble spots. Major Harris played little; Doug Flutie sporadically. The quarterbacks impressing the most were the young Rick Foggie and a rejuvenated Joe Paopao. B.C. attendance going into September was averaging around 34,000 but the Club had won only two games, by one and two points. When the Lions played a home and home series with Toronto the first week in September the light shifted. In a game which set a CFL record for points scored, the Argos defeated the Lions 68–43 in Toronto. In the return match before more than 36,000 at B.C. Place the Argos completed their rout by posting a 49–19 win. It was the end for Khuharich and Kapp. Young became Interim Head Coach; and General Manager; then Acting Head Coach and Vice President of Business Operations. Murray Pezim hired Bob O'Billovich to take over as Head Coach declaring that "the circus is over".[556] Not quite. Kapp lingered in the spotlight calling Pezim "an idiot"[557] and Jim Young "a hood ornament".[558] "I've been to Hollywood" said Kapp, "and I'll tell you there's nothing that compares with this zoo".[559]

When O'Billovich was announced as Head Coach it was necessary for him to return to Toronto, not able to take over as head coach until after a game with Edmonton. Young was named Acting Head Coach causing one reporter to comment that "there are two options here. Either Young is a football genius or he's one of Murray Pezim's favourite people".[560] When B.C. player Doug "Tank" Landry, a former Argo who had played for O'Billovich before being traded to Calgary, announced first he wouldn't play for O'Billovich and then he would, it was now left for "the Pez" to declare the Circus over. Some were doubtful: "At least that's what we think he said. It was hard to hear over the noise of the calliope".[561]

Aside from the turmoil in British Columbia, the Lions had a league wide impact in at least two other areas. On the playing field a style of play reminiscent of the late sixties and early seventies was making a comeback. Canadian football has always placed a premium on the mobile quarterback. Offensive systems incorporated straight drop back passes but in order to add another dimension, the roll-out pass was integrated into the scheme. That style of play was one in which the quarterback moved his pocket of protection and rolled out wide from the centre with depth before moving towards the line of scrimmage. Defensive personnel were uncertain as to whether the quarterback was intending to run or pass. The quarterback, for his part, did either one depending on the play of the defensive person's reaction. Eventually, defensive teams saw the manoeuvre so often that they developed predetermined reactions to it.

Offensive teams went back to the black board and developed what some coaches called a "dash" style of play. Russ Jackson in the sixties used it very effectively. The quarterback in this style dropped back in a normal way; the defence went into its drop back passing mode. After a five or seven step drop by the quarterback, he would "dash" to one side or another. In effect, it might look as if it were a "broken play", the quarterback being flushed out of the protective pocket. But it was a designed tactic, a prelude to a rollout style after first indicating a drop back pass.

The Lions' Flutie and Paopao were masters of the deceptive art, each one presenting a unique problem. Edmonton's coach Faragalli rated the two: "Each guy presents a different thing. Flutie scares you with his running ability. Joe has that quick release. He hits the seams.[562]

While that Lions' impact had a subtle effect, the fact that it had four good quarterbacks helped to make a league wide change. Much publicity had been generated with the courting and signing of quarterbacks Tony Rice of Saskatchewan, Doug Flutie and Major Harris of B.C. The Lions also had the veteran Joe Paopao having released Rickie Foggie who was picked up by Toronto. In Saskatchewan, Kent Austin and Jeff Bentrim were veteran quarterbacks. Tom Burgess had been dealt to the Blue Bombers in July. The result was that once the League settled into its season, players who were used to attract fans to the park, the "quarterbacks of the future", were not able to dress and gain any game experience. The CFL decided to expand its rosters to 37, allowing three quarterbacks to be dressed for each game.[563]

Some took it as another lost opportunity to develop a Canadian quarterback: "Ludicrous, absolutely ludicrous" was the way Larry Uteck, a former CFL player and Head Coach of St. Mary's Huskies, "Everybody in their right mind knows that no player is developed overnight. Yet here, when the CFL has an opportunity that would enable Canadians to develop at the quarterback position, they blow it".[564] Uteck expressed further that what the public really wanted to see "is local talent playing the game".[565]

The Argos' General Manager Mike McCarthy responded: "I'm supposed to pay a Canadian kid, let him travel with the team, and then just let him stand on the sidelines holding a football. Come on, get real. If the kid's good enough to play, he'll play. They could be Martians . . . Chinese . . . Irish . . . even Canadians but we've got to go with the best players available".[566] McCarthy was more concerned about the salary cap of $3 million. The Argos were the only team with two quarterbacks on their playing roster, Dunigan was injured. He had voted against the three quarterback proposal and criticized the "little guys", the Winnipegs and Saskatchewans who were "the first guys to bitch about the salary caps . . . they can have a bingo to get their money back. We can't".[567]

Controversy continued to swirl around the CFL in a variety of areas. Calgary Coach Wally Buono questioned the ethics of Argos' Coach Don Mathews and his "shoot the lights out" approach. In a game against Hamilton, the Argos set up for a field goal. Lance Chomyc, their place-kicker, ran towards the bench while calling out for his tee. The ball was snapped; Chomyc turned up field and caught a pass which resulted in a first down and, later, a touchdown. Buono was not impressed: "Although it was a great play, it raises the question of what's ethically right. That's why they got rid of the old sleeper play. You couldn't tell if the guy was leaving the field or not".[568]

In a move to create savings, the CFL was also planning to change its address. It had been at 1200 Bay Street since April 1, 1985 where it leased 8,000 square feet of floor space. During 1989, the cost conscious League sub let some 60% of its floor space to an advertising agency and was planning to shrink even more. The resulting space was too cramped. The CFL moved to the top floor of a five story building at 110 Eglinton Ave. West where it had use of 7,300 square feet of space.[569]

As the 1990 season progressed, it became obvious that the CFL was, once again, in trouble. Finances and perception had combined to portray an image of a "minor league". Attendance in two of the League's traditionally strong cities, Toronto and Hamilton was "down substantially. Torontonians have begun to whisper that the CFL isn't good enough for their 'world class' city and yearn for an NFL team, the prospect of which threatens the viability of a better Canadian product".[570]

It was a sensitive matter. Meanwhile a NBC news report had NFL Commissioner Paul Taglibue "pushing for an expansion franchise in Toronto". It went on to say: "The Commissioner has been humming a tune that sounds as lot like O Canada".[571]

Concurrently it was reported that even though Molson's had "invested more than $10 million in the CFL "in television and marketing rights, it was a trifle strange that former CFL Commissioner, Jake Gaudaur is on its payroll, aiding in the pursuit of an NFL franchise for Toronto".[572] Gaudaur who was inducted into Canada's Sports Hall of Fame was non-plussed. He had reactivated his management consulting firm. "More importantly, when I walked out of the Commissioner's office for the last time, driving home I took a look back on those forty-four years and felt sort of good about my life's work and decided that I owed the sport nothing and it owed me nothing. I still feel that way today and if that bothers anyone, that's their problem.[573]

Crump was assured that in spite of the NFL's exhibition game in Montreal and the movement of the WLAF into Montreal that the new spring league would honour CFL contracts and its own salary structure would be lower than the CFL's minimum scale. The Commissioner also met with NFL head Paul Taglibue on September 26. He was assured that the NFL had no plans to expand into Canada for at least 10 years.[574] Much of the uncertainty in the CFL relative to the NFL was due to the failure of the Argos to negotiate an exclusivity lease with SkyDome officials. The CFL wanted a lease which precluded NFL exhibition games; SkyDome officials were unwilling. The League passed a motion that the proposed lease "with the Argonaut Football Club includes an undertaking that the Corporation will not permit the Stadium to be used for professional football by any club that is not a participating franchise holder in the Canadian Football League or any successor League".[575] That was coupled with the good news that the Argos had earned a profit of $1,000,000, from 1989[576] with a season's ticket base of 27,600.

One solution advanced was to "sell the Canadian game as boutique football . . . to appeal to the true football aficionado".[577] It was proposed that the CFL

1. *Eliminate mid-season importing of players;*

2. *Reduce the numbers of imports at all positions to encourage the use of Canadian quarterbacks;*

3. *Concentrate CFL games on a single day (Saturday) with one feature game on Friday evening;*

4. *Eliminate the blackout rule;*

5. *Actively promote the game's distinctive features.*

Alison Gordon, writing in the Toronto Star Sports[578] had her own interpretation of what was happening.

She was asked by a reporter why Canadians were "so mad keen for baseball". Her "flippant response" was that it was so "because it is American . . . part of our famous national inferiority complex that we find more legitimacy in things that are hits south of the border than we do in our home grown accomplishments". She pinpointed the time when Torontonians went overboard for the Blue Jays. It was 1985 when "our guys beat the Yankees at their own game" winning the divisional pennant, the American League East. "The Blue Jays were at last, in the minds of those who love the phrase, 'world class'".

Relating how a "world class temple" was built for the "world class team", she wrote that "way in the back of those tiny minds was the hope that one day we would have a world class football team to play there too". She continued: "The Argonauts, of course, are not world class. The CFL is not world class. Everybody knows that the only world class football is played in the NFL. . . . The tiny minds who lust after and NFL franchise for the SkyDome just wish the CFL would hurry up and die so they can get on with their scheming". Gordon was also aware that the NFL was searching for new markets, part of what she called "sports imperialism". Exhibition games were being played in diverse areas such as England, Japan and Berlin as well as Canada wherever the American way was advancing or as she put it: "When democracy comes can NFL football be far behind?"

I would like to believe that Canadians are too smart to throw over their own, much more exciting, brand of football and embrace the phoney glitz and glamour of the American game, but on recent evidence, I can't.

. . . This city wouldn't be the same without the Argos. And the country wouldn't be the same without the Blue Bombers or the Tiger Cats or the Eskimos or the Rough Riders and the Roughriders. What wonderful names, quirky and anachronistic. The football they play is quirky, too. That's what makes it unique. That's what makes it Canadian. And that's what makes it worth protecting. Uniquely Canadian institutions are becoming endangered species these days. . . I plan to fight them (the schemers) with the only weapon I've got. I'm strolling down to the SkyDome and buying a ticket to watch the Boys of Autumn play.

Even Commissioner Don Crump seemed to be caught up in the "world class" syndrome. He had made the decision to increase the price of the best tickets for the Grey Cup game to $100, twenty dollars more than they were in 1989 at the SkyDome. He based his decision upon the awareness that the wanted to obtain a certain level of revenue with the number of seats at B.C. Place. When some complained that the seats were overpriced, Crump commented that: "This is a world class city and this is a classy event. A hundred dollars for an event like this is not a world class price".[579]

Crump was more and more centre stage as its CFL year wound down. He suspended Ottawa's leading tackler, Bruce Holmes, for one game, the play-off between the two teams, for twice taking "vicious swipes at Rickie Foggie's head as the quarterback stepped out of bounds. Holmes had been warned earlier in the season "when he hit a prone John Congemi, knocking the Argo pivot out of the game".[580] Crump defended his decision saying: "someone has to protect the quarterbacks" but Ottawa players weren't so sure of his motivation. Kicker Dean Dorsey typified their prevailing mood: "We have to beat Toronto, the Commissioner and everybody else. They've been screwing us since we signed the free agents".[581] The third place Rough Riders lost on all counts. Argos won the play-off game 34–25 only to lose the Eastern Division final to Winnipeg by a 20–17 score. In the west the second place Eskimos defeated Saskatchewan 43–27 and then the first place Stampeders by a 43–23 score.

It was the indifference of Vancouver and the host of empty seats at B.C. Place for the Grey Cup game that gave the impression of a League in disarray. "There were 13,000 unsold seats at B.C. Place and about twice that many remained empty".[582] Thousands of tickets were given away to youngsters who later overran the field so as to make the size of the crowd respectable. The CFL had always maintained that the League and the Grey Cup were important nation building forces.

> But at an event that is advertised as a unifying force in this country, the national anthem was roundly booed when part of it was sung in French. Think about that one for a while. This is what this sporting extravaganza has sunk to — some institution, eh?

In the game itself, Winnipeg, described as "an old-fashioned Canadian team", defeated the Edmonton Eskimos by a 50–11 score—scoring a record 28 point in the third quarter. "The outcome was a rebuke to changing styles in the CFL".[583] For Edmonton, it was an ignominious end to a controversial season. It had started the season at 9–3 and then stories of dissension and racism surfaced. There were rumoured to be rifts between white and black players and among different groups of black players. Late in the season, Edmonton Coach Joe Faragalli tried to put it all in context to illustrate the situation: "It's like this. When you win, it's daylight and when you lose it's dark and when it's dark the cockroaches come out. But now that we are winning again the cockroaches have disappeared".[584] "With some difficulty" it was reported, "(Hugh) Campbell and coach Joe Faragalli finally did get the lid back on . . . for clues about what really went on, watch to see who's replaced before training camp next summer."[585]

For Winnipeg, it was their second Grey Cup victory in three years. Much of the credit was given to a strong defence and the play of quarterback Tom Burgess, playing on his second consecutive Grey Cup team. Winnipeg's defence was anchored by Greg Battle, the linebacker who was selected as the League's Outstanding Defensive Player.

Other award winners were Toronto's Mike "Pinball" Clemons as the Outstanding Player, RB Reggie Barnes of Ottawa as the Rookie of the Year, Saskatchewan's slot back Ray Elgaard as the Outstanding Canadian and tackle Jim Mills of B.C. the Outstanding Offensive Lineman.

If the '90 season was a success on the field, it was not so at the till. The League decided at its February meetings to stop Club contributions to the League Stabilization Fund and to keep Club assessments at 1989 levels of $22,500 per month. The CFL itself was maintaining a deficit of $958,023[586] as it entered 1990. At the end of the year it had grown to $1,013,056. It had advanced loans of $1,000,000 to Ottawa, $600,000 to Calgary and $300,000 to B.C. from the Stabilization Fund which at the end of 1990 stood at $2,103,405. As far as the Grey Cup game, the revenue generated was $2,883,219. More than one million less than 1989's $3,947,625. When expenses were considered the net income was $707,409 in '90 compared with $1,928,844 in '89. Net income from play-off games were higher in 1990, $258,920 as opposed to $61,346 in 1989. The result was that Clubs received much less in '90 than they did in 1989. Hamilton, for example, which finished last in the east received 11% of the Play-off and Grey Cup games, $106,296. In 1989 as a Grey Cup finalist it received 14% or $278,627.

Gate equalization was still in effect too. There were five contributors: Toronto, $179,139; Winnipeg, $59,685; Saskatchewan, $88,850; Edmonton, $147,211 and B.C., $84,474. Three teams withdrew funds: Calgary, $111,988; Ottawa, $154,269 and Hamilton $293,102. At the end of the 1990 season one was still left with the impression that financial reality had caught up with the fans' perception. The CFL was in trouble.

Bob O'Billovich, coach, Argos, Lions.

Leo Cahill, Argos, Coach.

Ralph Sazio, Coach, G.M. Ticats, Argos.

Terry Greer, Argonauts 1983, first pro to gain more than 2000 receiving yards in a season, 1983.

LtoR James Zachery and Dan Kearns 1987
Grey Cup Edmonton 38 Toronto 36

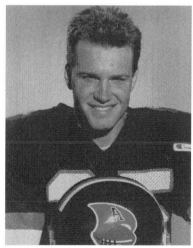

Gill Fenerty, Argos RB '88.

Tracy Ham, Eskimos 1989
communicating with coaches.

Chapter Five

By far the most publicity generated by a sale of a CFL team was when Harry Ornest sold the Toronto Argos on February 25, 1991, to a triumvirate - "Three Amigos" - of Bruce McNall, John Candy and Wayne Gretzky for a reported $5.5 million. A press conference called to announce the sale, attracted a "media turn-out, the likes of which haven't flocked to an Argo gathering since Green Bay Packers great Forrest Gregg came north to coach the Boatmen in 1979".[587] It was front page news. The "rich one", the "funny one" and the "great one" were seen to be the means of "reviving interest in the Argos and the struggling CFL".[588]

When the Argos were bought "there was a condition that the league Constitution would be amended to give each club its own television rights and in approving the transfer . . . the Board of Governors had accepted this condition".[589] The same reasoning was used for property rights, another area traditionally of a league-wide approach. The Argos agreed that while "national merchandising rights should be assigned to the League . . . a Club should have some control over local rights". . . the League would be entitled to match a local offer otherwise it would remain Club property.[590]

The area of gate equalization was also disputed by the Argonauts; a concept of "gate sharing" was worked out. Each Club would submit an audited statement showing its gross gates and net gate on a per game and season basis. The League Commissioner was then to figure out the 90% to be retained by the home Club and the 10% for the visitors and distribute that information. Within ten days each Club was to submit to the League payment of the difference it was to pay out to the visiting Club up to a maximum of $125,000. The total amount was referred to as the "Gate Sharing Pool".[591] A formula was then used to distribute the Pool: "A numerator equal to the amount of that Club's net entitlement and a denominator equal to the total net entitlements of all Clubs whose visiting Club entitlement exceeded their home Club obligations".[592] A team's "gross gate" was the total proceeds from ticket sales while its "net gate" was the gross gate less GST, Retail Sales Tax, per capita seat tax of stadium authority to a maximum of 50% of tickets sold, any legal or statutory sum directed by the jurisdiction in which the game was played. As a concession to the Argonauts, there was "an allowance for rental of the playing facility for each home game not to exceed 10% of the gross gate after the deductions above.[593]

Media interest received even more momentum when the Argos announced the signing of Raghib (Rocket) Ismail to a four-year contract which could "pay him $26.2 million for 1991–94. Of that, $18.2 million is guaranteed".[594] The former Notre Dame star spurned offers from the NFL and immediately set off publicity drums throughout North America. Hugh Campbell of the Eskimos was ecstatic: "It's a wonderful thing. (McNall) signed the guy less than 48 hours ago and already the CFL is on the map like it's never been before. Who wouldn't be excited? You'd have to be made of stone not to be. When have we ever had this kind of attention?"[595]

If there was any criticism of the deal it was that the spirit of the salary cap was violated. Ismail was to receive a guarantee of $4.5 million for the year; the salary cap was pegged at $3 million per team! The Argo solution was to pay Ismail a salary of $100,000 from the Club, the rest as a personal services agreement with owner McNall.

The first meeting attended by Susan Waks and John Candy "representing the new regime" was June 5, 1991, coincidently the one being chaired by Phil Kershaw of Saskatchewan; Roy McMurtry had resigned as Chairman in order to become Associate Chief Justice of the Supreme Court of Ontario, General Division.[596] Susan Waks suggested that the League allow Toronto to host the '92 and '93 Grey Cup games "as part of the new marketing strategy of the Toronto Club".[597] It was passed in two separate resolutions. Only Edmonton voted against the '93 proposal since it already had a group working to host it there. Again there was no news of applications or transfers of franchises. When the matter of expansion came up, Hamilton's David Braley spoke of Windsor, Candy acknowledged Montreal and inquired about the possibility of Halifax. After some discussion Candy asked a question which in retrospect has become a guiding principle for the CFL: He asked "Whether the League would consider U.S. cities close to the Canadian border which are not potential NFL franchise areas but would be large enough to support a team".[598] After discussion about a request from a Portland, Oregon, group to have an exhibition game played there and a similar request from Fargo, North Dakota, where a domed stadium was being built, it was agreed "that an Expansion Committee would be created under the Chairmanship of Mr. Candy with Mr. Braley and two representatives from the Management Council who could be named later".[599]

By September, Candy had reported that "he had met with individuals in Portland, Oregon, and Detroit, Michigan, and was informed that both cities were prepared to join the League in 1992".[600] At the next meeting, Candy reported that three different groups wanted a franchise in Portland and of some interest in Washington, D.C. But there were also some logistics to work out, e.g., playing rules, field dimension, import quota, expansion draft, franchise areas, territorial rights, scheduling revenue sharing, officiating, salary caps, currency for payment, broadcast regulations, property rights and player relations to name a few".[601] It was suggested that "a strategic expansion plan would be developed".[602]

By the end of October, the ardour had cooled somewhat perhaps because of all of the details to be worked out. "It was agreed to recommend to the Board of Governors that expansion not be considered until the 1993 season at the earliest".[603]

Candy also reported that he had been contracted by the Glieberman family about the Ottawa team, which at the time was still being operated by CFL, placing "a considerable burden on the League resources".[604] The Gliebermans proposed to take over the team for the remainder of the '91 season and continue in '92 "and subsequent years. The long range plan of the Glieberman family is to operate a team in Detroit and it would like the first opportunity in that area. At that time the Ottawa Club would be transferred to a new owner".[605] The same meeting unanimously passed a resolution moved by Susan Waks and seconded by Murray Pezim, "that the League accept applications for expansion to the new franchise areas effective if necessary in 1992".[606]

In his search for new US owners, Candy had inadvertently solved a huge and growing problem for the league. The Ottawa Rough Riders gave notice that it could not continue to operate. Its Board of Directors resigned en masse on Wednesday July 24, 1991 forcing the CFL to hold an emergency meeting at the Airport Marriott Hotel in Toronto on the twenty-sixth.

Ottawa had a history of financial losses in recent years. When Allan Waters sold the Club in 1987, it was estimated that he had lost $13 million over his 10 year tenure as owner.[607] He sold the Club for $1 to a limited partnership of 27 business men who injected $1.5 million to cover team losses in '87 and '88. They added an additional $450,000 for 1987 expenses.[608] The team's performance on the field matched its financial picture. Its 1988 record was the worst in CFL history at 2–16.

Bailouts were provided from a variety of sources. The City of Ottawa allowed the Club revenue from concessions, parking and rent to the tune of $600,000. The regional government provided an additional $500,000 relief for 1989. The CFL did its part too. As of December 31, 1990 it had provided $1,000,000 from the League's Stabilization Fund.[609] At the same time however, the CFL made arrangements to recover its short-term loan. The

1990 Grey Cup, gate and travel equalization along with 1991 season's tickets receipts were assigned to the CFL.[610]

Just three games into its schedule, its record 0–3, the Rough Riders had reached the crisis point. The League was told that "all of the directors and officers of the general partner had resigned and none of the limited partners was willing to advance any further funds necessary to operate the Ottawa Football Club. Consequently the Club is effectively not carrying on business at the present time with no one in command and with no one prepared to advance necessary funds".[611]

The CFL moved to fill the hole. Citing Article 3.08 of the League constitution, Ottawa's membership in the Canadian Football League was "deemed to be automatically terminated due to the fact that the Ottawa Football Club has disbanded its business organization and/or ceased to carry on its business".[612] In the next breath, the League granted a new franchise for a transitional period until a new owner was found. Numbered corporation 943399 Ontario Limited was created, a franchise in the CFL awarded to it "effective July 26, 1911" [sic].[613] League Commissioner Donald Crump went to Ottawa to oversee the transition. Jo-Anne Polack continued to direct the day-to-day operations of the Club reporting "directly to CFL controller Paul Mihalek and legal counsel John Tory".[614] She had been told "not to comment on the change of ownership because of sensitivity between the limited partnership and its creditors".[615] As far as the CFL was concerned, the Riders' debt to it had been wiped out but not all were pleased at the transaction. "Terminating the Ottawa Rough Riders", it was reported, "and then moving to establish a new corporate entity, under the same name, seems to be the franchise equivalent of putting the house in your mother's name".[616]

A procession of prospective buyers were mentioned as possibilities as the schedule unfolded. Toronto businessman Jim Manis and former New York Islander Denis Potvin were said to be interested as was a partnership of Ron Cassidy owner of Handyco Canada Ltd. of Vancouver and rock and roll entertainer Bobby

Curtola. Former players Larry Fairholm and Skip Eamon, two who were mentioned as possible Montreal franchise revivers were also courted.

By the end of September, the CFL was still operating the franchise. Its controller noted that "the net cost could be as much as $3.1 million without taking into account any possible revenues from concessions, television and the Grey Cup".[617]

More and more, it appeared that the League was looking to the McNall group for leadership. Sports and Entertainment Vice-President and Chief Financial Officer Susan Waks was suggested by Saskatchewan's Phil Kershaw as someone who could help sell the Rough Riders because of her knowledge of "a number of prospects in Los Angeles".[618] While the League was preparing a plan to operate as a seven team league, there was also a report from the Chairman of the Expansion Committee, John Candy, citing Portland and Detroit as possible members in 1992 - "If possible existing teams could be transferred to those cities".[619]

Not until October 18 was the Ottawa Club sold, the buyers Bernie and Lonie Glieberman, father and son, from Detroit, Michigan. There was controversy before the sale and after. The League was criticized for not insisting that debts prior to its takeover be cleared up.[620]

Three instances of poor resolution of outstanding debts were cited. Willie Gillus, now the Argonauts' back-up quarterback, was still attempting to get the 'Riders to pay a $2,000 medical expense from 1989 when he was a member of the Ottawa team. Ottawa's former offensive line coach Bob Weber, who was owed "more than $100,000 from the Riders' previous owners" sued the CFL and won his case in October. Head Coach Steve Goldman, fired by CFL Commissioner Don Crump on August 3, was issued one paycheque. He was "giving the League 10 days to pay him what's left of his $120,000 contract otherwise he'll pursue court action". [621]Goldman was replaced with Joe Faragalli who led the Riders to a 7–7 record after taking over. He too was the subject of controversy. When the Gliebermans formally took over the Club, their arrangement with the League was that it "would take over the existing stadium lease, player contracts, office premises and staff and would assume all obligations thereafter".[622] The CFL gave further protection to the Gliebermans declaring "it would be indemnified from charges incurred and applicable before the transfer date, in particular, salary claims by former coaches and players".[623] There was protection guaranteed should the former owners attempt to seize the equipment. The Rough Riders would also "become entitled to any share of the League revenues accruing to the Ottawa franchise after the transfer date".[624] Ownership of the Ottawa Football Club was transferred from 943399 Ontario Limited "to Ottawa Rough Riders Inc., a Michigan corporation owned by the Glieberman family of Detroit".[625]

One of the Gliebermans' moves at the end of the season was to hire Dan Rambo as the team's new Vice-President and General Manager of Football Operations. He promptly announced that he would "conduct a thorough search before hiring a coach".[626] Joe Faragalli, convinced that he had been told by the Glieberman family that he would be the coach, resigned in a huff: "I do not work for people I have no respect for. So there's no way they could get me back there under any condition".[627]

Another instance of the McNall group's influence was the sale of the Calgary Stampeders to friend Larry Ryckman. It represented another of the growing influences of the new owners of the Argonauts. Ever since the eighties the Club had been on the verge of collapse only to be rescued by the city or the province as a community owned and operated project. By the end of July the Club was in jeopardy again. It had a loan for $1.5 million from CIBC, another for $2 million from the Alberta Treasury Branch. Both were guaranteed by the province. Its creditors were questioning the health of the League. Cash flow was being severely strained early in the season when only two of its first six games were at home.[628] On the same day that the League terminated and resurrected the Rough Riders, "they also handed the Calgary Stampeders $270,000 worth of pogey, in effect. Another day at the office for Crump and the CFL, that most Mom and Pop of football Leagues",[629] wrote one disgruntled Ottawa reporter.

In a telephone conference call September 23, 1991 the Stampeders were sold to Larry Ryckman after club personnel advised CFL officials "that the only alternative to a sale to Ryckman would appear to be the collapse of the franchise. Approval in principle was given until a Board Meeting scheduled for October 2. Ryckman agreed to pay $1,500,000 to satisfy existing creditors with an immediate injection of $400,000 and to assume the $3,500,000 loan from Alberta. One condition was that the League forgive a debt of approximately "$450,000 arising from past advances".[630] A current advance of $150,000 was to be "repaid at the rate of $50,000 at the end of the years 1992, 1993 and 1994".[631] The new owner gave the CFL three undertakings: that the Calgary Club would notify the CFL of any change in ownership, that the Club would have the necessary working capital to carry on its League operations and that it would not support or encourage "the promotion, directly or indirectly an NFL franchise in Southern Alberta". The undertakings were binding only while "the CFL is in operation and the Calgary Club is using the McMahon Stadium for professional football".[632]

Television revenues have always been the pot of gold at the end of the rainbow as far as the CFL was concerned. It was to be the engine which could power the CFL to financial respectability. Prior to the 1991 season there was the expectation that each Club would realize $1 million or more from that medium. The CFL, still without a television contract for the '91 season turned to the McNall group even "before the signing of Ismail.[633] The Los Angeles based organization stated that "one of our goals was to become involved with the entire CFL not just the Argonauts, and to lend our expertise where we could, including marketing and the new television contracts ... an area where the League has had problems with the last few years and one where we had considerable success".[634] Once again, in addition to the Canadian networks, the CFL started looking south for television revenue to rescue it from its "sea of red ink". When the television contract was announced, it was without a major rights holder. CBC was to telecast 25 regular season games plus exclusive rights to play-offs and the Grey Cup game. TSN was to show 28 regular season games; CTV was shut out as was the League's Canadian Football Network which was too expensive for the CFL to operate. The League also decided to lift Argonaut blackouts in an effort to appeal to sponsors in the largest market; all in the hope of earning $1 to $1.25 million for each Club.[635]

At best, however, there was a certain amount of wishful thinking. CBC was paying $1.7 million to the League and was providing technical facilities costing $4 million. All advertising revenue generated would be the CFL's property. TSN was paying the League $800,000. Molson, even though it was not assuming its role as rights holder, was still substantially involved. It would buy $800,000 of advertising for the CBC and $250,000 for TSN games. In addition, should the Nielsen ratings reach a predetermined level, it would pay CBC a bonus of $150,000. For the lifting of each blackout of the Toronto games, the Argonauts would receive $200,000. The lifting of the blackout games in Hamilton would result in the purchase of 500 home game tickets by Molson. As well, Molson would contribute $100,000 to each of the eight CFL Clubs. The cash gift would be supplemented by $30,000 in services for each CFL member. Each Club would receive $1 million only if the CBC production costs were included. The big winner in the deal was the Argos who could receive a maximum of $1.8 million extra should all the home games be televised and the blackouts lifted.

Indeed, it was later demonstrated that the CBC was playing hardball with the CFL. The League owed the network $3,000,000 for 1991 production costs.[636] League Chairman John Tory offered to "phone CBC to request deferral of payment until the end of January".[637] In the meantime, he suggested a payment of $200,000 be made "as an act of good faith". The CBC gave its answer that it wasn't interested in faith; it wanted good works. CBC wanted its money by March 10, 1992. It also stated "it will not make a proposal for the 1992 season until the 1991 matter is settled".[638] The

CFL had no alternative. It authorized "a payment of $675,000 forthwith and a payment of $75,000 prior to February 4, 1992 and the balance of $1,600,000 prior to March 10, 1992".[639]

Television negotiations, always an important consideration for the CFL, were also another area of influence by the McNall group. In effect, they brought a business-like approach to a League which was more used to operating with greater informality. Clearly the McNall group was not pleased with the television contract negotiated for 1991. In order to finalize the deal with its largest rights holder, CBC, "it was necessary to agree to blackout lifts of CBC games played in Toronto and Hamilton".[640] The CBC had been "adamant on this condition".[641] While the McNall group agreed that the League had little choice in the matter, it did object to a blanket payment to Hamilton "for lifting the primary blackout for four home games. McNall added that the amount should be determined by the extent of the monetary damage to the home gate receipts which can be directly attributed to having lifted the blackout".[642]

Hamilton owner David Braley replied that the announcement of the lifting of the blackout for the Toronto area resulted in an immediate "900 seasons ticket cancellations from long-time subscribers" and a halt to new subscriptions. The loss of fans per game was estimated at 4,000 to 8,000 per game.[643] Braley was ready to withhold his approval for the lifting of the blackout, unanimity was required, should Hamilton not be compensated.[644]

Subsequently the matter surfaced once again. Susan Waks was "disturbed that payments had already been made to the Hamilton Club for its agreement to lift the blackout on four of its home games".[645] Her understanding of the television agreement was that such compensation should be at the end of the season "based on provable damage to the home club".[646]

Commissioner Don Crump "advised that the absence of a major rights holder had a damaging effect on the League's television revenues in 1991".[647] The League was forced to hire an "outside agency" to sell advertising for its televised games. Commissions and CBC charges were such that there was a "net for each Club in the estimated amount of $285,000".[648] Not only that, "the nature of the advertising business is such that the revenue is received long after the event".[649] The outcome of all of this was that Susan Waks "advised that the Toronto Club would like to have income contracts and expense commitments approved by the Clubs beforehand",[650] another implied criticism of Crump. After some discussion the League passed a unanimous resolution that "a contractual commitment or expenditure by the League in excess of $25,000 shall require the prior approval of Mr. John Tory on behalf of the Board of Governors".[651]

Because of the extraordinary number of Argonaut televised games, the publicity generated by the McNall group, the signing of Raghib Ismail and the tough business-like approach taken at the League level regarding funds and blackouts, there was a certain amount of nervousness in Hamilton. There, the Tiger Cats were undergoing financial strain. Fans were staying away; the season ticket base was being eroded. The Hamilton-Toronto rivalry seemed to be spilling over from the field. Hamilton Mayor Bob Morrow was "told by reliable sources that the Argonauts are trying to drive the Tiger Cats out of Hamilton[652] . . . and absorb the entire Canadian football market in Southern Ontario».[653]

Of course, the Argonauts denied it. But the Hamilton officials might have thought so just because of the overwhelming amounts of publicity generated by the Toronto team: The arrival of McNall, Gretzky and Candy on the scene, the signing of Ismail and the marketing surrounding him (the Argo's seasons ticket campaign kicked off with a half page and with the simple message on a plain background "Put a Rocket in Your Pocket"). Television seemed to be hooking its coverage to the Argonauts: the CBC was telecasting 7 of their 10 home and four away games; TSN was carrying five Toronto games.

True to the people's impression that the California trio would bring glitz and glamour to the League, the Argonauts showcased Mariel Hemingway and the Blues Brothers at the opening League game. Sports Illustrated, The New York Times and a host of American media were featuring the upstart Canadian Football League which had attracted Ismail and Flutie and the deep pockets of Bruce McNall. Suddenly, the game was being noticed once again by Canadians. Some didn't see the whole scenario as unusual:

> *Nineteen ninety-one may go down as the year the Americans discovered Canadian football. While at home the papers and the airwaves are full of stories about financial woes of the teams, it's left up to American publications and TV networks to come up with upbeat news about our game. . . . Grasping for American approval—isn't that the Canadian way?*[654]

Indeed, there seemed to be a thirst for American approval, which of course, it was hoped would pay off in much needed revenue from television. When it was announced by McNall representative Roy Mlakar "that Prime Ticket wished to carry the game live to its 254 million viewers in the U.S.A.",[655] no financial consideration had been mentioned. League officials in discussing the proposal "agreed that while the exposure itself was a benefit to the League, there should be some more tangible receipt such as a contribution to the cost of the AFCA (American Football Coaches Association) reception in Dallas on January 7, 1992".[656] It was obvious that League officials were anxious to defer immediate revenue in the hope of the long sought after major American television contract.

Rightly or wrongly the League was committed to its evolving widening of the door to the United States. As a result, rule changes for the '91 season were minimal, confirmation that the game was exciting, would be accepted in the US on its differentiated merits and needed only tinkering.

There were changes in the coaching ranks. In Toronto, Don Mathews left the team mid-way through his 2-year contract, citing "philosophical differences" with Argos' General Manager Mike McCarthy.[657] Mathews had come to Toronto with a promise to bring a "shoot the lights out" approach to football. He delivered. In spite of injuries to all of his quarterbacks, Matt Dunigan, John Congemi and Rickie Foggie during the course of the season, the Argos set a CFL record by scoring 689 points. Mathews moved to Orlando where he was announced as the Head Coach for that city's World League of American Football team, surfacing later as a mid-season appointment as Saskatchewan's Head Coach. Mathews was replaced in Toronto by assistant Adam Rita.

There was an even greater surprise in Winnipeg. The CFL was losing its Coach of the Year. Again, the newly created WLAF was the culprit; Mike Riley signed to become the new Head Coach of the San Antonio Riders just five days before he was announced as the Canadian Football League Coach of the Year. If seemed as it was "deja vu all over again". After 1988, Riley was selected the Coach of the Year and took a job as an assistant at Stanford University where he was to be offensive co-ordinator. Two weeks later he returned to Winnipeg to coach the Blue Bombers. This time, however, Riley was determined to see his decision through. It was an "opportunity to build something that's not there. A chance to start from the ground floor".[658] Riley's decision was aided by a reported salary income of $100,000–$125,000 (US), more than the $90,000 he earned with Winnipeg, plus a new car, a share of the Club and membership in a Country Club.[659] Winnipeg responded by signing former NFL coach Darryl Rogers to replace Riley for the 91 season.

A third major change in coaching took place in Edmonton. On February 4, 1991, the Eskimos announced that they were replacing Joe Faragalli with Ron Lancaster. There had been rumours that former quarterback Tom Wilkinson had been offered the task, "accepted it and then turned it down after further thought".[660] For Lancaster, the quarterback turned sportscaster, it was a second chance at coaching, his first one at Saskatchewan having been a disappointment.

In League play, both Hamilton and Saskatchewan ended up in last place in their respective divisions. Hamilton, with a 3–15 record, replaced its coach David Beckman with fired Saskatchewan coach John Gregory who was himself supplanted in mid-season by Don Mathews. At the other end of the standings, the Argonauts and Eskimos finished in first place at 13–5 and 12–6 respectively to earn byes. In the East, Winnipeg hosted the Rough Riders and subdued them by a 26–8 score; in the West, the visiting British Columbia Lions were edged by Calgary Stampeders with a 43–41 score. In the finals, Toronto handled Winnipeg easily 42–3 while in the west Calgary, rapidly gaining a reputation as the "Cardiac Kids" defeated Edmonton by a 38–36 score, punctuated by a 20 point 4th quarter comeback.

Winnipeg, the site of the 1991 Grey Cup game, was a welcome relief after the disastrous 1990 Grey Cup game in Vancouver. it was obvious to all that the game was being played, that it was important to the community, that it would attract over 50,000 paid spectators as opposed to the 26,827 who bought tickets for the 1990 game.[661]

Weather and the comparisons with the covered stadiums of Vancouver and Toronto were the topic of conversation. Any report about the game was sure to include references to "bone-chilling . . . sub-zero temperatures and brisk winds".[662] Stampeder middle linebacker Alondra Johnson was quoted as having said that his "working for six months in an ice cream packing plant in Los Angeles"[663] helped him to prepare for the Winnipeg weather. Just two days before the game, one estimate of the game day temperature was "the mercury slumping somewhere between 8 Celsius and death from exposure"[664] . . . the artificial turf will be frozen and the ball will be like a rock».[665]

There were two camps forming. On the one hand, Calgary Coach Wally Buono was in favour of the Grey Cup site moving around the League: "The CFL is steeped in tradition because of climate",[666] he said. "You're doing a disservice to the smaller cities of Canada if you don't allow them to host it".[667] There were some who disagreed saying that an era was coming to an end. The 79th Grey Cup game was to "bring to a close a chapter in national sports history".[668] Some passed it off as just another case of Hog Towners thinking the world started and stopped there when the writer mentioned that

> *the Grey Cup will be played at SkyDome for the next two years. It will likely never again be played outdoors or in a smaller city. Like the Super Bowl, it will become primarily a television-driven exercise, a 'culmination event' (as the WWF calls Wrestle mania), an excuse to squeeze the maximum exposure and maximum dollars out of a single football game.*[669]

Winnipeggers seemed to be oblivious to the developing dictum that "the CFL can evolve or die".[670] Indeed they seemed to revel in the developing mystique about "Winterpeg". Among the many souvenirs offered to the public was a teddy bear "named Shivers, appropriately".[671]

At the awards evening Thursday before the Sunday game, the west won four of the five categories, B.C. Lions players winning three of those four. Doug Flutie was selected the Outstanding Player over Winnipeg's Robert Mimbs. Lions tackle Jim Mills won his second consecutive Outstanding Offensive Lineman Award. Chris Walby of the Blue Bombers was runner-up. The third B.C. winner was running back Jon Volpe selected as Rookie of the Year ahead of the Argonauts' high profile Raghib Ismail.

The Outstanding Canadian Award was won by Edmonton's fullback Blake Marshall. Lance Chomyc of the Argonauts was runner-up. Winnipeg's Greg Battle was the only eastern player selected, winning the Outstanding Defensive Player Award over Calgary's defensive end Will Johnson.

When Volpe won over Ismail, it prompted one reporter to write that "deeds won out over dollars",[672] a not so subtle reference to the huge contract being paid to the "Rocket". There was no question that Volpe was a deserving choice. He had rushed for 1,395 yards on 239 carries and scored 20 touchdowns, a record for a rookie. The "Rocket" had his defenders and detractors. He scored 13 touchdowns and had 2,959 all-purpose yards mainly from pass receptions and returning kicks. Throughout the League he was an attraction that the public wanted to see. There were "several incidents with crowds on the road that resembled scenes out of Beatlemania".[673] At home, the Argonaut ticket revenue was "up 40 per cent, advertising and sponsorship up 144 per cent and concessions up 92 per cent".[674] Evidence of how the Argonauts and the CFL benefited from his status as a "marquee player" can be gained from the Eastern Final. Season's ticket holders were not forced to buy tickets for the game and because of that "the Club had no real idea of how many people would show up".[675] In addition, the TV blackout was being lifted; there was no headline entertainment being provided; only the Argonauts and Blue Bombers and the game were being offered. Fifty thousand spectators packed the Dome to cheer the Argonauts to their one sided win and entrance to the Grey Cup game.

But not all were pleased with the Rocket. Earlier in the season, Calgary linebacker Dan Wicklum hit Ismail with what some called a "late hit" while others saw as a normal defensive tackle. It caused the Rocket to be "woozy". Tempers flared. Commentators fretted about run of the mill players acting as "hit men", robbing the League of excitement and drawing power. The Commissioner reacted by sending a missive from his office to all teams "about the value of the marquee players to the CFL's health in general. Translation: lay off the high priced talent".[676] Argonaut partner Wayne Gretzky was also critical about the Calgary player's hit. To show that there were no sacred cows, "Wicklum responded calling Gretzky's comments 'ignorant and ill-informed'".[677] Calgary receiver Demetrius "Pee Wee" Smith, who caught the last minute pass to propel the Stampeders past the Eskimos in the Western Final, was also critical of the Argonauts in general, ("Toronto's spoiled. They don't want to come outside and play") and the "Rocket" in particular ("So he's a marquee player and can't be tackled hard? Every time he's hit hard, it seems there's a flag. But he's got a uniform on, just like me").[678]

The Toronto club seemed eager to protect their young 21-year-old who at times did not show up for engagements. During the early morning "Meet the Players Breakfast" on Friday of Grey Cup week Ismail was absent. It was the second incident in a week. He was a half-hour late for the Eastern Final workout at SkyDome, saying that he had gone to the Exhibition grounds where the Argos normally practiced. On this occasion, "a publicity bonanza for the game . . . to thank everyone who contributed to the Club's success and hopefully impress some buyers of the television time next year",[679] the Argos were embarrassed. It was a mandatory event; the Argos sent word to him. Ismail "did honour them with his presence briefly and then took off".[680] Publicly, the Argo players seemed less concerned with the Rocket's absence. Said quarterback Rickie Foggie: "He sleeps more than anyone I know. He also runs faster than anyone I know".[681]

Foggie might have been right. In the Grey Cup game it was a dash by Ismail, 87 yards on a kick-off return, that provided the spark and deflated Calgary. It made up for two earlier plays by Ismail. In the first half he fumbled after a 67 yard punt return. In the second half, his objectionable conduct penalty early in the fourth quarter contributed to Calgary scoring a touchdown which put them only one point behind, 22–21. A Toronto recovery of a Calgary fumble on the subsequent kick-off culminated with a touchdown pass to Paul Masotti from Matt Dunigan to clinch the game 36–21. The game was also a testimony to Matt Dunigan who directed the Argonaut attack in spite of a broken collarbone, the pain and feeling deadened by novocaine. An attendance of 51,985 sat in temperatures of -17°C and winds from the north west blowing at 13 kph. It generated receipts of $3,246,180. It was the first Grey Cup game ever played in Manitoba. The CBC's live Grey Cup broadcast was "the top rated Canadian produced TV show of the year-it drew an average audience of 3.531 million"[682] It was a continuation of the good news that the league had received from its Western Championship game between Calgary and Edmonton. The A. C. Nielsen ratings for that game showed "an average minute audience of 1.4 million, an increase of 30 per cent from last year's game".[683]

In Toronto, where a parade was held to honour the Argonauts, there were the inevitable comparisons with the Blue Jays whose fans were prepared for a world series berth but were disappointed when three home games in a row were lost. The season long improvement of the Argonauts, their growing acceptance by the public was reflected in the chants of "Rock-et", "Rock-et" and "Broooce" paying recognition to Ismail and McNall. It gave credence to the idea that "when owner Bruce McNall signed Ismail, he was paying for an idea, the veneer of the big time, the kind of American celebrity validation that seems so important in the Southern Ontario Market".[684]

The revival of the Argonauts, the successful Grey Cup game, the excitement created by the play of the injured Mike "Pinball" Clemons and Matt Dunigan who served as the delivery system for the "Rocket" created a sense of optimism about the CFL for the first time in years. Stephen Brunt wrote:

> *The challenge now is to bottle that excitement, to sell it, to keep the league on an even, disaster-free, keel this winter, to present a united front, get some games on television in the U.S. and press on for expansion.*
>
> *That's a helluva task.*
>
> *But look at where things are to day, then look at where they were a year ago. The worst is over.*[685]

On the surface, it appeared as if the new WLAF would be a thorn in the side of the CFL. Underneath, however, there was really no threat at all. The WLAF as a spring league, had a low salary structure; it would honour CFL contracts; allow a player to play in its league in the spring, gather experience and move on to the CFL in the fall. In addition the placing of a franchise in Montreal would serve to keep football alive in that city and provide a barometer of acceptance for the CFL.[686] Ever since the Alouettes left Montreal, the League was searching for ways to re-enter the Montreal market. The Montreal Machine franchise would be a good indicator of the Quebec city's appetite for football.

Once the World League of American Football collapsed the only real competition to the CFL for the American players was the NFL. Expansion of the CFL into the United States was obviously becoming a cornerstone for league success and in keeping with the new Argonaut owners' vision. Suddenly, interest was revived in Montreal. It was Canada's 125th year; the Quebec market of more than 6 million was not being served; there was interest but no application as yet for league membership. There were two camps, the one wanting expansion to occur in the Canadian markets first; the other seeking the United States fields. Murray Pezim was for the latter. "The only basic problem you have with expansion is Canadian content and that's a big hurdle to overcome".[687] Perhaps he was thinking of the new agreement which had to be negotiated with the players prior to the '92 season. The CFL governors decided to test the market in Portland scheduling an exhibition game in June between the Lions and Argos, two teams which had good players who would be recognized by the American public, Doug Flutie and "Rocket" Ismail.

In the end, it was the McNall formula and acceptance that spelled the end for Commissioner Don Crump. In spite of ratings improvements, television revenues for the '91 season would result in approximately $200,000 per team. Even then, that figure was considered to be more the result of McNall's entrance on the negotiating scene rather than Crump's. The league was hoping to have its '92 schedule finalized before the end of the current year in order to capitalize on the high ratings. There was a consensus however that Crump would not be in charge, that he would "jump or be pushed"[688] from his lofty perch.

Crump did not seem to fit in to the image the CFL was attempting to promote. The new owner of the Calgary Stampeders was described as having "nice hair, nice suit, talks smart and talks business with the right amount of new-age missionary zeal";[689]on the other hand, Don Crump appeared to be uncomfortable in his role. There were problems in public relations: "It seems all I do is answer questions that there aren't any answers to. I don't know".[690] His answers at times were considered by some to be irrelevant. When asked to "explain the tough season the league had just weathered" Crump answered that "When we started the year there was the recession and we were in a war and three teams were in trouble".[691]Reporters were puzzled as to what the Gulf War had to do with the CFL, one wondering, tongue in cheek but nonetheless indicative of some of the feelings toward Crump: "Did he think former Montreal tight end Nick Aragki was Nick Iraqui?"[692]

Crump seemed to be a reluctant passenger. He didn't help his credibility when at a media conference during Grey Cup week, he referred to the possibility of expanding to Portland but placed it in Washington rather than Oregon.[693] But it was the television contract and the entrance of McNall into the CFL which sealed his fate. From that point on he had "been on the outside looking in as the Californians began to recast Canadian football in their own image."[694]

On December 11, Donald Crump announced his intention to step down as Commissioner once a successor was found. "I think my general feeling was that every time I had to go to a board meeting, it was like walking across a mine field. I guess I just don't want to put my foot on another mine,"[695] said a beleaguered Commissioner. The committee to find a successor consisted of Phil Kershaw of Saskatchewan, Hugh Campbell of Edmonton, Toronto's Susan Waks and Ottawa's Bernie Glieberman.

The CFL had succeeded in restoring the title of "Commissioner" to its titular head in 1991 but ever since it had struggled with the type of Commissioner in office. Don Crump had an astute financial background, was able to ride shotgun for that "Maverick Mule" Harold Ballard both with the Toronto Maple Leafs and Hamilton Tiger Cats, but there was also the growing realization that the Commissioner was first and foremost working for the Clubs and doing their bidding. In the end, Crump was done in by his inability to perform as the League's Board of Governors, the owners, wished him to perform.

Television revenue was one of the major areas of concern. Whereas Clubs had targeted revenues of $600,000 to more than $1 million each, there was $240,752 for each one at the end of the '91 season.[696] Crump "insisted that several of the governors did not understand the difficulty he had in attracting potential advisors. 'Some people thought that there was a hole in the ground full of money. And I guess they blamed me for not finding that hole', said Crump".[697] Some thought that the CFL was still living in the past, in those heady days when it had the large television contract with rights sponsor Carling O'Keefe. The more than $1 million per club from one source was a healthy slice of the revenues each Club had to generate. Cash flow had been pretty well guaranteed; front offices had more time to spend on other areas. All of that was in the past said Crump: "it's not just a matter of getting someone to sign on the dotted line and getting the money from them up front. It doesn't happen that way anymore".[698]

Crump also refused to look upon expansion to the United States as the road to greater revenues through American television contracts, something which brought him solidly in conflict with the Los Angeles group which owned the Argonauts. He compared American interest in Canadian football to that of Canadians' with Australian Rules football. He downplayed the effect that adding one or two American teams would have on American television saying "the only viable medium is the CBC. And they have fixed costs, so they aren't going to budge on their financial demands. So its up to the CFL to go out and sell advertising".[699]

In some ways Crump suffered from the same image problems as the CFL. Some thought that "he could have been sent to California for a buff and polish... it was as much a matter of style as much as anything else that made a change necessary especially in the new veneer conscious CFL of Bruce McNall and his pals where there are no dweebs allowed".[700]

As for Susan Waks, the McNall group's Vice President, Crump was "more of an individual player"[701] in an area where a team approach was needed. As a member of the League's Executive Committee which was charged with spearheading the search for the new Commissioner, she felt he should be "a strong business person and communicator".[702] Phil Kershaw, President of Saskatchewan and also a member of the CFL Executive Committee, thought that "the Grey Cup and the television contract are the two most important areas under the Commissioner's jurisdiction. Ultimately, he's judged on his performance in those two areas".[703] There was a perception problem, said Kershaw. Crump "was overblamed and under credited for the things he did during his two years as Commissioner. But the perception problem almost became a problem in itself".[704]

When Crump resigned on December 11, 1991, he offered to stay on as long as the League wanted him to, up until the new Commissioner was named if necessary. The League declined. "The members of the Executive Committee felt that December 31, 1991, was most appropriate in all of the circumstances".[705] The Board of Governors' meeting, held via a telephone conference call, was considered so confidential that even long time League Secretary Greg Fulton along with Controller Paul Mihalek, were asked to leave the line. John Tory kept the minutes relating to the discussion about the Commissioner".[706]

The meeting also decided to use a "head hunter", the firm of Heidrick & Struggles Canada Inc. to assist with the selection of the new Commissioner. Contact had been made between the company, a Toronto based "executive search firm with experience in the sports industry"[707] and member of the Executive

Committee, Hugh Campbell, in a letter to Campbell dated December 18, 1991.[708]

The "executive search consulting firm" made its report at the Board of Governors meeting in Edmonton on January 29, once again in camera with only Governors and alternates in attendance. It was reported that as many as 30 and as few as 15 applied, or were considered. Among the most notable names mentioned were Tony Gabriel, Leif Petterson, John Michaluk and Larry Fairholm, all former players and now successful business men, former Ottawa Mayor James Durrell, Insurance executive Ron Barbaro, former BC Lions General Manager Bobby Ackles and Senator Norm Atkins.

After the report by Heidrick and Struggles representative Bruce Ward, the CFL decided to expand the selection committee to include one member from each club "not represented on the Executive Committee, plus League Counsel"[709] in order to interview candidates, select and announce the choice at the League's Annual Meeting in Hamilton, February 27, 1992.

That choice, announced at 7pm in Hamilton's Football Hall of Fame, there among the love and tradition of the game in Canada, was Larry Smith. "When we interviewed him, we said, 'Stop right there' - we knew he was our man," said Ottawa Rough Riders owner Bernard Glieberman, a member of the CFL's search committee".[710] Smith had impressive credentials. He had been a first draft choice of the Alouettes as a running back and tight end, played in 140 consecutive games, appeared in 5 Grey Cups and won two. He retired after the 1980 season. As impressive as that was, he maintained that he was "not coming in to be a jock. I'm a business man. I was a jock 20 years ago".[711] His business credentials were equally impressive. A graduate of Bishop's Economics and Business program in 1972 and Mc Gill's Civil Law in 1976, he was a president and head of the frozen bakery products division of Olgivie Mills Ltd., a division of John Labatt Ltd.

Reaction was almost totally positive; there were many comparisons between the old and the new. Noting that the announcement was made in the Hall of Fame at 7pm, "too late to make the dinner hour television newscasts", the inevitable comparison was made:

> *Lots of history, lots of nods to the ancients, and a stupid organizational botch: that's the CFL Past in a nutshell.*
>
> *And the CFL Future? Well from the current confusion, amidst the fallout from last year's McNall Revolution, emerges a guy who talks like a business school textbook.*[712]

Larry Ryckman was another owner who was pleased saying that Smith was "a contemporary man, someone who is disciplined, confident and one who can handle any distractions. I'm not criticizing Donald but perception ultimately becomes reality. Larry is the perfect individual at the best time. He has been given total authority by the governors".[713] Brian Cooper of the Argonauts was equally supportive: We've always maintained that we need a person who has ties to Bay Street. Sport is a business and there's no disputing Larry's business sense".[714]

At his first press conference, Smith's impression on the media was positive and immediate. His quick quips caused one wag to report that "for once the critics were laughing with a Canadian Football League Commissioner instead of at him".[715] He answered a variety of questions dealing with problem areas in the League. He stressed the importance of financial viability, gaining partnerships with the corporate sector and aggressive marketing. On League expansion, Montreal was high on the list but expansion to the United States was a distinct possibility since "as a business you have to go where you can grow... with a plan in place but... your house in order first".[716] Other priorities were stabilizing the Hamilton Tiger Cat franchise and the unique blend of privately and community owned clubs that was the CFL. Television of course came up and the new Commissioner was for continuing the lifting of the blackout as the Argonauts had insisted: The Argos proved last year that lifting blackouts works.

You have to deal with each market separately. Obviously a good TV deal is essential".[717]

The CFL was a League with serious financial problems both from a collective and individual club perspective. It owed money to the CBC; operation of the Ottawa Club prior to the Glieberman sale from July 26 to October 19 "cost approximately $2.1 million".[718] The Stabilization Fund was gone, its money used mainly "to recover the funds expended by the League in the operation of 943399 Ontario Limited to maintain the Ottawa franchise"[719] before it was sold. At the end of 1991, the CFL's deficit as a league was $1,954,724 having grown from $1,162,673 at the beginning of the year.[720] The League had attempted to eliminate the deficit by increasing Club assessments from $14,500 per month in 1989 to $36,935 in 1991. It was too large an increase for clubs to handle. At the June 5, 1991 meeting in Regina, the assessment was cut back "to the 1990 rate of $22,500 per month plus GST".[721]

Television which was always hoped to be the "cash cow" to save the League was generating revenue but the League's costs in manufacturing that revenue were high. The Canadian television Rights Fee was $1,603,000; the U.S., $113,260. The League earned a bonus of $123,000 because of good ratings. Advertising revenue was $6,470,992 but it cost $1,539,821 to generate that amount. Other costs were Administration ($4,478), Blackout compensation ($500,000), consulting ($8,200) and telecast charges ($4,323,913). The total remaining from television was $1,933,840 or $241,730 per club.[722] Fortunately the net revenue from the Grey Cup game in Winnipeg was high, $1,748,732 as opposed to $707,409 in 1990. But net income from playoff games in 1991 was only $4,942, down from $253,873 in '90.[723]

It was in the midst of this financial upheaval that Larry Smith gave his first major presentation to the League's Board of Governors.[724] Aided by a visual display, he stressed the need to attract revenues from "gate receipts, television and marketing ventures"[725] in addition to having a good on-field product. He wanted to re-organize the League office "to make it more responsive to the clubs, the media, the business community and the players". His vision for the League in 1996 was to have

- *nine profitable Canadian franchises with solid, committed ownership*
- *three profitable U.S. franchises*
- *four to six major national sponsors, five to six major regional sponsors and 5 - 10 minor national sponsors*
- *a successful licensing business with a 15% market share generating revenues in excess of $3,000,000*
- *a self-supporting League office regarded as an innovative, dynamic organization with strong management and player relations*
- *a success story integrated into the community with a new generation of supporters*[726]

While the Commissioner was commended for his long-range view, it was the short-term which was the immediate concern of most. Edmonton, saying that the deficit could not be swept under the rug, wanted that addressed before any other proposals were considered. Toronto, represented by Rosanne Rocchi "complained that the figures in the presentation (were) misleading". She was particularly concerned that the "potential liability of the League with regard to its operation of the Ottawa Club has been understated, which could impact on the distribution of revenues to other clubs".[727] Saskatchewan's Phil Kershaw "asked whether it would be feasible to seek out a source of bridge financing to ensure that the Clubs and the League survive the season".[728] Nothing too insignificant failed to come under the scrutiny of the Board members in their effort to search for ways to cut costs. Hamilton's Braley, noting that the League's budget for officiating was $768,400, asked how much of that was attributable to the use of a seventh official on the field. It was "approximately $72,000".[729] Even the office space costs, which were higher in 1992 because of a "rent free period during the early months of

1991" were considered high by the Argonauts' Rocchi who pointed out that office space was available in downtown Toronto at $8.00 per square foot.[730]

In the words of Calgary owner Larry Ryckman who was described as the "personification of the new guard" of the CFL owners,

> *There's really been a change of the tides here".[731] The new appointment was at a critical point in the life of the CFL. Changing tides, a watershed, the end of the beginning of the beginning of the end: the fate of Canadian Professional football whatever it turns out to be, will certainly be decided during Larry Smith's five year term in office. The traditionalists might as well get used to the jargon, get used to the new style and hope like hell there's genius somewhere.[732]*

In some ways the idea of the McNall group as a boon to the league was wearing thin. They seemed to have caught the feeling that individual clubs were to look out for themselves first rather than having a league perspective. When the McNall group bought the Argonauts from Harry Ornest, there were "certain understandings reached" which included the "awarding of the 1992 and 1993 Grey Cup games to Toronto, the exclusive marketing rights in the Toronto area, the granting of local television rights to the Toronto Club and exemption from gate equalization".[733] On its part, the Toronto Club provided a trade-off. It "would make available to the League and the other Clubs its marketing expertise and the public relations services of its high profile personnel".[734]

Apparently the "understandings" were not written down. Clubs balked at incorporating them into the League regulations. Ottawa's Bernie Glieberman said he was "disturbed by what he has learned since his purchase of the Ottawa Club".[735] The League struck a committee of Gary Campbell of Edmonton, Larry Ryckman of Calgary and John Tory "to meet with a group from the Toronto Club to clarify what was agreed to by both the League and the new owners" of the Argonauts.[736] The Argonauts had also exerted a not so subtle amount of pressure for resolution of the issue. It presented the League with an invoice for $422,000 related to travelling expenses for public relations performed by its high profile leadership on behalf of the League. The cost to each Club would be in excess of $50,000.[737] At the same meeting, the Toronto Club reported that John Candy had asked to be relieved of the Chair of the Expansion Committee "because of his heavy professional commitments".[738] Apparently Candy still wished to stay on the Committee.[739] The League replaced him both on the Committee and as Chair with Calgary's Larry Ryckman. It also offered the Argonauts a "settlement of the outstanding public relations account with payments of $125,000 per year for two years which amounts to $15,000 per club.[740]

The Argonauts had other complaints. Its rental of the SkyDome was $70,000 per game. Not only that, the lease arrangement "provided that the landlord must be compensated in the event of a blackout lift".[741] Such compensation had been "waived in 1991 because of the ongoing negotiations".[742] The SkyDome and McNall were at odds over the collection of receipts from the restaurants overlooking the field during Argo games: The Argos wanted revenues; the restaurants were unwilling to pay it. When McNall was buying the team "he was told that he would be allowed to sell advertising but... found out the Sky Dome's exclusivity with some advertisers means he can't sell to the competition".[743] McNall wasn't complaining about the exclusivity. Rather, he was upset about not being told when he was negotiating to buy the Argonauts saying he "would have asked to have it made up in other areas such as lower rent or more of a percentage of concessions".[744]

McNall was also venting his frustrations with the lack of progress he was making with the league on items that he thought were agreed to when he purchased the team. "The attitude seems to be that 'don't worry, they've got deep pockets".[745] He was critical of the other CFL owners who spoke of "revenue sharing" but not "cost sharing". "No one, he said, offered to pay a share of Ismail's $18 million salary, although everyone agreed his presence helped rejuvenate the CFL last season".[746] Not only the CFL, but the Argonauts whose average attendance rose by "more than 14,000 per game".[747] McNall was more critical of his fellow league members rather than new Commissioner Smith who "has a lot of people yapping at his heels".[748] But it was obvious that McNall was "disheartened to the point where he talked about the possibility of releasing marquee wide receiver Raghib (Rocket) Ismail to the NFL's Los Angeles Raiders and even selling the team".[749]

In the end, the League adjusted and a compromise was effected. The television arrangement in effect in 1992 was to continue through the '94 season as "a transitional provision".[750] Beginning in 1995, the League would select five home games from each Club's schedule and have the right to include those in the national television package "with the proceeds to be distributed equally".[751] The remaining games would be the priority of the home Club to be used to generate television revenue, all of it being retained by the home Club".[752] In the future any constitutional amendments regarding the television arrangements would have to be approved by 6 of the 8 Clubs or its equivalents.[753]

Only the Hamilton Club voted against the motion. Calgary was not represented at the meeting. It carried by a 6-1 vote, the stipulation being that it would be for the 1992 season and reviewed at the Annual Meeting in 1993.[754]

Hamilton was clearly not pleased with the developments. Its crowds were falling off. Owner David Braley had lost some $5.2 million since he became owner of the franchise. He had most to lose by the changes in the new "gate sharing" formula. Under the existing formula, his Club would have received $410,398 in 1991 whereas that would have been $250,603 on a 90% - 10% home/ visitor ratio and $202,603 if television blackout money was factored into the equation in the same way.[755]

Braley was actively trying to sell the Club. He was having problems with the municipality which was refusing to continue with a payment of $300,000 per year for advertising and trademark rights at Ivor Wynne Stadium, although it had offered to cut the rent from $100,000 to $50,000.[756] When Braley threatened to move, the city issued a termination notice. The Club would be forced to vacate Ivor Wynne Stadium by July 7 although permission was given to play the opening game on July 9 against Winnipeg.[757] Braley was frustrated. He needed cash flow; the League was slow in coming forth with money it owed from the 1991 season; he also resented the fact that the League had supported Ottawa and Calgary out of CFL revenue and thus created some confusion as to "the question of unlimited liability: Is it $1.5 million? Or is it $3 million"?[758] For newly acquired quarterback Damon Allen, it was deja vu, "the Ottawa Rough Riders of '91 without the fans".[759] The situation stabilized itself somewhat when an announcement that the club was to become a "not for profit" community based Club headed up by lawyer Roger Yachetti and former player and banker John Michaluk. The announcement was greeted with temporary relief all around. It was "no longer third and long (but) the win isn't secured either".[760]

As serious as the Hamilton situation was, the B.C. Lions' was even more precarious. The Hamilton change cost the League no money. That was not the case with B.C. Lions and their flamboyant owner Murray Pezim.

The 1990 Lions of Murray Pezim and quarterback Doug Flutie led the CFL with an average attendance of 40,000. B.C. supporters had forgotten about the circus atmosphere of the early Pezim years; Coach Bob O'Billovich seemed to have brought some stability to the organization. But the unquestioned attraction to all was the play of quarterback Doug Flutie. Under his leadership, the Lions had a 11-7 record; he threw a record number of attempts 730, completing 466 for 6619 yards and 38 touchdowns. He was selected as the CFL's most outstanding player for the '91 season. Flutie was also in his option year in '91 earning a reported $350,000[761], set to become a "free agent" on February 15.

Discussion between Flutie's agent Bob Woolf and Murray Pezim became rancorous. Negotiations broke down. Flutie threatened to go back to the NFL; Pezim called it a ploy. "I'm not prepared to go any further; I can't go any further", said Pezim. "Bob Woolf won't listen. We can't afford anymore. I've said this before and I'll say it again. Doug Flutie works for me. I don't work for him. And I don't intend to work for him".[762]

Pezim said that he had offered Flutie a three year contract of $600,000, $600,000 and $700,000; Woolf was seeking $600,000, $800,000 and $1 million in U.S. funds.[763] Negotiations broke down completely. Flutie announced that he would not return to B.C. to play football. Enter Calgary and owner Larry Ryckman. The Stampeders announced at a press conference on March 23, 1992 that they had signed free agent Flutie. In what was de-scribed as a "creative deal" Flutie could earn $5 million in a four year contract, bonuses included, with partial ownership which the quarterback said "was a major, major part of my decision".[764]

Ryckman was gushing over his new quarterback. "Doug is the Wayne Gretzky of football, that's what he is"[765] and "the greatest of the great, the best player in the history of Canadian football"[766] Calgary fans and media trumpeted the team's new acquisition. But B.C., the Lions, O'Billovich and Pezim were more than mild-ly upset. Pezim demanded that the Stampeders trade him Dan-ny Barrett as compensation. He described the Calgary owner as "that chicken Ryckman"[767] when he refused.

In the wider context of the League, comparisons between two franchises were made: In Hamilton where David Braley was sell-ing the Club, a proposed consortium of local business people bowed out, able to raise only one million of the $3 million price tag for local ownership; meanwhile in Calgary, Flutie had signed for $1 million per season. "The Calgary situation... a perfect ex-ample of what Bruce McNall and his progressive pals want the League to become. The Stamps sign a "marquee player"; inter-est in the franchise is sure to peak; the veneer of big time, deep pocketed ownership is maintained".[768]

Barrett was traded to the B.C. Lions in return for Offensive Tackle Rocco Romano and first year Centre Jamie Crysdale. "The deal also included a cash payment estimated at $250,000 and the right to play an exhibition game in Portland, Oregon, against the Toronto Argonauts".[769] Pezim, a stock promoter, paid the $250,000 to Ryckman with shares of a Jamaican gold property, the value of which dropped from $1.27 to 24 cents.[770] Ryckman was furious, threatening to not bring the Stampeders to Vancouver for a July 23 game. Media in both cities ridiculed the whole exercise. Pezim countered by saying he would "hand out rubber fowl so the fans can pelt Chicken Ryckman".[771] Even the Calgary media was upset, one report calling the whole scenario "a circus run by clowns" and chastising Stampeder owner Ryckman whose "remarks ruined the credibility of his cause, not to mention the credibility of those of us who want to treat the CFL as a professional league".[772]

By mid-August, the Lions were 0-7. Whereas in 1991, they averaged 40,000 spectators per game, 26,000 was the largest crowd that they drew in 1992. Pezim announced that the team was for sale, that he wouldn't "put another dime" into the Club.[773] When no takers were available at the $1 price and assumption of team debt, the League decided to act. It rescinded Pezim's franchise owned by Prime Sports and awarded a new one to Vancouver Football Operations Limited.[774] Once again, the CFL was forced to use its funds to operate a club. It was estimated that $180,000 per week would be the cost. The B.C. Pavilion Corporation offered to contribute $100,000 per week up to six weeks; Canada Safeway was set to contribute $25,000 per week.[775]

Realizing that "the temporary operation of the B.C. Club would impact on the total distribution of revenues at year end",[776] the time limit for the League's involvement was set at 30 days. During that time, It was decided that the Commissioner and two Board of Governors members would be a management committee; that private and/or government funds would be sought to relieve the League's financial burden; that all suppliers and associates, (i.e.) the CFLPA, were to be approached to secure "substantial cost reduction or revised financial arrangements"; that the maximum amount of funds advanced for the operation at any one time be $200,000.[777]

The Player's Association was to be contacted since Prime Sports had not remitted contribution to the CFL Player's Pension Plan.[778]

As per arrangements, another conference call was held seven days later to review the situation. One hundred thousand dollars of the estimated $1,600,000 needed was spent in the first week. Canada Post joined Safeway and the B.C. Pavilion Corp. in offering "cash contributions". It appeared "that no matter who becomes the new owner, the League may have to be responsible for up to $1,000,000 in charges".[779] The League decided to continue the bailout "until September 19, by which time it must have transferred the franchise to a new owner or terminate the operation".[780]

When the Board of Governors of the CFL met at the Delta River Inn in Richmond, B.C. on September 16, 1992, it was with the idea that "the meeting had originally been called to ratify the sale of the B.C. Club to the Pattison Group as the new owner".[781]The deal fell through, "the main reason... a concern about the financial viability of the League more so than the recent history of the B.C. Franchise".[782] The proposed "sale" had called for financial arrangements whereby the Pattison Group, the B.C. Pavilion Corporation (PAVCO) and the League would be one-third partners for the balance of the 1992 season.[783] In return for its involvement, PAVCO was expecting the 1994 Grey Cup game to be played in B.C. to help it recover its costs, tougher cost control measures by the League, a lower salary cap and reduced administration costs.[784] Indeed, the clubs passed a resolution that on all monies owed to them by the League as of September 15, an interest rate of prime plus one percent be added.[785] On September 23, the CFL, by means of telephone conference call, met again and under similar terms as would have been the case for Pattison, named Bill Comrie as the "new member". Comrie, the owner of The Brick furniture chain, a former director of the Edmonton

Eskimos and co-owner of the San Diego Gulls, was the new partner with the League and PAVCO for the 1992 season, and to be sole owner for '93.[786] Throughout the League, there appeared to be a collective sigh of relief. A commentator reported: And so ends The Crisis That Could Have Killed The Canadian Football League, Chapter XXVII.[787]

If the salary demands of Flutie and his subsequent signing by Calgary were contributing factors to the B.C. turmoil, the move of Matt Dunigan from Toronto to Winnipeg played a similar role in Toronto. Dunigan played out his option in 1991 and quarterbacked the Argonauts to a Grey Cup victory while playing with a separated shoulder. The Argonauts, contending that Dunigan was injury prone wanted to structure a contract based on the number of games played by the quarterback. Dunigan refused, arguing that the Argonauts' system called for minimum protection on passes with a maximum number of receivers being released in the pattern. When running back Mike Clemons at 5'6 and 180lbs was kept in to block, he was responsible for a defensive lineman who might weigh upwards of 250lbs. The overall effect, said Dunigan was that the quarterbacks in the Argonaut system were underprotected and more likely to be hit and therefore injured. Dunigan who was offered a reported $250,000 with the Argos, had missed 20 of 36 games since joining them in 1990. Prior to that he missed only 11 of 120 regular season games in Edmonton and B.C.[788]

Dunigan was seeking a guaranteed salary per year; owner McNall would not authorize more than $450,000 unguaranteed for the year. In the end, Dunigan signed with the Blue Bombers. His contract called for a guarantee of $500,000 for each of two years with an option for a third season at $500,000. Winnipeg also "took out an insurance policy - for a premium of $100,000 - that will indemnify them for the full $1,000,000" if Dunigan suffered a career ending injury.[789] The move was not without great pressure on the club. General Manager/Head Coach, Cal Murphy contacted a bank "to arrange a loan in order to meet Dunigan's demands".[790] The bank refused his request citing the $1.1 million deficit and the $800,000 in playing contracts for this year.[791] Murphy approached Winnipeg Enterprises Corp., the operators of the Stadium and Arena. They agreed to the loan with the stipulation that "Murphy had to promise... to raise ticket prices by $2 across the board for 1993".[792]

The moves had predictable results in Calgary and Winnipeg, two cities which were to meet in the 1992 Grey Cup game, and B.C. and Toronto. The latter two teams ended up in last place in their respective Conference.

In Ottawa, the Rough Riders created ongoing controversy with the signing, at the Gliebermans' insistence, of former NFL stalwart Dexter Manley. Prior to that, they decided to change the team's logo. Normally there would be a year's notice required to do so since all CFL teams might be left with obsolete merchandise in their stores. The requirement was waived since there were "possible legal consequences of using the old logo which the previous bankrupt owner might claim as its property".[793] The new logo a flaming "R" generated some controversy but not nearly as much as the "football toting beaver with skull and crossbones across its jersey". It was just another in the seemingly endless number of pratfalls performed by the Ottawa Club with its "new ownership, new management, no quarterback and salary problems".[794]

Indeed, it was later revealed that the team had been able to circumvent the salary cap going back to 1990. That year, the team signed "a gaggle of high priced free agents". It was an attempt to get the fan interest back but, said Jo-Anne Polack, "Now how are we going to get away with it".[795] Polack wasn't aware that the Salary Cap wasn't going to be enforced when she first joined the Rough Riders. Having signed the "free agents" however, the club expected that it would be monitored. It set up an elaborate scheme to escape detection. A moving company issued cheques to players to "help disguise a player's bonuses".[796] The moving company issued the player a T4 slip for Income Tax purposes and "would then invoice the team 'for services', Polack said. The same thing was done with an Ad agency and a printing company".[797] Polack stated that the practice was done "in case an auditor came in and started to go through the payrolls; that they couldn't trace it - from the League's purposes". She also mentioned that the practice was stopped "because after 1990 we realized no one was going to check anyway, so why bother".[798] Polack also said that only about 3/4 of players' contracts addendums that contained bonus clauses were filed with the League office. The rest would be held back. All of this was designed to give the impression that the Rough Riders were within the League's "competitive expenditures" ceiling. She also said that "the Riders filed all the contract addendums they had been holding back in the weeks before the team's board resigned en masse in July of '91. The concern was that the players get paid their due, she said".[799]

The year was also one where the League's collective agreement with the Players Association came up for negotiation. It promised to be tough bargaining for the League since it was strapped for cash. It decided that "a specialist in labour law" would be hired to help it prepare for the negotiation.[800] At a subsequent meeting, Warren K. Winkler Q.C. of the Toronto law firm of Winkler, Filion and Wakely, specialist in labour legislation was introduced and hired on a retainer basis "to assist the Player Relations Committee as its chief negotiator and spokesman".[801] Winkler was also to submit a "bi-weekly confidential report to the League by telephone conference on the progress of negotiations".[802] The Players Relations Committee consisted of the Commissioner, Hugh Campbell, Alan Ford and Mike McCarthy. It was evident however that Winkler, Campbell and Smith were most involved. Winkler, in his report to the League after successful conclusion of the pact, reported that as "a person outside the League", he had observed a change in attitude on the part of the Players' representatives "from one of extreme antagonism and distrust to the other extreme of understanding the League's problems and the desire to co-operate in solving them".[803] Winkler concluded that the reason for this was "the high level of credibility which the Commissioner and Mr. Campbell presented on behalf of the League".[804]

Not all felt the same way. Indeed, Mike McCarthy complained at the League's meeting for the ratification vote that he "had not been consulted during the negotiations on key financial issues which affected the Toronto Club, such as disclosure of financial statements and the release dates for veteran players".[805] The League had in fact been successful in having the Association's financial demands withdrawn. Pre-season compensation was improved to $325, $425, and $525 per week for 1st, 2nd and 3rd year veterans.[806] Pensions were also improved. Players were to contribute $1250, $1350 and $1500 in 1992, 1993 and 1994 while the clubs would add $1050, $1150 and $1300. In addition, $200 per player would also be contributed from the Grey Cup receipts to the Players' Pension Plan. The League also agreed to double its life insurance premium to provide $60,000 coverage per player and to allow a meal and travel per diem of $55, except if the Club provided a pre-game meal in which case the per diem was to be $40. No meal/travel allowance was to be paid if on the return trip after an away game, the team departed prior to noon local time and did not have a meeting or practice that day.

The agreement also called for the Association to aid the League in its move towards the salary cap or as it was formally called, the Competitive Expenditure Cap; for the President of the Players Association to be a member, ex-officio, of the League's Expansion Committee; "for each Club to provide two pairs of shoes to each player".[807] This latter stipulation generated a great deal of discussion and "considerable objection" by the member clubs. In the end, the Association and the League compromised: the Association withdrew its two pairs of shoes demand; the League agreed to limit its right of recall of waivers to "two occasions during a year".[808]

Much of the criticism regarding the CFL seemed to be emanating from Toronto where the initial enthusiasm for the Argonauts, their owners and the "Rocket" had subsided dramatically. The Argos had a dismal season; they suffered under the red glare of the Rocket's diminished performance on and off the field. In the aftermath of the success of the Blue Jays and their World Series triumph, the ultimate validation for a city wanting to be known as "world class", the Argonauts, their owners and the CFL suffered in the comparison. It was "fashionable to ridicule the ownership of the Toronto Argonauts... their crime is that they saved the CFL and therefore hindered Toronto's chances of getting an NFL franchise".[809] Noting that outside of Toronto the League was flourishing, particularly in the west where "to many of its inhabitants, the CFL is an important aspect of life... (McNall, Candy and Gretzky) don't deserve abuse for that. They deserve the Order of Canada".[810]

There was also some consternation within the League. The Argonauts, as part of the McNall group's purchase, would host the 1992 and 1993 Grey Cup games. It was expected to be a source of revenue for the Club and the League. After all, the 1991 game in Winnipeg had shown a profit of $1,748,732 for the League.[811] It was reported that Winnipeg in addition to its CFL share of $218,592 also reaped $800,000 from its hosting the game. The League's Grey Cup budget was "based on the agreement with the Toronto Club guaranteeing a gross gate after taxes of $3,700,000".[812] Together with other incidental Grey Cup related revenues, it was anticipated that $3.9 million would be generated which with expenses of $1.9 million would leave a profit of $2,000,000 for distribution among the teams.[813]

Not all were enthusiastic about the Toronto plans for the national celebration. Two longstanding institutions, the Grey Cup Parade and the Miss Grey Cup Pageant, were abolished. There were objections from the other clubs but Argonauts' Executive Vice President Brian Cooper prevailed: "When times change, we have to change as well... (the Pageant) is just no longer politically correct and beyond that, it's just something I personally wouldn't want to do".[814] The Parade, which dated back to the 1948 arrival of the Calgary Stampeders and their chuckwagons was cancelled because it would have been held 2 weeks after the Santa Claus Parade. It was felt that people would "not come back two weeks later (after the Santa Claus Parade) when its colder, and do the same thing".[815] Grey Cup tickets were priced at $85, $115 and

$125 for the game to be played November 29 in the Dome. The Argonauts also decided to surround the Grey Cup game with a variety of appropriate events. The club put $500,000 into "Fanbowl", an interactive theme park". Running from November 26 to 29, the Fanbowl included such items as a 30 yard field goal kick, a 40 yard dash against a row of lights timed to simulate the speed of "Rocket" Ismail and a quarterback challenge (i.e.) throwing a football to a "sensor driven target in a game simulation". In addition there were exhibits of a football factory, a film with some of the Grey Cup's great moments, the opportunity to sit in a CBC director's chair to direct camera angles plus some 5000 square feet for exhibitors to merchandise their wares. Social events included an indoor tailgate party on game day, a black tie gala featuring Celine Dion who would also headline the half-time show, a casino at the Convention Centre, mass parties at the St. Lawrence Market with Michelle Wright and Prairie Oyster, a "power breakfast" hosted by the Junior Board Of Trade on November 25 in addition to traditional "flapjack" breakfasts hosted by Calgary and Edmonton on November 26 and 27. The Argonauts were optimistically looking forward to a full house of 52,000 and a gate of $5 million.[816]

Meanwhile, as some predicted, the teams with the high profile quarterbacks, Calgary and Winnipeg prepared to meet in the 80th renewal of the Grey Cup game. Calgary had finished in first place with a 13-5 record having defeated Edmonton 23-22 in a close western final. Edmonton itself had barely squeaked by Saskatchewan, edging them 22-20. Winnipeg ended up tied for first place with Hamilton in the Eastern Division but was awarded 1st place on the basis of having outscored Hamilton in their four games played with each other. The Tiger Cats staged a great come-from-behind victory in a snow storm at Hamilton to defeat Ottawa 29-28 but were no match the following week for the Blue Bombers who earned a decisive 59-11 victory. It had been a traumatic year for the Blue Bombers who had seen their coach and general manager, Cal Murphy, undergo a heart transplant operation early in the season, and return as an observer in time for the Grey Cup game. Assistant Urban Bowman took over as the interim head coach.

Murphy received a standing ovation from the assembly at the Bassett Theatre at the Metro Convention Centre when he presented the Outstanding Player Award to Calgary's Doug Flutie. It was the Calgary quarterback's second consecutive MVP award. He defeated the Eastern representative Angelo Snipes of Ottawa. Western division players won three of the League's five awards. Ray Elgaard of Saskatchewan was chosen the Outstanding Canadian over Hamilton's Ken Evraire; Edmonton's Willie Pless was chosen over Ottawa's Snipes as the Most Outstanding Defensive Player; Winnipeg's running back Michael Richardson was chosen as the Outstanding Rookie over Calgary tackle Bruce Covernton; Ottawa's tackle Rob Smith won the Outstanding Offensive Lineman Award over Saskatchewan's Vic Stevenson.

In the end, the Grey Cup was won by Calgary 24-10 on the strength of game MVP Doug Flutie and his pin point passing. Flutie's 480 passing yardage was only 28 yards short of the Grey Cup record set by Montreal's Sam Etcheverry in 1955. Flutie completed 33 of 49 passes including touchdown passes to Allen Pitts and Dave Sapunjis who was selected as the Outstanding Canadian in the game.

While there was celebrating in Calgary, there was consternation throughout the CFL. The official attendance was announced as 45,863. Only three days prior to the game, the Argonauts Brian Cooper "reported that 38,000 tickets had been sold for the Grey Cup Game.[817] The CFL's Record Manual for 1993 decided not to list Grey Cup Receipts for the first time. There was disappointment. Various reasons were advanced: There was no Ontario team in the Final; the Argos' poor season, "fallout from the euphoria over the Blue Jays", general economic conditions, overpriced tickets, and poor distribution methods.[818]

When Commissioner Larry Smith reported at a year end meeting that there was a "shortfall in Grey Cup Revenue", he was asked by the Edmonton representative "how there could be a shortfall on Grey Cup revenue if the gross gate was guaranteed by the Toronto Club".[819] It was Brian Cooper who responded that "the guarantee was conditional upon a sell-out, which did not happen. The Commissioner stated that the Toronto Club lived up to its commitments".[820]

The Argonauts' wanted to sell the rights for the 1993 Grey Cup game to Calgary. The attempt was questioned since prior approval by the Board of Governors of the CFL was neither given nor sought. League Chairman John Tory replied that there were "extenuating circumstances" revolving around the '92 and '93 games. He might also have mentioned '94 and the awarding of the game to Vancouver. "Otherwise", he agreed "the Game is the property of the League and the site must always be determined by the Board".[821]

The 80th Grey Cup game should have been a happy occasion for the CFL. Yet there was a strange pall which had fallen over the League, much of it due to the uncertainty over the announced expansion plans.

Chapter Six

Without a doubt, the major CFL news of 1993 revolved around the issue of the expansion of the League. It had always been a possibility but the emphasis was mainly in Canada. Cities such as London, Halifax, and Windsor were among those mentioned most often. There was always a hankering to move back into the Quebec market ever since Montreal left the League. Any talk of expansion south into the United States was met with a combination of fear and suspicion. The experience of the early 70's and subsequent government intervention opposing expansion of the American leagues into Canada and the Canadian Football League into the United States was an object lesson for the League to chew upon.

The status quo of this state of affairs continued perennially. There were occasional glimmerings of hope that the Halifax-Dartmouth area would enter a team, that the Montreal franchise would be revived, that an exhibition game in Saint John might stimulate Maritime interest, if not in expansion, at least in awareness for television and merchandising revenues. The closest the League came to expansion to the United States was when a possible franchise was considered for Windsor, Ontario, its closeness to Detroit considered a plus in the drawing power should a team be located there.

Through all the turmoil of 1992, the League took concrete steps towards a very new future for itself. They culminated in an announcement at the end of the year to expand into the United States. It was only with the sale of the Toronto Argonauts from

Harry Ornest to Bruce McNall, John Candy and Wayne Gretz-ky that expansion into the United States was pro-actively sought after. It was no secret. "The long range plans of the Toronto ownership included expansion into the U.S. when it acquired the Club", said Brian Cooper.[822] Indeed John Candy became Chair-man of the Expansion Committee of the League; he took his position seriously, making contacts extensively throughout the United States. The League had parameters: It would only seek out those cities which would never gain an NFL franchise and which preferably were in proximity to the Canadian border.

The first target was Portland, Oregon. Interest had been demon-strated there. The League decided to showcase itself with an ex-hibition game between the Argonauts and the Stampeders. Both had marquee players who would be familiar to the fans, Ismail with Toronto and Flutie with Calgary. As the June 25 game in Portland neared, Commissioner Larry Smith and the members of the Expansion Committee were to meet with the potential franchise applicants. With all of the attendant publicity, Bernie Glieberman expressed the opinion that in Ottawa he "sensed an attitude that the League is becoming Americanized with ref-erence to two American owners and the talk of expansion into Portland".[823]

Such talk was something that the League wanted to avoid. It wanted the U.S. market, its fans and its revenues but not at the expense of alienating the Canadian public. The U.S. was the des-sert; Canada, the meat and potatoes. Glieberman felt that "such attitude could be partly offset by stories of a revival in Montre-al".[824] Along the same theme Calgary's Larry Ryckman, also Chairman of the Expansion Committee, was reported to have "received overtures for a team in Halifax".[825]

At the first meeting after the Portland game, won by Calgary 20-1, Larry Smith reported to the CFL's Board of Governors: He "was pleased with the result of the game in Portland, which drew 16,000 fans and the sponsors of the event had indicated their interest in having a franchise media response was favourable and he expects a formal application to be filed in support of an expansion franchise".[826] Indeed the possibility of expansion into the U.S. was more probable than at any other time, so much so that Smith asked for directions as to "how the League would react to such an application".[827] The question of non-import players was discussed. Smith had "received an opinion from CIAU officials that a U.S. player in Division II would be comparable to a CIAU player and suggested that might become the equivalent non-import status for a Portland player".[828] It was the first real discussion of the practicalities of expansion. Interestingly enough, it was Ottawa's Glieberman who defended the status quo regarding the League's import non import ratio, suggesting that "the League should stick to its present eligibility rules unless it is forced to change by U.S. government action".[829] Winnipeg's Cal Murphy wasn't that enthralled by the proposal either. He argued that if Portland were able to classify Division II players as non-imports, so too should other CFL Clubs.[830] The matter was referred to a committee to be formed by the Management Council for review and a report.

With the British Columbia Lions ownership problem dominating much of July, August and September, expansion became a less urgent topic. At the CFL meetings in October in Hamilton, the Commissioner's strategy was outlined to the League in a presentation which would serve as the dry run for one to the media on November 12. There were questions by the owners: Would there be a reaction by the NFL? Would they retaliate by moving in to major Canadian cities? Would expansion clubs make a firm commitment to the CFL and not use their acceptance as a stepping stone to somewhere else? Had surveys been done to determine the acceptability among Americans of Canadian rules? Should the League play its games earlier to avoid conflict with the NFL and U.S. College football? What would be the position of the Federal government? Would their existing level of support be maintained or diminished? To these latter questions, it was League Chairman John Tory who "replied that expansion would be regarded as an export of Canadian culture and would likely be encouraged".[831]

The League decided to form two working committees to assist the Commissioner. Hugh Campbell, Mike McCarthy, Wally Buono and Greg Fulton were to "study the logistics of expansion including inter alia, expansion draft, negotiation lists, territorial rights, college draft, import status, scheduling, officiating and other operational matters".[832] The other group formed to screen expansion candidates was Bernie Glieberman, Bill Comrie and Bruce Robinson.[833]

The same meeting saw the report of Hugh Campbell's committee, which had been formed at the June 29 meeting. Its purpose was to review "the status on the non-import category in the event of expansion outside Canada".[834] The consensus was that current CFL players were of higher calibre in ability than those of the World League; that "experienced non-import players are capable of playing in an expanded League" but the feeling was that new recruits (of non-imports) "may find it difficult". As a result, the committee made its major recommendation: The present total number of non-imports on the eight teams (8x20) "be required in the expanded league spread over a greater number of teams, with a plan to phase out the non-import category in two or three years".[835] It was a major step. There had been restrictions upon the number of imports in Canadian football since 1936. It had been brought into effect after Winnipeg won the Grey Cup game of 1935 with 9 Americans in its line-up of a 28 man roster. Governing body officials did so because they wanted the game to be an expression of Canadian talent thinking that Canadian genius would be blunted by the importation without restrictions. To that end, an American would only be eligible to play in the Grey Cup if he had been in the country for one year. In fact, the 1936 Grey Cup game was not played between the east and west because the Regina Roughriders' American players had not been residents of Canada for the one year period.

Interestingly enough it was the Saskatchewan and Hamilton Clubs, two organizations which had a history of local talent, which inquired about the recommendation. Saskatchewan's Phil Kershaw noted the political nature of such a decision: Various levels of government had supported the League; "any action to diminish participation by Canadian players could be controversial".[836] He was in favour of forcing U.S. teams to use local talent. Hamilton's John Michaluk feared a reaction from CIAU and high school leagues "if they feel their players are being deprived of an opportunity to play in the League".[837] Roger Yachetti suggested that the League offer "some greater financial incentive to universities and junior leagues to produce players".[838]

In response, the Commissioner noted that the 1936 import regulation "a protectionist rule for Canadian Players" had served its purpose. The expansion of the League into the U.S. "would provide an even greater incentive to produce players of a higher standard".[839] Campbell suggested that the Canadian rules on a "Canadian field to the extent possible" would provide the alternative, different game from the NFL. It was left for the Chairman, John Tory to respond. Tory had been appointed League Chairman of the Board of Governors February 28, 1992; he also had ties to the Conservative party in power. He responded to the "political controversy" comment.

> *When Canada entered a Free Trade Agreement with the U.S. in 1988, the national congenital inferiority complex became manifest with ominous predictions of loss of sovereignty, cloning of industries and being swallowed up by the American giant. Although these did not come true, the same reaction might be expected when expansion is announced.*[840]

After announcing that he "would discuss the proposals with the Players' Association in order to defuse possible public reactions from this source",[841] a motion was framed to help diffuse some of the Governors' reactions. "It was moved by Bernie Glieberman and seconded by Hugh Campbell that approval in principle be given to the proposal to phase out the non-import status as the League expands outside of Canada provided that the League continue to support minor football in Canada".

It was carried by a 7-1 vote with Phil Kershaw asking "that his dissenting vote be recorded".[842]

On November 12, 1992, Commissioner Larry Smith met the media at the SkyDome to discuss the expansion of the Canadian Football League. The media were there en masse; TV cameras whirred; reporters were busy scribbling notes; the "Fan Radio" was live. It had been years since the CFL had attracted such attention.

With the help of his visual aids, Smith made the presentation in favour of the League's expansion posture. Potential sites were identified: Portland, Montreal, Halifax, Sacramento, San Antonio, Orlando, San Jose, St. Petersburg, Las Vegas, Birmingham and Hawaii. The CFL had isolated "four hot buttons": Portland, Montreal, Sacramento and San Antonio. These were "the most serious" possibilities. Indeed Smith had instructed Greg Fulton to prepare schedules for 10 and 12 teams for 1993. Smith explained that the recent demise of the WLAF provided a "window of opportunity" for the CFL to move into areas not served, nor likely to be served by the NFL, with a "differentiated product".

Expansion had not occurred in the CFL since 1954 with the entrance of the B.C. Lions. In the meantime, the League had lost the Alouettes; It had two choices: remain stagnant with the status quo or expand into new markets. As what Smith called "the oldest professional League in North America", it was able to trace its roots back to 1892 without difficulty. The CFL was attractive to American investors because of its competitive expenditures cap and its business "run as a business". Not only that it was providing a model whereby the "breakeven" point was 25,000 to 27,000 fans; the League was driven by gross gate and local sponsorship. Television was not the financial necessity for its franchises although it was expressed that ultimately it would generate high revenues.

Smith emphasized that the NFL was fully aware of the League's plans and that there was no intent to compete with the acknowledged #1 in the United States. Rather, the CFL was pursuing the "Wal-Mart" strategy of going into smaller markets and being a "major player" there. Football interest was portrayed as being such that the public would embrace the distinctive "differentiated" Canadian game. He maintained that "if its not done right we're not going to do it for '93". Describing the League as a "low cost producer with a high quality product", Smith detailed the five criteria by which prospective applicants would be judged. Quality of ownership (i.e.) financial worth; Sport management experience personnel; local expertise (since it was gross gate and local sponsorship driven); Stadium capabilities of 30,000 to 50,000; sharing the League's version of growth ("understanding the big picture").

Smith also listed the benefits of expansion for the CFL. The value of the base franchise would increase; the economic benefits to a community with a CFL franchise in Canada had been shown to be in the range of $25-$30 million; there would be jobs created as the fan base expanded.

There must have been a certain amount of confidence on the part of Smith about the "four hot buttons". He discussed the ownership groups involved. Portland's bid was spearheaded by Paul Allen, the owner of the Trail Blazers NBA team. He was finalizing negotiations with the city of Portland for a planned $205 million entertainment facility to house his basketball team. Once that was finalized, it was anticipated that Portland would turn its attention to the CFL franchise. Smith's presentation was bilingual. The former Alouette had conversations with the Olympic Installations Board and with Roger Dore owner of the Montreal Machine of the WLAF. It was obvious that Smith wanted Montreal back into the League and recognized that involvement by the Francophone community was a must. It could not be "run as a large social club for a small part of the community".[843]

Sacramento's ownership group was headed by Fred Anderson, owner of a large Pacific Coast Construction company, while San Antonio's Larry Benson, described by some as being wealthier than any of the present CFL owners was doubly valuable as a prospective owner since the new state of the art facility, the 65,000 seat Alamodome was due to open in '93 and could accommodate a Canadian sized field.

During his press conference, Smith also brought up the issue of Canadians, or non-imports, playing in the expanded CFL. Noting that it was the "$64 question", he said that the League had struck a Committee to look at it; that immigration lawyers were being consulted and while no decision had been made, a "philosophical position" had been taken "to support Canadian University football". He made it clear however that the prevailing free market economic mentality would govern; the "1936 protectionist rule" had "served it time". It was a "new market", a "new time"; there was a need to be "more competitive".

> *I'll be honest with you. When I played, I thought I played because I was a good football player not just because I was a Canadian. And when I knocked the crap out of somebody who was bigger than I was, I didn't care where he came from as long as we were going to win the game. I can't see how people like Mike Soles or Blake Marshall wouldn't play on any team in any league, anywhere...".*[844]

As might be expected, the CFL announcement elicited a variety of responses. The Globe and Mail in a generally supportive editorial called it the "CFL's Hail Mary pass".[845] Its readers had already been primed for the news. One of its columnists, Marty York, had already written about the expansion two days before the conference. He highlighted the major points which would be made and commented on the import/non-import ratio. Citing League Secretary Greg Fulton "who considers himself a nationalist... not hot and bothered about the imminent changes", he reported that "Canadians to-day seem more global minded, particularly the younger generation. I'm sure that it has a lot to do with television. Look at baseball. People didn't seem to be complaining that there were no Canadians on the Blue Jay roster". York opined that "the bottom line is that most Canadians covet the best talent possible, regardless of origin. Hey, nationalism is great, but it doesn't pay the bills".[846]

York's cohort, Stephen Brunt, scooped all other reporters. One day before the press conference Brunt, in what Larry Smith described as "getting the award for investigative journalism", listed the four main possibilities for CFL expansion, Montreal, Portland, Sacramento and San Antonio, detailed their owner, stadium, history and intangibles and even organized the proposed 12 team CFL into "the new look: Eastern: Toronto, Hamilton, Montreal and Ottawa; Central: Winnipeg, Edmonton, Saskatchewan and San Antonio; Western: Calgary, B.C., Sacramento and Portland".[847] Another Globe and Mail reporter, James Christie, speculated that the Canadian Football League, as it is known and loved, will move towards extinction to-day"[848] with Smith's announcement.

In the Toronto Star Jim Proudfoot wrote that the '92 Grey Cup game signalled the "end of an era for the CFL".[849] While there would certainly be others in the future, "as an expression of something uniquely Canadian, the game's institutions are dead - or certainly will be if things work out as planned".[850]

Proudfoot acknowledged that Larry Smith felt that it was the Canadian rules which gave the game its feature, which would as a "differentiated product" make it marketable in the United States and thus the Canadian game would never change.

> *But sceptics wonder. What if it turns out just a little tinkering here and there could enhance that marketability? Why would the CFL, having bitten the expansion bullet hesitate to go one step further? And what*

if the Texans, Californians and Oregonians decide they absolutely detest this strange looking sport? Will the CFL pick up its marbles and go home, or try to adjust? You know the answer, eh?[851]

A sceptical Alison Gordon wrote of the CFL's "Wal-Mart approach" of competing only in non NFL markets:

I wish it didn't sound so much like settling for less. I mean, do people who can afford NIEMAN MARCUS shop in Wal-Mart by choice? Of course not. They shop there because they haven't much choice and they take no particular pleasure in it. Is that the image Smith is building for the CFL?[852]

She too commented on Smith's assertion about the rules of the game being the distinctive Canadian feature:

And that's non-negotiable? I wonder. What if, a few years down the road, more American cities want to get in on this good deal, this exciting Canadian Football League that's such a success. Except that, gee, it's tough to revamp the stadium, and we're not talking a really big deal, just lop off a few yards here, another few yards off there. Is that asking too much?

And gosh, its kind of hard to get anything going with just the three downs. It's not like real football, know what I mean?[853]

On Grey Cup weekend, the Citizen published an article by former Rough Rider great Ron Stewart.In "Bye Bye Canadian Football",[854] Stewart acknowledged that with the financial woes of the CFL, the decision to expand into the U.S. had been made and "any discussion on the merits of the decision at this point is no more than an exercise".[855] After advancing his opinions on the increasingly declining number of Canadians which would invariably be part of the proposed Open Market CFL, Stewart proposed that

When the CFL goes south, all that tradition, all that history, all that East-West glue will subside into the realm of old memories. Sad and unnecessary.

I believe that someday, the Canadian Football League will rise again. It has been too big and too important in our country, to disappear forever.

Until then, let's return the Grey Cup to Rideau Hall and retire it with the honour its place in our history deserves.[856]

The depth of feeling of Canadians was evident in letters to the editor.[857] Not only were they saying that the Canadian Football League was important; they also wanted to insure that there would be continued opportunities for Canadians in the expanded version.

In Winnipeg, acting General Manager Lyle Bauer, expressed a view which was to be heard often: "From a strictly business point of view, it makes sense. But it would mean taking away a lot of the emotion and the tradition for the sake of business. I don't think you can do that with the Canadian Football League".[858] It was reported that in Winnipeg, which some liked to refer to as "the land of the dinosaurs"[859], "perhaps one in a hundred calls (to the Blue Bombers offices) is in favour of teams in the United States. The local radio seers and most of the press is dead set against it".[860]

Winnipeg's Cal Murphy, recently allowed to leave London's University Hospital where he had undergone his transplant operation in order to attend Grey Cup Week festivities in Toronto, also opposed expansion to the United States "not based on patriotic fervour... strictly a matter of dollars and cents".[861] After noting that the NFL injected $30 million into the WLAF which also had a television contract and the League still failed, he asked "What makes us think we can go in and be the grand poobah?"[862] He mentioned that travel costs from Winnipeg to San Antonio and Sacramento would cost $40,000 a trip". Three days would be necessary since it would be impossible to get red-eye flights back to Winnipeg". San Antonio, he said was the site of the Houston Oilers' training camp in session "for six of the first eight weeks of our season". Mentioning that Houston would probably play a couple of exhibition games there as well and after September 1, high school football Friday nights, college football on Saturday afternoon and the NFL on Sundays, he asked: "When are we going to play our games?" Canadian teams, he said, were not good draws in the United States illustrating his sentiment with examples of the Edmonton Oilers even with Wayne Gretzky, the Blue Jays and Expos. San Antonio, Sacramento, Orlando and St. Petersburg were too close to NFL cities, he reasoned. More could be done to sell the game in Canada, he argued, and "until all Canadian avenues have been explored, a move to the U.S. should not be contemplated".[863]

Murphy reacted to the $3,000,000 franchise fee from expansion teams and the "suggestion that the new teams would be able to pay that amount off over five or six years", each team realizing "$125,000 to $130,000 a year" with a huff: "You could make that in a bake sale".[864] Murphy said he "might" listen to talk of expansion if the $3,000,000 fee was paid up front to the League which in turn would operate its office from the interest and use the principle to bail out any team that ran into a financial crisis" similar to Ottawa in '91 and the B.C. Lions in '92.[865]

Expansion and the side issues generated from it continued to evoke strong sentiments in the post Smith press conference days. CIAU coaches, feted only six days later by the CFL at its annual luncheon recognizing the winner of the Frank Tindall Trophy as the CIAU Coach of the Year, were overwhelmingly opposed to the removal of the "quota system". They instructed the CIAU executive vice president Mark Lowry "to lobby on behalf of maintaining the quota".[866] Liberal MP Lloyd Axworthy of Winnipeg announced that he would introduce a private member's Bill to prevent expansion of the CFL into the U.S. While the tactic was successful almost 20 years earlier with a Liberal party in power, there was no chance that it would be so well received with the Conservative government of the day.

Former university quarterback Jamie Bone, described as an example of "even the best players in Canada have trouble finding jobs in the Canadian Football League, especially at the quarterback position" commented: "its a sad day if they can't include Canadian content".[867] He might have been thinking of St. Mary's outstanding quarterback Chris Flynn who was unsuccessful in his attempts to make the Ottawa Rough Riders and later the Toronto Argonauts. Two Toronto residents of the same street, St. Clements Avenue, each playing a large role with the Stampeders were opposed to the CFL plan. Dave Sapunjis and Andy McVey could agree with expansion but not with elimination of the quotas. Sapunjis called for the League to continue with "community based players":

> I know there's kids in Calgary that look up to me because I'm playing in the league. And I know there's a lot of people in North Toronto that follow the CFL because I'm playing in it.[868]

Sapunjis was selected as winner of the Dick Suderman Award as the Canadian player of the 1992 Grey Cup game for the second consecutive year. The slot back who grew up in Toronto and attended the University of Western Ontario had confirmed his status as one of the outstanding players in the game. That "status as top Canadian" however was said to be "probably on the endangered species list when the league expands to the United States".[869]

McVey was more blunt: "It hurts me to hear Larry Smith say the CFL no longer needs that Canadian rule. If it hadn't been for that Canadian quota, Larry Smith would not have played nine seasons with the Montreal Alouettes after he came out of Bishop's University. He wouldn't be Commissioner of the Canadian Football League to-day if he hadn't spent those years with the Alouettes".[870]

Hamilton's non-import receiver Nick Mazzoli speculated that while he thought that he could play in the new non quota league, "you'd see a steep reduction (of Canadian players) I don't think there'd be many Canadian offensive linemen and guys like Ray Elgaard, Jeff Fairholm, Dave Sapunjis and I would be fighting for jobs. And without Canadians the CFL would be 'a very anti social thing - It's not going to be a fan's game'".[871] Former player Peter Dalla Riva echoed those sentiments later when it was announced that he would be inducted into the Hall of Fame: "Being a Canadian, that rule got the door open for me. It gave me the chance to try. If they decide to change things and some Canadian kids don't ever get the chance to try, that's sad."[872]

Those sentiments were echoed later on during the preparations for the 1994 Grey Cup game. BC tackle Vic Stevenson addressed the issue:

> *A good coach will see the raw talent but why keep the guy around for two years when you can bring in a kid from an American school who'll be a lot closer to being ready? Coaches get paid to win to-day. They might not be around in two years.*[873]

Calgary linebacker Matt Finlay was even more to the point.

Content rules were needed because:

> *American coaches are prejudiced. They don't want to play Canadians. You can see the look on their faces whenever they have*

to deal with the ratio. When all this start-
ed, when American teams were brought
into the league, a lot of people thought one
year and it would be all over. American
teams would win everything. Well, Sac-
ramento's been in the league for two years
and they haven't made the playoffs. Ca-
nadian teams still dominate. Four teams
missed the playoffs - three American and
one Canadian. . . . So what's the problem.
It's not like they're winning everything.[874]

During that same '94 Grey Cup week the Toronto Star's Mary
Ormsby reinforced the point:

So don't curse the Baltimore All Americans
for ruining a cherished moment of Cana-
diana today. Canadians have managed to
do that all on their own. . . The CFL, long
before Larry Smith bounded aboard as
Commissioner, compromised its Canadi-
an identity. This is a league, after all, that
gives US quarterbacks the benefit of the
doubt even when they clearly don't under-
stand the Canadian game. . . Meanwhile,
such Canadian Pivots as Dan Feraday, Ja-
mie Bone, Chris Flynn and countless oth-
ers didn't even get a second glance and still
don't. The CFL's moribund quota system
did not protect their dashed dreams - nor
will it protect those of Laurier hero Bill
Kubas - because their breeding is suspect.
This is also the league that stereotypes the
precious homegrown talent it is supposed
to nurture and display.

The unwritten rule is that Canadian play-
ers anchor the offensive line, kick, punt,

fetch coffee, fill in at linebacker, give hap-
py face interviews to grumpy reporters on
off days, log a few downs at receiver, block
for the star running back, squeegee the
training table, run errands, attend union
meetings, wash the coach's car and answer
phones. Glamour positions are reserved for
Americans.[875]

In Calgary, a Winnipeg fan at a sports bar "trying to smile away the abuse he took from the Stampeders faithful" said "We have to keep this game Canadian. You don't get this excitement in the States".[876] There was also some humour injected. At the 1992 Grey Cup game, a sign announced "CFL Expansion 1994: Gander Guppies", while another proclaimed "My Canada includes Portland".[877]

Indeed, it appeared that Canadian life in general, and the CFL in particular among the youth, was taking second place to that of the "American way". A sociological study by Reginald Bibby of the University of Lethbridge offered verification. Twenty-two per cent of Canadian youth followed the CFL while 26 per cent were more interested in the NFL. A breakdown of the total percentages allowed more insights. In the west, 40% of teens followed the CFL. That figure dropped to 25% in Ontario, 20% in the Atlantic region and only 10% in Quebec.[878] The study of 4,000 youth offered as one of its conclusions that "Canadian youth are choosing American in virtually every area of life in the face of the unprecedented presence of U.S. media".[879] It appeared that talk of expansion of the CFL into the American market might be as much a case of "if you can't beat them, join them". For others, the concept of expansion which was just beginning to surface in November as a viable option was the only way: "You can keep the CFL the way it is and have a truly Canadian failure or you can expand into the United States, see the game regain some of its stability and then find ways to re-establish a greater Canadian presence".[880]

Bibby's study of teens in Canada and their embracing of "American heroes in every sphere of life" was widely reported. Michael Jordan, Beverly Hills 90210, Guns and Roses, Julia Roberts, Stephen King, Dan Rather and George Bush were all ranked at the top in their various categories. Bibby also said that there was only one category, "one Canadian institution that has managed to keep up with the American competition - the Canadian Football League".[881] Of the 4,000 teens surveyed nationally, 26% said they followed the NFL closely while 22% indicated the CFL. His national adult survey of 90-91 indicated that of those 18 and older, 16% followed the CFL and 11% the NFL.

To Bibby, this "something of a cultural miracle",[882] could be explained in three ways: The CFL was "surviving the American television onslaught" in spite of telecasts of American networks, such as CBS, NBC, ABC, ESPN and TNT, received in Canadian homes, were "bigger than life" when compared with lower budget CFL telecasts on CBC and TSN.

Secondly, Bibby pointed out that "as if the NFL needed help, two of our indigenous channels, Global and TSN, supplement the five American networks in piping NFL games into Canadian homes".[883] In addition, news of NFL scores, injuries, comments, pre-game hype, and post game discussion was taking time up on sportscasts and sports pages.

> *These first two factors alone should virtually bury the CFL. Our findings suggest that they combine to bury our national hero nominees in virtually every other area of life. Surprisingly they don't annihilate the CFL. But that's only two-thirds of the miracle.*[884]

The third reason advanced by Bibby was the "strangely sadistic Canadian media". The football season "signals open season on the CFL. Make no mistake about it, perception is reality".[885] He said that the media "annually go out of their way to contribute to the perception that the league is fragile and probably near death".[886]   He acknowledged that there were "objective problems"; some unstable franchises; promotion lacking but nonetheless "sport types, rather than contributing to calm, have - in John Candy's words - been like sharks smelling blood".[887]   He referred to references of the CFL a "minor league", "Triple A", "financially troubled", "beleaguered" and "cash strapped" all appearing "with reckless abandon". After listing examples to expand on this theme, Bibby concluded:

> *If the CFL ever fails, let's be clear about something: its failure will in large part reflect the failure not merely of the league but of the Canadian media to neutralize the impact that their American media counterparts are having on this century-old sports institution of ours. The CFL might be Canada's ugly duckling; but a remarkable duckling it is in an age when most things distinctively Canadian have gone the way of the U.S. cooking pot. Who knows what the CFL could look like if ethnocentric Americans could be persuaded to give it a closer look and masochistic Canadians stopped trying to put its head on the chopping block.*[888]

When the CFL met in Calgary January 12, it was a foregone conclusion that it would expand into San Antonio and Sacramento. While the announcement was made in Calgary, the details were left for a press conference called the next day, January 13 in Toronto. Only Winnipeg Blue Bombers voted against the plan. Describing the Club as "pro expansion in Canada" the Blue Bombers' President Bruce Robinson declared "we're a Canadian game. We're proud of our Canadian players and our Canadian heritage. We felt we had to take a stand and make our point".[889]

As much as anything however, the Club's objection was based on its perception of the revenue accruing from the expansion fees. With the League keeping half of the monies to dissolve its deficit problems, there would only be $75,000 for each Club which "wouldn't be enough to offset travel costs".[890] Winnipeg said the Clubs were to put up $600,000 a year for two years and the balance of the $3,000,000 to be paid from profits.[891] Winnipeg's cost of expansion predominantly in travel was estimated to be $200,000.[892] When the press conference was held in Toronto, much to the chagrin of Calgary media who pressed for details after the announcement of League expansion to San Antonio and Sacramento was made there, Robinson declined to attend. Some dubbed the Blue Bombers' management as "dinosaurs", but they claimed they had the "facts to back up their arguments".[893] Other representatives who were wavering about the concept of expansion to the U.S., Bill Comrie and Phil Kershaw in the end voted "yes". Kershaw said: "We see this as an experiment... we need a little bit of sizzle back in the CFL".[894]

The CFL move generated publicity and comments throughout the land. It was a milestone decision. The American flag accompanied the Canadian as the CFL made its historic announcement. The media conference in Toronto was telecast live by TSN from Ontario Place. Players' Association representatives while voicing apprehension about the player quotas problem which had not yet been addressed, were enthusiastic. Dan Ferrone of the Argonauts describing the announcement as "absolutely fantastic... this will make the League better". George Reed said it would "bring some stability and growth to the League and get away from the death watch". Politicians were less enthusiastic: "the end of the CFL as we know it" was Bob Kilger's opinion. The MP from Cornwall was the Liberal sports critic. The NDP sports authority John Brewen of Victoria gave a blunt response: I can't imagine very many issues in which I would have no comment but this is it. I've joined that great group of Canadians who probably don't care one hit". Annis Stukus, the coach of the last expansion team in 1954, the B.C. Lions said he knew it was coming and hoped "they watch the budgets... I just hope Hamilton isn't dead". Queen's University Coach Doug Hargreaves guessed that "there will be fewer jobs for Canadian players... However the move to expand to the U.S. was strictly a business decision".[895]

In San Antonio, a press conference was held at the 65,000 seat Alamodome, the playing home of the new San Antonio Texans. Hard hats were issued to all, not as was suggested by one reporter because of "the weaker mentality that has long prevailed among the League governors", but because the stadium was still under construction.[896] There were sceptics who say this is just another of the many football teams and leagues who had passed through. Former Winnipeg Head Coach Mike Riley resurfaced as the New San Antonio coach. Referring to the city's "bundle of teams", he spoke prophetically of the ever present "death watch for these football teams". Civic officials and the "movers and shakers above Riley (were) considerably more optimistic".[897] But there were also warning sounds: unpaid bills from the World League team contributed to the perception that owner Larry Benson "doesn't seem to be revered locally... (he was) advised to keep a low profile".[898]

Perhaps the indicator as to what could transpire should have been taken from a local businessman and one of Benson's partners, Paul Sides who ventured that "it's like being married. You make that commitment, but I don't know if it always lasts".[899] And it didn't. The whirlwind romance courtship and marriage was over in two weeks. The Coach of the Year Dinner in Edmonton should have been a joyous occasion celebrating the two week honeymoon and the announcement of Wally Buono as the recipient of the Annis Stukus Trophy. Sacramento Gold Miner president Fred Anderson "broke the news to reporters... Moments later Larry Smith announced that the San Antonio franchise had been put on hold until 1994.[900] No members of the Texas based team had attended the League meetings in Edmonton. There was speculation as the what had happened: Team officials were said to need 25,000 season tickets as a base to operate in the Alamodome and it was obvious that it wasn't going to happen. The San Antonio Express News suggested that the situation deteriorated when the team's "Board of Directors was re-figured giving

Benson less say in the team's daily operations".⁹⁰¹ There were some who said that Benson's brother Tom, owner of the New Orleans Saints, influenced the pull out. Both Larry Benson and Fred Anderson had received $2 million each in a settlement with the NFL over the WLAF, that money to be used in financing the CFL franchise fee. Larry Benson had left "a lot of unpaid bills". Benson was not available for comment "having gone away on a little vacation to try and regroup himself".⁹⁰²

When Benson did surface to make a comment, he blamed "the Alamodome's management commitments to events in 1993" for his withdrawal. Stadium officials were upset; they had spent "nearly $250,000 (U.S.) preparing the Alamodome for CFL play". The General Manager of the city-owned facility was irate in denying the charge: "I'm very very disappointed if that's his view. We stuck our necks out for him. We supported him every step of the way".⁹⁰³

Amid all the furore, a Gallup poll taken prior to the San Antonio decision showed that Canadians were still divided on expansion to the United States. Nationally, 33 per cent disapproved; 31 per cent were in favour, the rest were undecided. Sentiment against was higher in the Prairies where 43% were opposed and 36% for with 22% undecided. At the same time, nationally, 65% favoured returning to Montreal; 56% of Quebeckers were also for the CFL returning to the former league city.

While all of this might have caused Winnipeg's Cal Murphy to say "I told you so", he didn't, publicly. He was concerned that no money was paid by Benson for his franchise causing one reporter to write: "getting in and out of the Canadian Football League is easier than getting in and out of matrimony - and a lot cheaper".⁹⁰⁴ Murphy did however announce that the Blue Bombers would no longer send assessment cheques to the League.⁹⁰⁵ On March 3, the Portland group announced formally that it would not pursue a franchise in the CFL saying that "building a new arena for basketball in more important; our staff would have had to spend an inordinate amount of time focussing on the CFL's business affairs".[906]

It was a disappointing turn of events for the CFL and for Larry Smith. His "four hot buttons" had been reduced to one. Montreal, Portland, San Antonio had one by one not responded. Only Sacramento Gold Miners would answer the call to start as the CFL's first new franchise since 1954 and the first American one ever. The League announced that a "hold" would be put on U.S. expansion for 1993. Since the San Antonio decision, interests from Ohio (Nick Mileti) and Florida (Sal Biondo) had been pursued but by February 8, the CFL decided to proceed with an unbalanced schedule of 18 games over a 20 week schedule.[907]

At the CFL meetings in Toronto, with the Grey Cup finished, the League's Governors met to finalize the year's discussions. The issue of Import quotas was still to be resolved. It boiled down to two points of view. The League had made it known that it wanted to phase out what it called "the Canadian quota". Larry Smith had informed the Players' Association "that 160 non-import positions would be guaranteed over the next two years regardless of the number of teams".[908]Winnipeg, Saskatchewan and Hamilton all chose to address the non-import question as part of clubs' remarks on expansion.. Winnipeg expressed "genuine concern about the status of the Canadian player whose role may be considerably lessened in direct competition with more readily available and better trained American players".[909] Saskatchewan noted that its club relied heavily upon non-import talent and took its commitment to develop football in the Province seriously. He wondered how various levels of government support would be "affected... if it can be perceived as a denial or diminution of opportunities for Canadian players".[910] Hamilton wanted "the present import ratio maintained and to enhance the supply lines of Canadian talent, the League should increase its support at the Amateur levels".[911]

There seemed to be two ways to go:The League could insist on all teams adhering to the ratio of Canadian to American players; on the other hand American based teams would be made up entirely of American players; Canadian teams would continue to operate with 20 non-imports. The Argonauts General Manager Mike McCarthy was opposed: "By mid season, when the Americans begin to learn our rules, we'll get our butts kicked. With all those Americans, we'll definitely be at a disadvantage".[912] One of his players, guard Dan Ferrone did not share McCarthy's view. Ferrone was also an executive with the Players' Association which was holding firm to its Collective Agreement. "There are a lot of guys in this league who believe there is a misconception when it comes to the ability of Canadians".[913] Ferrone repeated what had been advanced by others (Leo Cahill on the Fan Radio and articles in the Globe and Mail November 24, 1992). As long as the salary cap was in place and adhered to, the type of American attracted to the CFL would be the same as currently and Canadians had demonstrated their ability to compete with them. Ferrone laid out the CFLPA position: "As players, we are totally for expansion, provided the ratio isn't altered".[914]

Regardless of what was being said, economics was dictating the League's stance. The CFL salary cap for 1993 was to be $2.5 million, it was previously $3,000,000. It included Players' salaries, coaches salaries, those on the injury list, practice roster, signing bonuses, performance bonuses, any extra training camp salary costs, vehicle expense/gasoline and anything defined as salary or salary benefits under the Canadian Income Tax Act.[915] Not only that salaries of marquee players presently in the League were to be "grandfathered"; the new salary cap for marquee players was placed at $250,000. "Rocket Ismail, Doug Flutie and/or other marquee players over the $250,000 amount" were to be exempted for '93.[916]Salaries in '1993 would have to be trimmed. Unlimited imports were the solution, especially with the demise of the WLAF and the huge market of football players in the United States who would play for less than what CFL teams had to pay for their talent currently.

A comparison using salary, exchange and taxes illustrated the problem graphically:

	American on American team	American on Canadian team
Salary	$85,000	$85,000
Income Tax	28% - 23,800	38% - $32,300
Net	$US $61,200	Can$ $52,700
Net		@.73 exchange $38,471

As far as the players were concerned, "the answer is clearly defined in the collective bargaining agreement".[917] Twenty non-imports were required by each team even among expansion teams "except where such a restriction would be unlawful".[918] The contract ran through the 1994 season and the Association wasn't budging from its position in vowing to protect the Canadian players, Ferrone, the Association's second Vice President saying "if we don't, it will be an insult to those who fought for it".[919]

Smith had always maintained that "your top Canadians are going to play even if the League is on the moon. It's the fringe players, the ones on the practice roster, the ones who aren't on the active roster" who would be affected.[920] Some weren't impressed. Jim Proudfoot, calling Canadian players an "endangered species" wrote:

> please drop that sanctimonious claptrap about Canadians remaining competitive under any circumstances. CFL coaches wouldn't trouble themselves with Canadian players at all if they weren't compelled to dress some for each game. They're a colossal pain in the neck. Always have been. Recruiting Americans is easier and cheaper and they come fully prepared".[921]

In an effort to speed up the process of Sacramento becoming ready for the '93 season, the League tentatively approved its expansion draft of Canadian talent. There would still be 160 non-imports required among the nine teams. Eighteen would be the number for each Canadian team and 16 for the new Sacramento club. As far as the American team was concerned, it would select 8 non-imports from a pool provided after each club protected 5 players. A second round of eight selections was to be made after the Canadian Clubs protected one non-import after the first round.[222] The draft would not take place.

Negotiations continued with the Players Association about the number of Canadians on each team. The CFL proposed that the non-import ratio be reduced to 0 after a five year period decreasing the number from 160 by 40 each year. At the end of five years, it was proposed that competition be open, that market forces determine who would play. The Players Association balked; it wanted the existing contract to apply for two years as per the agreement, after which negotiations could occur. On February 11, 1993, Smith suspended talks with the players. The existing contract would be honoured until it expired after the 1994 season; after that the league would push for no non-import quotas.

Players were critical of Smith: "I hope Larry Smith understands he'll be recognized as the Commissioner who killed the Canadian in the CFL",[923] said the Argos' Dan Ferrone; Winnipeg's player rep. Chris Walby, lamented that the game was becoming "too much like a business. There's no concern for the guys who make the League".[924] The players were upset that the talks were suspended without warning, that the League was attempting to make a unilateral decision. Walby continued: "Larry has got to realize he's the Commissioner not the judge. There's a guy who forgot where he came from. This is a black day".[925]

From the perspective of the League, it appeared to be strictly a business decision. Clubs had already decided to drop the salary cap to $2.5 million from the $3 million of '92. There was also the "ultimate life saving goal of Smith and the American owners to bring the salary cap down to a mere $1.5 million".[926] It could be done by removing the non-imports and their salaries from the equation and concentrating on the huge talent pool in the United States where the supply would dictate lower salaries for players. The WLAF, for example, "set up a salary structure based on position. Quarterbacks earned $25,000 a season; running backs, receivers and linebackers would earn $20,000 a season; linemen, blocking backs, specialty team players, kickers and defensive backs earned $15,000 a year".[927] Under such a threat, it was in the CFL's imports best interests to support the Players' Association's attempt to maintain the non-import regulations.

Reactions were swift. Media lined up on either side. In Winnipeg, veteran columnist Hal Sigurdson tied the League's decision to the larger political issue: "the blueprint was sitting there in Ottawa all along. You save the league the way we're saving the country. Turn it into a minor league U.S. branch plant".[928] He blamed "the transient professionals, the coaches and general managers... predominantly American" for turning the CFL "into the bag lady of professional sport".[929] He labelled Smith's assertion that "import restrictions were first established in 1936 to protect Canadian jobs" as "Codswallop". He explained that nobody had a "job" playing football in 1936. "They played for team jackets".

The real reason, he said, for the import rule passed by the Canadian Rugby Union (CRU) in 1936 was to "accelerate the development of Canadian football" but at the same time "to prevent some egomaniac with deep pockets from importing a winner". Sigurdson supported his view by citing long time Winnipeg observer Vince Leah "who was there... the original intent was to gradually phase out imports as the level of Canadian football improved".[930] Sigurdson maintained that

> the number of imports gradually increased, not for the betterment of Canadian football but because some American coach thought it might save his job. The fact a Canadian Commissioner is not being lynched for taking a decision that will ultimately remove all import restrictions tells you how far the league has strayed from its original concept.

*It also tells you it is dead. It may continue
to twitch for another few seasons, but rigor
mortis is already setting in.*[931]

On February 26, Smith made the announcement that Sacramento would be allowed to play with whomever it wished. The League's regulations concerning imports and non-imports would not apply to the American team. As well, the draft on non-import talent would not be held. Players Association President George Reed was fuming because Smith made the information public "without first consulting his Association".[932] Smith said that "he had spoken to Reed about what he was going to announce... would eventually like to see some sort of local content rule".[933]When the Sacramento Gold Miners were ready to play their first exhibition game, it was eagerly anticipated for a number of reasons. It was against Winnipeg, the team which was so opposed to expansion into the United States. The Blue Bombers, however, recognized a business opportunity when they saw one. That game was promoted as "U.S. vs. Us" and "Us vs. Them". It was a great chance to draw a good crowd when expenses were at their lowest because it was an exhibition game. On the wider front, there was the potential for all sides to say "I told you so!" There were those who felt that Sacramento with its unlimited imports would prove too much for the non-import laden Blue Bombers. On the other hand, it was an opportunity for those who believed that Canadians could play with the American talent attracted to the CFL's expansion team.

The game attracted a good sized crowd of 23,191. Sacramento won 21-15 but nobody really had the chance to crow. Quarterback Matt Dunigan was ejected from the game, just three minutes into it; he took exception to the play of Sacramento's Randy Thornton and Basil Proctor, ripping Thorton's helmet off his head, throwing it downfield.[934] Winnipeg finished the game with untried rookie Keithen Mc Cant. The Bombers came under criticism from its public and media: The team was criticized for playing the Star Spangled Banner after O Canada since it was "standard operating procedure to play (the American National

Anthem) first".[935] Dunigan, thrown out after 2 minutes and 11 seconds "the million dollar man... four-for-four for 55 yards before he lost his cool".[936] "Words like 'pitiful' and 'pansies' were echoing from the West side stadium crowd"; the customers who paid up to $24 a ticket "were not referring to the U.S. guys who had been to-gether for a mere nine days".[937]

When the Gold Miners moved into Ottawa to open the '93 CFL regular season, they had a perfect record in the exhibition season, having defeated B.C. 38-20. Sacramento was less than excited about its early schedule, meeting first Ottawa and then Hamilton in less than 72 hours. Again the game was a matter of conjecture. It was billed as the "first international" CFL game. Russ Jackson, the former Ottawa standout ventured an opinion that the ground rules would change. "The name of the game in football is injuries. And when a Canadian gets hurt he's difficult to replace. But the Gold Miners have an entire country of not-ready-for-the-NFL players from which to choose".[938] Ottawa owners, Bernie and Lonie Glieberman, decided that the local TV blackout would be lifted for the TSN telecast saying "This is a historic game and we think everyone should be able to see it".[939] Twenty-four thousand showed up to watch the Rough Riders win the game 32-23. When the Sacramento team returned home after losing its first two games in the CFL, it was to play the Calgary Stampeders and Doug Flutie. There was a crowd of 20,082 in attendance; Calgary won 38-36 and there were a host of positives. The game received superb publicity in the Sacramento Bee, one columnist calling the game "an improved version of an old game that was a crashing bore",[940] another writing that "It works. The CFL has built a better mouse trap".[941] Larry Ryckman, Calgary owner and head of the CFL's Expansion Committee, perhaps thinking of the prospects invited to the game to witness CFL football first hand was delighted: "I think we could sell three franchises off that one game alone".[942]

The fact remained however that Sacramento was 0-3 after its first three games. By mid August, Sacramento had one victory and was on the verge of its second against Hamilton but was still in last place in the Western Division.

It was reported that the move to four teams in the playoffs rather than three was made "in order to provide the expansion Gold Miners with a better shot at generating interest in their market".[943] It was necessary because apparently the gild was tarnishing for Sacramento. Owner Fred Anderson estimated he would lose $3.5 million in 1993.[944] Average attendance of 15,000 was inflated. The Club was giving away about 2,000 tickets per game. For the Edmonton game, season ticket holders were given two free tickets. He lamented that "tax write-offs don't make up for the kind of losses I'm taking. This is a very hard hit, take my word for it".[945] Sacramento needed at least 25,000 fans per game to break even. Several reasons for the team's lack of success were offered. The NFL and college football, especially San Francisco 49ers and Stanford University were attracting most of the interest. The team was in last place; CFL players were not well known. Even David Archer's abilities as a quarterback were being questioned: "he's not a good CFL quarterback. He just stands there and gets sacked while other CFL quarterbacks roll out of the pocket".[946] Anderson was critical of the lack of assistance from the CFL: "almost nothing in the way of marketing support...they don't have even one person here (in the U.S.)".[947]

Failure might be too strong a word but it was evident that CFL franchises were struggling throughout the League. In Hamilton, attendance had fallen off. Financial resources were low. Long-time General Manager and former player, Joe Zuger, resigned in early January. The Club had traded its "marquee player", quarterback Damon Allen, to Edmonton and pinned its hopes on second year quarterback Don McPherson. When he was unable to generate victories the team turned to non-import quarterback Bob Torrance who started two games, the first non-import to do so in the CFL since Greg Vavra in 1987. Purchase inquiries came from Americans Sal Biondo from Washington, Paul Snyder of Buffalo and Nick Mileti from Cleveland. The Club was forced to approach the CFL for advances in income. When the CFL was requested to assist in a bail out, there was refusal. Memories of the expensive costs of the B.C. and Ottawa franchises were still fresh in everyone's mind. Calgary's Larry Ryckman contributed $100,000 to assist the Tiger Cats in meeting their payroll.[948]

While Ryckman's money was appreciated, some later comments were not. He suggested that there was a possibility that the Tiger-Cats might move to Halifax "if Hamiltonians were not more supportive".[949] An unsigned circular was distributed during the Tiger Cats Labour Day game with the Argos suggesting that "Ryckman's involvement in the Ti-Cats was insulting and unnecessary and that he should be received with scepticism".[950] Hamilton's Chairman Roger Yachetti in interviews with the CBC and the Globe and Mail also took on Ryckman calling for him to be more discreet in his comments: "I don't see why he would say this. Perhaps it's wishful thinking by Mr. Ryckman but I haven't heard anything about the Ti-Cats going to Halifax".[951] Ryckman countered that "when Roger goes on TV and says everything is okay in Hamilton that's wishful thinking, in my opinion".[952]

When the CFL's Board of Governors met in Ottawa on September 14, the Hamilton situation had deteriorated to the point that the Tiger Cats requested $1 million in aid from the League. The League refused, but in the end it was the new franchise of Las Vegas and Nick Mileti which came to the rescue. In return for early payment of the remainder of his franchise fee, the League gave Mileti a discount fee of $500,000. His payment of $1.5 million U.S. gave the Tiger Cats their share of $150,000, enough to see them through for yet another while.

In mid October, the haemorrhaging was stopped. Toronto financier David Mac Donald, put in touch with Hamilton by Ryckman, surfaced with a plan to inject $1.5 million in '93 and a further $1.5 million (less commissions and royalties) in early '94. It guaranteed that payments on the Club's debt of close to two million dollars over the past two seasons would be made and that the Tiger Cats would remain in Hamilton at least through 1994.

In Toronto, there was turmoil of another kind. The Argonauts seemed to be in the business of "divesting". It sent eight of its players to Edmonton to join former Argonaut Coach Adam Rita. It dispatched "Rocket" Ismail to Los Angeles Raiders. It gave up its rights to the Grey Cup game, selling it to Larry Ryckman and the Calgary Stampeders. It gave up its "exclusivity clause" to football in the SkyDome to allow an NFL exhibition game to be played there in August. It was to be the first pre season NFL game, Cleveland Browns vs. the New England Patriots, in Canada since 1961. Cleveland's record was 7-9 in 1992; New England's 2-14, prompting Dan Barreiro of the Minneapolis St. Paul Star Tribune to give them the "Give it up and join the CFL Award".[953] The game was sponsored by Molson's and was advertised as "the football event of the year in Toronto". Cleveland defeated New England 12-9 before a "turnstile count" of 33,021.[954]

The Argonauts also replaced Brian Cooper, the Club's Executive Vice President. The announcement was made in an "Argo release datelined Los Angeles rather than Toronto".[955] Chris Flynn, seeking to gain a spot as a backup quarterback was also released, his football days as an aspiring CFL quarterback over. The Argos had also lost their first draft choice in the university draft plus $50,000 for having gone over the League's salary cap of $3,000,000 in '92.[956] Further changes were made By mid season f with the Argos sporting a 1-9 record. Ron Barbaro, former president of the Argonaut Playback Club and a successful insurance executive was named President and CEO of the Argonauts. His moves to resurrect the floundering franchise were swift. The man who was proclaimed for having saved the Toronto Zoo and the Santa Claus Parade moved to replace General Manager Mike McCarthy, re-assigned Head Coach Dennis Meyer to defensive co-ordinator, fired offensive co-ordinator "Mouse" Davis, and hired former Argonaut and B.C. Lion Coach Bob O'Billovich - all within 48 hours of his appointment. He gave some indication of his approach when during the team's first game in the Dome, September 19 vs. Winnipeg, he had the play by play televised on the Jumbotron so that fans could enjoy and see the game as they would as if they were at home. It was the first time it had been done. Apparently Barbaro had not inquired about the Club's right to do so: "It's easier to say I'm sorry rather than to request permission", he philosophized.[957]

In a further effort to attract past season ticket holders, the Argonauts offered two free tickets for the October 31 game with Saskatchewan to all 1992 subscribers who didn't renew for '93. The team's average attendance which was 20,000 in 1990, Harry Ornest's last year as owner, rose to 36,304 in the Grey Cup year of '91, fell to 32,053 in '92 and was averaging 25,334 in '93.[958] At the same time as the attendance fall-off, the team was losing and missed the CFL playoffs with a 3-15 record. Rumours started when the team lost its last game of the season to Winnipeg 12-10. A guest of Barbaro at the Saskatchewan game was newspaper magnate Ken Thomson. Was he being courted as "part of the group Barbaro is trying to put together to take the Argos off Bruce McNall's hands?"[959] McNall denied a story that he was trying to sell the Argos but it was in couched terms: "As long as the people of Toronto indicate they want the Argos, he's 'here to play'".[960]

McNall's partner, Wayne Gretzky was convinced that time had come. "The fact is, people in Toronto don't want the CFL... I've told McNall, I think it's time (to sell)... As far as I'm concerned, time's up".[961]

A "dance" of a different type was underway in Ottawa. Some called it a "soap opera season".[962] It had its start early in the year. The Rough Riders announced the signing of John Ritchie as CEO on the recommendation of Brian Cooper of the Argos.[963] Ritchie had formerly been with Alpine Canada and had no football experience. When General Manager Dan Rambo "balked at reporting to Ritchie, he was fired June 2. His position was not filled. Ron Smeltzer was given the title of Director of Football Operations reporting to Ritchie in addition to his duties of Head Coach. It was an attempt to address the business side of football with a business man "to run the business side rather than" an ex-player.[964]

While there was some uproar, it was minor. Rambo had made few friends among the media; the Gliebermans seemed to be trying to develop a strong team. Indeed, the decision was made to bring in import Mike Graybill, the first import lineman in 10 years, as a means of strengthening the team. It meant changes had to be made elsewhere. Reggie Barnes, a popular and talented running back was released, finances and the "quota" cited.[965]

On August 16, the Riders at 1-6, owner Bernie Glieberman announced that J.I. Albrecht would be hired as a "consultant to the President/Chairman" and that Dexter Manley would be brought back as quickly as possible to start at Defensive End.[966] The announcement about the arrival of Manley was said by Irv Daymond, Centre, to have "taken the Riders down to the level of Professional wrestling".[967] Don Campbell wrote that "there was no possible better backdrop than that provided by the ongoing preparations for the opening of the Super Ex Midway"[968] for the Club's announcement. Daymond was even stronger in his criticism: "Not only is Lonie insulting the players in this dressing room, he's insulting the football fans of Ottawa who want honest to goodness football, not cheap marketing crap".[969] "Why do we take pay cuts when (the Gliebermans) have that kind of money to throw around. It's a slap in the face to every player in this room. He's not going to help" said linebacker Gregg Stuman.[970]

When the Rough Riders defeated the Argonauts on August 26, their one point victory, without Dexter Manley, propelled them into third place and gave the coaches a stay of execution but the guessing game of when the firings of the coaches would take place continued. Ottawa's Gliebermans seemed to have replacements at hand. George Brancato, Ottawa's last coach when the Grey Cup was won was hired to work with the Defence. As was John Salavantis, former offensive co-ordinator with the Tiger-Cats, who assumed the same role with the Rough Riders.

When Bernie Glieberman gave the directive that Manley had to dress and start against Toronto on September 25, two assistant coaches, Jim Daley and Mike Roach, quit in protest. Fights among players became commonplace. Angelo Snipes and Danny Chronopoulos on the field; Ken Walcott and Michael Allen in the parking lot; Andrew Stewart and Glenn Kulka in the locker room. When Dexter Manley was suspended and fined by Glieberman for calling Coach Ron Smeltzer a "liar", it was described as "just another day at the nuthouse that goes by the name Ottawa Rough Riders".[971] The Gliebermans responded by suspending Manley "for conduct unbecoming a professional athlete".[972] They had previously ordered Smeltzer to start Manley for the October 30 game against Winnipeg in spite of the head coach making "it clear he was not only opposed to playing Manley but didn't even want him in camp".[973] In Manley's first game against the Argos, he left after 16 plays with a hyper extended elbow and slight tear in his knee. His team-mates disputed the injuries, irritated further that Manley was being paid handsomely for not being able to play while they had taken pay cuts in order to contribute to the team.

Owners said the players were jealous. Players responded by calling the situation "the Season from Hell".[974] Still, the Rough Riders had a chance to salvage their season. Going into the last game of the season, tied for third with the Argos with a 3-14 record, they had only to see Argos lose or the Riders win their final game against Hamilton. They won 27-26, ironically enough aided by a hit on quarterback Todd Dillon by Manley late in the fourth quarter. Dillon, somewhat rusty, had just joined Hamilton, having spent the year at graduate school in the U.S. He fumbled, Ottawa recovered and went on to score the winning touchdown. It was Manley's "first statistics in the CFL - a tackle and fumble recovery"[975] and enough to prompt him to speak of his "disfigured helmet" and how he would have three sacks and cause the quarterback to lose the ball at least twice as a result,[976] in the playoff game rematch. Manley also "revealed" that he was fined for saying that the "Riders had offered a pre-game reward to the player who could knock Dillon out of the game, as Manley did".[977]

In the eastern semi-final, the Tiger-Cats led again by Todd Dillon, ended the "Riders' Nightmare Season" defeating them by a 21-10 score. Manley was still on everyone's mind. "For the record, Manley had no sacks yesterday. No fumble recoveries. No tackles. No nothing".[978] On November 15, Albrecht, Brancato and Salavantis were told that they were no longer needed. Lonie Glieberman said that he intended to bring Manley back in '94. On November 22, "one hundred and three days after owner Bernie Glieberman first threatened to fire Ron Smeltzer, the axe finally fell".[979] Smeltzer was informed over breakfast by John Ritchie who then went to Lansdowne Park to fire assistants Harry Justvig, Jim Clark, and Dick Maloney. Only secondary coach Larry Hogue, whose contract had expired November 30 was invited to apply when a new head coach, the Riders' 9th in 10 years, would be selected. The "soap opera season" had come to an end.

But the Playoffs continued, Hamilton moved to Winnipeg for the eastern final eager to make amends for the twin embarrassments of having lost the play-off game of '92 to Winnipeg by a 59-11 score - a game which saw the Tiger-Cats' bench pelted by snowballs from some Winnipeg fans resulting in some Tiger-Cats invading the stands to search them out - and then losing twice to the Bombers in '93, the game in the Manitoba capital by a 61-10 score. The Blue Bombers had their share of adversity. Cal Murphy after his return from heart transplant surgery broke a hip and arm in a fall early in the season. He coached practices from a golf cart and from a press box perch for games. Then the Bombers lost quarterback Matt Dunigan with a torn Achilles tendon during the team's 33-26 victory over Sacramento. Quarterback Sam Garza, also the son-in-law of Murphy, would have two games to hone his quarterbacking skills before meeting Hamilton. And as successful as the Club was on the field it was having financial woes. It was into its $1.2 million line of credit from the Winnipeg Enterprises Corp., the Club's landlord, had a second line of credit with the corporation and an outstanding loan of $500,000 from the Royal Bank. The province approved a loan of $1 million in September.[980]

"Nonetheless, the Bombers beat Hamilton in the Eastern final for a second time by a 20-19 score ."

The CFL had decided in March to change its play-off format in the West. It moved from three teams, the traditional 1st place bye while 2nd and 3rd played off, to four teams in the play-offs, First vs. Fourth and Second vs. Third, the winners to meet for the Western Division Championship. As a sweetener, the League announced that the second and third place teams would still receive $1800, the fourth team $1300 and the first place one $2500.[981] The change however had to be approved by the Players Association. By the time the matter was ready to be voted on, training camps had broken. Such matters were not to be negotiated during the season according to the contract. By August, the announcement was made once again. Calgary players whose team was solidly ensconced in first place were upset. The Calgary public initiated a boycott of the play-off game. Eventually the League agreed to a vote by the Players' Association for their determination. Only by the first week in November was the change ratified.

In the west, the expanded play-offs took place. The Saskatchewan-Edmonton game between the second and third place teams was expected to be a close one. When the game was over, however, the Eskimos behind a confident Damon Allen, defeated the western 'riders by a 51-13 score. In the other game, 15,407 showed up for the game which had originally been the target of a fan boycott; Calgary thought that its team should have been awarded a bye for having finished the season in first place. The Stampeders were victorious over the B.C. Lions by a 17-9 score.

The western final was, once again, "the battle of Alberta". Calgary, which according to sources had paid $350,000[982] to Bruce McNall's Argonauts to buy the rights to the game, was gearing for its own Grey Cup party. It had promoted the B.C. Lion game as a type of film with the billing: "How the West will be won. Part I of a two week mini series. Starring Doug Flutie, the Ultimate Weapon as the Rifleman, Co-Starring the Wild Bunch Alondra Johnson, Marvin Pape, and Matt Finlay. Directed by Wally

Buono. A Larry Ryckman Production. General Warning: Some scenes will not be suitable for the opposition".[983]

When Larry Ryckman bought the rights to the 1993 Grey Cup game from Bruce McNall's Toronto Argonauts, he fully expected that his Calgary Stampeders would be playing. It was a gamble but a calculated one. Published reports had him paying $350,000 plus $24,500 GST to the Argos and a further $350,000 guarantee to the League.[984] It was not stated whether the latter was above the $3,000,000. guarantee the Argos had given when they were awarded the '92 and '93 games. Calgary City Council approved $390,000 worth of services while an additional $1.1 million was to be spent to bring McMahon Stadium capacity close to 50,000. All in all, it was estimated that some $13 million would be the total cost of all activities.[985] The Grey Cup Festival had a non profit arm, the Calgary Heritage and Community Foundation; Ryckman maintained that he wanted only to "break even". Calgary would benefit from any surplus of funds. Of the $1.1 million spent to improve the seating capacity, approximately $450,000 was allocated to "an auxiliary press box to accommodate 300 media" Ryckman's plan was to convert that area into 13 luxury suites for the '94 season hoping to recover his money over a four year period by renting them to corporations and individuals.[986]

All seemed to be proceeding smoothly and according to plan - until that fateful Sunday, November 21, when the Eskimos spoiled the Stampeders' plans, defeating them by a 29-15 count. The Stampeders finished the season at 15-3; their fans had been assured through the Club's advertising that the "west would be won". The playoffs were only a necessary nuisance. Only 20,218 spectators showed up for the game which was played in -20 temperatures, winds of 24 kph and blowing snow. Conditions were so hostile that the beginning of the third quarter was delayed an extra 15 minutes to clear the snow from the field. Flutie's hands were "frozen" to the point where he had no feeling in them and was forced to miss a play at the end of the game while trying to thaw them out. It was a disappointing end to the season for Calgarians who attended the game, some saying it was the coldest they had ever been to, enduring frostbite on their uncovered skin, staying "until the last second waiting for the Flutie miracle."[987]

Stunned Stampeder fans faced the reality that they would be hosting a Grey Cup celebration for their rivals from the north.

Calgary became "the city of the big hurt."[988] Grey Cup plans were in jeopardy. Some 20,000 seats had been sold prior to November 19; they included those purchased by Safeway for its family huddle section "where admission is cheap".[989] An additional 30,000 were still to be sold and in one week.

The emphasis was now on attracting Edmontonions; Calgary fans were not about to cheer for their northern rivals - not after spending anywhere from $84 to $115, plus service charge and GST. Two columns of classified ads offering Grey Cup tickets for sale appeared in the Calgary Herald as late as November 26.

After having been defeated by a Calgary team in the 1991 and 1992 western finals, Edmonton and its self proclaimed City of Champions descriptor, had become the butt of Calgary jokes. Not this year though! In spite of recent -30 C temperatures, only smiles were frozen on the faces of its citizens as a result of the Edmonton win. Monday morning at work saw people "laughing and happy. It was like someone won the lottery."[990] The tables were turned and Edmonton loved it. News reports chortled that Calgarians were "still numb from the loss." An Edmonton newspaper asked its readers for their favourite Calgary jokes ("What's the difference between a loonie and Calgary quarterback Doug Flutie? You can get four good quarters from a loonie").[991] "There's no word", poked the Edmonton Journal, on what Doug Flutie is going to do with the twenty tickets he purchased. But who knows? He may have placed an ad too!"[992]

At a reception and send-off at City Hall in Edmonton, the Edmonton euphoria at Calgary's expense, continued. "What more could we ask for? Calgary's throwing a big party and it's just for us", said Mayor Jan Reimer. Her bet with Calgary Mayor Al

Duerr meant that Edmonton's City of Champions sign on the outskirts would be polished by her counterpart. Clearly, she was enjoying the moment: "I'd like to personally thank (the Eskimos players) for saving me from the embarrassment of riding in the Grey Cup parade wearing a Stampeders' sweater,"[993]she continued.

Fears of the weather inflicting its wintry grip on Calgary's Grey Cup game, particularly because of the 3:30 P.M. start, were unfounded. Temperature at game time was 6 C, positively balmy in comparison with the previous week. Regardless of the warming breezes, there were still some disgruntled patrons who booed the playing of the American anthem prior to the game. It was played along with O Canada in recognition of Sacramento's membership in the League. In the press box, though, "not a single regular media person from Sacramento was among the approximately 300 accredited writers and broadcasters."[994] It remained for Gold Miners' quarterback David Archer to represent the team, sending "a scene setting column to a newspaper and radio clips for three stations, so at least they're getting some coverage down there."[995] Archer was also hired as the colour commentator for the Telemedia radio broadcast of the game.

The Edmonton Eskimos, aided by seven uncharacteristic Winnipeg turnovers, won the Grey Cup contest by a 33-23 score. Damon Allen was selected the MVP. The Calgary jinx continued. David Yule, the Referee, tore a muscle in his right calf late in the first quarter and was unable to continue. The Calgary native was replaced by alternate Ken Lazaruk. It was an especially happy victory for Edmonton's defensive end Jed Roberts. Twenty-five years ago earlier, his father, tight end Jay Roberts was a member of the Ottawa Rough Riders' Cup winning team

It was obvious that the CFL was still rooting itself in its traditions; it was equally obvious that it was bent upon creating new ones. Doug Flutie was selected the most Outstanding Player for the third consecutive year, a league record. He was chosen over Winnipeg's Matt Dunigan, who because of a severed achilles tendon, would not be ready to play in the Grey Cup game. Flutie, whose 1993 league statistics included a record 6,092 passing yards and 44 touchdowns in 18 games, was a near unanimous selection. Fifty two votes were cast for him, one against with one spoiled ballot.[996] Other award winners, their margin of victory and runners-up were: Outstanding Non-import, Dave Sapunjis by a 51-1 margin over Gerald Wilcox of Winnipeg; Most Outstanding Lineman, Chris Walby of Winnipeg, 40-14 over Bruce Covernton of Calgary; Outstanding Defensive Player to Saskatchewan's Jearld Baylis, a 37-17 winner over Winnipeg linebacker Elfrid Payton; Rookie of the Year to Hamilton's Michael O'Shea who edged Calgary's Brian Wiggers, a receiver, by a 29-25 margin. In another break from the past, the winners and runners up received no monetary prizes, instead being rewarded with "rings, trophies and prizes from the league and Grey Cup Festival organizers."[997]

The League also made known its all time "dream team". Voting was conducted by ballot by fans attending CFL games and at sponsors' outlets during the '93 season. The All Time CFL All Stars were:

DEFENCE
Cornerbacks: Joe Hollimon, Edmonton, Dickie Harris, Montreal.
Halfbacks:Garney Henley, Hamilton, Dick Thornton, Toronto.
Safety:Jerry Keeling, Calgary.
Outside Backers: James Parker, Edmonton, Mike Widger, Montreal
Middle Linebacker: Wayne Harris, Calgary
Ends: Herb Gray, Winnipeg, Bill Baker, Saskatchewan.
Tackles: John Helton, Calgary, John Barrow, Hamilton
OFFENCE
Tackles: Frank Rigney, Winnipeg, Roger Nelson, Edmonton.
Guards: Roger Aldag, Saskatchewan, Tony Pajaczkowski, Calgary
Centre: Ted Urness, Saskatchewan
Receivers: Ray Elgaard, Saskatchewan, Tony Gabriel, Ottawa

Hal Patterson, Hamilton, Brian Kelly, Edmonton.
Running Backs: Leo Lewis, Winnipeg, George Reed,
Saskatchewan.
Quarterback: Ron Lancaster, Saskatchewan.
Specialists: Punter, Lui Passaglia, B.C.
Place Kicker, Dave Cutler, Edmonton.
Returns, Henry Williams, Winnipeg.
Coach: Bud Grant, Winnipeg
General Manager: Norm Kimball, Edmonton
Most outstanding Player*: Jackie Parker, Edmonton.

* Parker played quarterback, halfback, wide receiver, place-kicker and punter in his career.[998]

When Commissioner Larry Smith delivered his "State of the
League" address followed by a question and answer session,
some obviously pent-up emotions were vented. Among other
items, Smith revealed that 1993 would probably be the last year
guaranteeing an east-west final. With expansion into the United States proceeding, a north-south final was being positioned
and advice from American teams was beginning to flow. Seeded
playoffs and wild cards would probably evolve as would pressure
for a league name change. Indeed, Smith noted, Sacramento had
already requested one, substituting North American for Canadian. It was reasoned that such a name change would make the
league "more attractive to U.S. investors".[999]

Las Vegas, Nevada, was the home of the CFL's newest team, the
"Posse." It was announced with all the glitter and glitz that Vegas
could muster. On July 27, 1993, the CFL had awarded a franchise to Cleveland business man Nick Mileti after presenting the
League with a cheque for $1 million. It was a down payment on
the $3 million U.S. franchise fee. Smith stated that the League
was still looking to add two more teams for the '94 season. Nash-
ville, Portland, Montreal, Orlando and Jacksonville were considered possibilities.[1000] It had been rumoured that the Montreal
franchise would be operated by the Expos which "would share its
front office staff" in an effort to defray expenses.[1001]

There were detractors in Las Vegas. The Record-Journal's sports writer Stephen Nover reported that the NFL was the game of choice; College football drew about 8,000 per game. The Canadian sized field would mean "pads on the walls" and end zones of 17 yards depth rather than 20.[1002]

The announcement continued to draw editorials and comments. The Toronto Star, after sympathizing with the CFL and its problems suggested that

> *had the energy poured into the pursuit of franchises in 3rd rate American cities been put, instead, into resurrecting the Alouettes in Montreal, re-invigorating the Tiger-Cats in Hamilton and the Argos in Toronto, and creating a team in Halifax, maybe we could have kept a distinctive Canadian League.*[1003]

Smith was the object of some criticism. One reader wrote "Commissioner Larry Smith, if he's remembered at all, will be a footnote in sports history as Canadian football's Brian Mulroney".[1004] Meanwhile, in Vegas, the" First Lady of Magic", Melinda, was placed in a cannon carrying a blank banner. When it was fired and the smoke cleared, she was standing on the other side of the stage. She unfurled the banner to reveal the team's name and logo. The colours were light brown (sand) black and white; the logo silhouetted black horses on a sand background with white lettering.[1005] The CFL had arrived in Las Vegas, "The Entertainment Capital of the World".

Two other American teams arrived in time for the 1994 CFL season. Each, in its own way, was a result of some form of rejection. Each was in a city which the original CFL vision had not included. Baltimore had been an NFL market. Its team, the Colts, had left, some said, in the middle of the night, for Indianapolis. It also left a community embittered. After a long association and identity with the NFL, it had been unceremoniously dumped. The CFL was to be the benefactor of the civic animosity. The city collectively was anxious to show its former associates that a mistake had been made. The second American team was from Shreveport, Louisiana. In its original approach to expansion into the United States, the CFL wanted to go into markets which were too small for NFL consideration. A bi-product would be that the CFL was demonstrating that it was not in competition with the NFL.At the same time, the non NFL cities were expected to be in major television markets, the search for a television contract being an ongoing objective of the CFL. The arrival of the league in Shreveport was tied directly to the Gliebermans who decided to take their "circus" from Ottawa and travel to Louisiana. When the Gliebermans had purchased the Ottawa franchise in 1991, they had a written agreement that at the end of the three years they would be allowed to place a club wherever they chose. The Ottawa franchise would remain for new owners. The long range plan of the Gliebermans was "to operate a team in Detroit; it wanted the first opportunity in that area. At the same time, the Ottawa club would be transferred to a new owner."[1006]

Unlike the Baltimore Colts, the NFL and Robert Irsay, the Gliebermans did not go quietly in the night. Already the butt of much criticism in Ottawa because of the 1993 season, they were the centre of increased controversy both inside and outside the city. From a league perspective, there were fears that the Ottawa franchise, a 118 year tradition in that city, would cease to exist. If the league were going to have a team in Shreveport, it "preferred" that it be an expansion franchise and therefore generate the $3 million fee. The Glieberman family was insistent about the move: "the ideal situation would be for part of the (Ottawa) team to move with him to Shreveport as a new team and a buyer for the Ottawa team could be found to keep the franchise in Ottawa."[1007]

Tempers began to heat and flared into fisticuffs when Lonie, along with his body guard and girl friend, found themselves in an argument with patrons at the Yucatan Liquor Stand on a Saturday night. "A patron of the bar slugged the 300 pound (Steve) Wilson", Lonie's bodyguard/friend. According to the patron:

"Glieberman's popularity plummeted with the crowd at the bar. Last year. . . no one would harass him. But this year is a different story."[1008]

The furore continued. The Gliebermans had only recently signed a ten year lease to play in Frank Clair Stadium. At the same time, they had investigated Louisville, Lexington, San Antonio, Columbus, Memphis, and Richmond as possible sites before settling on Shreveport. It appeared as if they were ready to act without the "due process" insisted upon by the league.[1009] Equipment manager Jim Rempel had been instructed by Bernie Glieberman "to pack up the equipment bags and prepare for a move."[1010] Special consultant J.I. Albrecht had "already set up shop as the Gliebermans' front man for the possible new club, the Pirates".[1011]

The new franchise and the sale of the Ottawa club were tied together. There would be one more team in the CFL; the $3 million price tag had to come from somewhere, either from the Gliebermans for the Shreveport franchise, the new owners of the Rough Riders or a combination of both. In addition, there were Ottawa's debts, estimates ranged from $1.2 million to $1.4 million, that had to be addressed. As a consequence of all of this, the CFL sought to develop more strict guidelines which would ensure that teams would not move to greener pastures. There was some speculation that the NHL by law 36.5 would be used as a model causing one scoffing reporter to state that if that were the case "we already know how 'protected' our Canadian asset is going to be at crunch time."[1012]

All of this seemed to be a continuation of the carnival atmosphere which had prevailed during the 1993 season. Former General Manager, Jo Anne Polack sought and was granted an injunction to prohibit the Gliebermans "from taking any Rider assets out of Ottawa".[1013] She was seeking $15,000 owed her; the Gliebermans' lawyer countered that the money, mostly from vacation pay, was owed by previous owners and that if Polack wanted the money "let her sue the CFL".[1014] The injunction was lifted as soon as the Gliebermans' lawyer appeared in court to contest it. The CFL was getting nervous. It had a schedule to draw up. Ottawa City council entered the equation. It proposed that it spend $3 million to upgrade Frank Clair Stadium. It seemed to be the key to attracting former Ottawa Senator owner Bruce Firestone. Before that key could be turned, however, the city wanted a guarantee that it would be paid the $340,000 it said that the Gliebermans owed. In a convoluted arrangement which included the Gliebermans, Firestone, the City of Ottawa, Bretton Woods Entertainment and Toronto financier/Ottawa fan/Ottawa Senator/Hamilton Tiger-Cat investor/CFL consultant, David MacDonald, who assisted in the raising of the money necessary, the accommodation was arranged over a two day period. Bernie and Lonie Glieberman gave the CFL $1.7 million for the right to field a team in Shreveport. A further "$1.85 million in deferred payments. . . from ticket surcharges and a share of Ottawa's take on future expansion fees"[1015]made for what Smith labelled "a hybrid situation. It's an exit for Bernie Glieberman and an entry for Bruce Firestone."[1016]

It set the wheels in motion to finalize a number of pending announcements. Firestone, while serving on the CFL's expansion and marketing committees was to remain in the background. Phil Kershaw was to take over as the operational manager of the Club, much as Paul Robson had done when he moved from Winnipeg to Ottawa and Norm Kimball when he left Edmonton in an attempt to resuscitate Montreal. Kershaw in turn hired Mike McCarthy and Adam Rita, the former as a player personnel consultant, the latter as head coach. The following day, February 18, CFL Commissioner Larry Smith announced at a press conference in Shreveport the acceptance of the Gliebermans' Pirates as the twelfth team in the league, the fourth American club for the 1994 season. The team, whose colours were purple, orange, silver and black, also took with it five members of the Rough Riders, Gregg Stumon, linebacker, quarterback Terrence Jones, wide receiver Wayne Walker, cornerback Joe Mero and defensive end Dexter Manley. J.I. Albrecht became the Executive Vice President/Football Operations. It was apparent that his hand was present in the selection of other personnel. John Huard was appointed Head

Coach; George Brancato was to be an assistant in charge of the offensive back field and quarterbacks; Albrecht's son Dean,, an agent who had Huard as one of his clients, was named the team's General Manager and director of Player Development. The other assistant coaches were Steve Dennis, former defensive back with the Argonauts and Roughriders, Bob Surace, the offensive line coach was from Huard's Maine Maritime Academy as was Mark Hedgecock, an assistant listed as "'quality control coach' . . . a post created by the NFL Dallas Cowboys a few decades ago. . . considered one of the most important factors in professional football today."[1017]

Controversy continued to follow the Gliebermans. John Huard was fired before the season began and replaced with former Argonaut coach Forrest Gregg. "Philosophical differences"[1018] were cited by Lonie as the reason. There had been complaints about training camp conditions and Huard's military style approach, "abrasive at the best of times and he was arguing with everyone."[1019] Gregg was placed in full control of football operations, a situation which made the Albrechts' and all of their appointments' positions tenuous. They were later relieved of their duties. By September the purge was complete. George Brancato and Bernie Ruoff, in charge of special teams, were fired.[1020]

On February 17, the third American franchise, had been awarded. Baltimore, Maryland, spurned by the NFL, proposed to the CFL and the League accepted. it was a calculated gamble. After all, this was an NFL market, an abandoned one but at the same time one which would have preferred to carry on the relationship. Was the CFL simply being espoused on the rebound? How would the Baltimore public respond to Canadian Football? Owner Jim Speros was betting heavily that the public would be overwhelmingly in favour of the team which he would name the Colts. Others weren't so sure. They saw the NFL as perhaps an inferior game but played by superior athletes; the CFL might have been a superior game but it was played by inferior athletes. A letter to the Baltimore Sun put it more pragmatically: "

There are three reasons why we should support Speros. The first is the number of 3-0 games the CFL had last season. The second is the CFL Colts have a chance to make the playoffs before the end of the next century. The third is that if we got behind the CFL Colts the NFL would be more likely to award us an expansion franchise the next time.[1021]

There was no doubt that the former NFL team had left a long and storied legacy in Baltimore. Speros tried to evoke that by naming his new team Colts. The NFL would have none of it. It sought and received a court injunction to prohibit the CFL team from using the name. It seemed to be one more reason for the fans to support the new team. Royal blue, white, black and silver were adopted as club colours. A horse head with a flowing mane emulating stripes with stars interspersed was the team's logo. Don Mathews, who had resigned from Saskatchewan, was selected as head coach. He sought to surround himself with people knowledgeable in the Canadian game: Steve Buratto became the offensive co-ordinator while Joe Barnes became the quarterback coach. One of Mathews' first moves was to sign former Argonaut quarterback Tracy Ham. Marketing of the club revolved around the animosity toward the NFL, Robert Irsay, and to some extent, Indianapolis. A season ticket theme was the "Indy Challenge". In 1993, the NFL team had sold 36,112 tickets The goal for the Baltimore Club was to exceed that. Animosity towards the NFL increased when a court ruled that the club could not use the term "colts" in their name. Even "CFL Colts" was prohibited. The decision was made to call them the Baltimore "CFLers".

Meanwhile, in Las Vegas, the smoke and mirrors began to clear as the hype faded into the background. Owner Nick Mileti arranged for Las Vegas Major League Sports Inc. to be on the Boston Stock Exchange. The NASDAQ listing at $8. per unit was expected to generate $4.7 million in operating revenue in addition to paying off the $2.5 million he borrowed to buy the club.[1022] The innovative and successful approach caused other CFL clubs to look closely at duplicating the venture as a means of eliminating their debts. Las Vegas continued to be innovative by announcing that they would begin their training on a specially built field in a parking lot behind the Riviera Hotel. Twelve hundred tons of sand topped with grass sod were to be used to build the 70 yards by 80 yards area complete with bleachers to seat 600 fans who were to receive free vouchers from the Casino in the Riviera.[1023] A four storey banner hanging from a parking garage in the background proclaimed it to be the "Field of ImPOSSEable Dreams"[1024] Ron Meyer, a former NFL coach with Indianapolis and New England was named the head coach with assistance from former Ottawa mentor Ron Smeltzer. Fans from around the league made arrangements to join excursions to Las Vegas to watch their team and visit the self proclaimed "entertainment capital of the world."

If it all seemed to good to be true, it was. By June 30, the Club's quarterly report was showing a loss of $2.24 million.[1025] Attendance was dwindling. Ticket prices were cut. Much of the problem, according to one local source, was that "the town is based on a major league perception. People bet on major league sports all the time and they perceive the CFL as minor league."[1026] By the end of August, Mileti had resigned as Chairman and CEO. He was replaced by Los Angeles investment banker Glenn Golenberg.[1027] The controversy surrounding the Posse refused to fade. In a game with Shreveport, Las Vegas was ahead by 34-21, having scored with 16 seconds left on the clock. Gamblers had made Las Vegas 14 point favourites. A decision was made to attempt a two point conversion. It failed but it was obvious that someone had bet that the Posse would cover the spread. One of the fears that CFL followers had when a decision was made to encourage CFL games to be listed by gamblers was becoming realized.

Financial concerns were such that when Hamilton and Las Vegas, two teams strapped for cash, met on September 25, Ron Meyer suggested that the game "should be called the Bankruptcy Bowl. Whoever wins the coin toss should keep it."[1028] Things had gone downhill from the first home game, July 16, when the Posse defeated Saskatchewan 30-22 in overtime. The temperature was 96 degrees F at half time but more notable was the singing of the Canadian national anthem by Dennis K.C. Park. The words were wrong; the tune was more like O Tannenbaum and it was sung off key. And all before a national CBC television audience. The rendition set off an immediate reaction. The Ottawa Citizen invited its readers to "call Touchline at 721-1990 and on your touchtone phone, select code 7505 to hear this original rendition of O Canada."[1029] Nick Mileti wrote an apology to PM Jean Chretien. Even Vice President of the United States, Al Gore, was aware. On a visit to Ottawa, he remarked "I was certainly glad to see that the US players reacted so strongly and better than the singer".[1030] Park was immediately sought after by a variety of talk shows and television programs in Canada. The Hamilton Tiger Cats, keen to seize an opportunity to sell more tickets, invited him to sing the national anthem once again, this time correctly, before one of their home games.

By the end of the season, it was obvious that the Posse had ridden into the sunset. After a combined total of 5,000 watched two home games, the final one was "moved to Edmonton and league officials perform(ed) euthanasia."[1031]

In Sacramento, meanwhile, the Gold Miners was burdened by its second straight season of missing the playoffs. The small crowds it was drawing at Hornet field contributed to large financial losses and the team made plans to move to another locale in search of a new life.

It wasn't only the American teams that were struggling. In Toronto. the triumvirate of Gretzky, Candy and McNall was conspicuous by its absence. By February, the club had an estimated $1.3 million in debts and according to SkyDome officials, owed $300,000 in rent.[1032] It was a large comedown from the hectic media-fanned promotional days when the "Big League" veneer was bandied about. Interest was in decline and the Argo ownership had left a lonely Ron Barbaro to manage as best he could. It seemed as if all were in a holding pattern. Barbaro's approach, a complete switch from the early heady days, was announced at a buffet breakfast meeting for the media and sponsors. A jazz trio played in the background; the Argo Sunshine Girls would be replaced by "fresh faced university style cheerleaders."[1033] Plans were announced to have the players "ride out to centre field on a float shaped like the good ship Argonaut."[1034]

An attempt was made to attract youth and families. Day care, face painting, pre game parties, appeals to university football programs, tickets for high school students in the upper level, a revival of the Argo Playback Club and inexpensive tickets, were all part of attempting to recapture the public's interest. The Club had gone from a high of 51,000 for the eastern final game in 1991 to a low of 16,000 for the game with Edmonton in '93

The path towards re-vitalization became more difficult. In the midst of all of this restructuring, Gretzky and McNall announced that they were selling their shares. John Candy proposed to put together a group to buy the Club. The news continued to get worse before it got better. John Candy suffered a heart attack and died March 4, 1994. The 43 year old was on location in Mexico. Aside from his great status as a film star, he was described as "the most supportive in the Argo organization. . .the strength of the ownership in Toronto. . . one of the positives of the CFL."[1035]

Gretzky, on a visit to Winnipeg, elaborated to Winnipeg Free Press columnist Scott Taylor:

> *When John Candy died, it was a devastating blow for a lot of reasons. Most importantly, he was a great friend but he was going to buy out Bruce and I and take over the Argos. . . We don't believe the CFL has a future in places like Toronto and Vancouver. In Canada, the CFL is a league for community owned teams that don't pay rent and get government help The business of the CFL doesn't work in places like Toronto*

And Vancouver. Those are major league cities that expect a major league product. The CFL, now that it has expanded to second tier markets in the United States, is perceived as minor league football.[1036]

By early May, the Argos had been sold to TSN, a subsidiary of Labatt's. Paul Beeston, president of the Blue Jays, was named to head up the football team. Some cynics suggested that Labatt had bought the Argonauts in order to obtain the rights to an NFL franchise since "whoever owns the Argos also owns the rights to professional football in the SkyDome." Beeston was clearly irritated by the insinuation: "Do you think that we want to be associated with something that won't work?"[1037] What was referred to as the "Blue Jays-ization of the Toronto Argonauts"[1038]continued when Bob Nicholson, vice president of the baseball club, took a similar position with the Argos. In an effort to reconstruct ties with the past, the club returned to the traditional logo of "a football shaped ship with oars sticking out the side and a sail."[1039]It was stylized in an effort to make it more contemporary, riding on a rippling sea, all enclosed within a circle. Toronto was on the top, Argonauts below; the sail was white rather than blue and outlined with black. The football was black; previously, it had been brown. Designed by Stanford Agency, the logo "would adorn the team's letterhead and program but not the side of the helmets."[1040] The letter A would remain on the helmets since a year's notice was needed because of merchandising contracts. Bob O'Billovich was retained as General Manager and Coach.

The four American teams had contributed approximately $14.3 million (CDN) in expansion fees: $3 million US from Sacramento, $2.5 million US each from Las Vegas and Baltimore and $2.8 Million CDN from the combined sale of the Rough Riders and the creation of the Shreveport Pirates.[1041] It was money that was sorely needed. The league was in debt to the tune of approximately $2.5 million and called upon the various clubs to eradicate it. But in spite of the improved cash situation, clubs were still having financial problems as the season evolved. The Blue

Bombers were beginning the year with a debt of $2.6 to $2.8 million. Included was "the existing deficit of $1.8 million, a payment towards the league's debt of $450,000 and a projected loss of $800,000 for 1994.[1042]

In Edmonton, the Grey Cup champion Eskimos released a financial statement showing a loss of $171,269 for 1993, some $36,000 less than the previous year. The BC Lions reported an operating loss on the 1993 season of $2.6 million. "The real loss, said Bill Comrie, after taking into account the receipt of expansion fees, was $2.19 million." [1043] The BC owner was angry that his words were being challenged by a columnist in the Province. He sent out an open letter to the media in which he admitted that his team spent over $3,000,000 on coaches' and players' salaries. In addition, he said, the club spent $300,000 on equipment and training room supplies, more than $100,000 for general manager Eric Tillman, $70,000 in wages and car expenses for personnel director Bill Quinter, $60,000 in salary and expenses for two secretaries, $135,000 in medical coverage, $60,000 for UIC and CPP and $55,000 for the Players' pension fund. Travel costs were $430,000 plus $30,000 for ground transportation, $150,000 for hotels and $120,000 in per diems for players on away trips. Training camp expenses were an additional $350,000.[1044]

Comrie was determined that the team would stay within the salary cap for 1994. When former player Mike Gray was "hired" as a defensive line coach, he was taken on with no salary. The only way that he could travel with the team on a road trip was if one of the normal travelling party, usually the manager or player personnel director, decided not to go.[1045]

The CFL Players' Association, fearing that its members would be trapped by the public's perception that they, the players, were the cause of the clubs' financial woes, decided to make their salaries public. The vote of the Association was 15-3 in favour. The three dissenting votes were by Winnipeg's Chris Walby, Edmonton's Randy Ambrosie and Saskatchewan's Dave Ridgeway. All were year round residents of their community, one of the reasons given for their reluctance. They were not convinced that neighbours reading in the paper of their salary would say "Darn, I didn't know that you played for so little." Another reason given for the disclosure was the hope that "general managers could no longer mislead players and agents in contract negotiations."[1046]

Finances continued to be a problem with almost every team in the league but particularly Hamilton, Ottawa, Las Vegas and Sacramento. All suffered from poor attendance during the season. The possibility of expansion continued to be the anticipated elixir which would solve the money problems: the league decided that the next round of expansion, in time for the '95 season, would double in fees to $6 million per team.[1047]

Speculation was rife that Larry Smith would be asked to resign. The hectic pace of old franchises with problems, new franchises, potential new sites for expansion, settling disputes plus the need for day to day hands on business decisions all contributed to a search by Smith for a lower profile. It was noted that "Smith had distanced himself from the media, becoming increasingly more difficult to reach. Club executives have long complained that keeping track of Smith's travels and finding him has been tricky." The suggestion was made that the initials CFL stood for more than the name of the league: "The new phrase: Can't Find Larry".[1048] In time, the dust settled and the season began; attention was more focused on league play. Criticism subsided. There were still kinks to work out but Smith was named "Marketer of the Year" by the Toronto chapter of the American Marketing Association "for his success in reviving the CFL despite the many obstacles facing him both financially and in terms of fan appeal."[1049] As if to recognize that Smith couldn't be everywhere at the same time, the League announced that it had hired Jeff Giles as its chief operating officer, a "newly created position (to) focus on the day-to-day business dealings" of the CFL.[1050]

"Smith and the owners are apparently getting what they want; one wonders if they can handle it."[1051] So asked Doug Smith of the Canadian Press early in the new year. The CFL had been a folksy group depending more on informal contact. Now it would find itself having "to communicate with media not familiar with the league."[1052] The reporter's story was triggered by a press release announcing a serious expansion bid from Orlando, Florida. He had tried to contact the League but Larry Smith "was at home recovering from a hernia operation. . . VP of Communications (was)in a car on a snow bound highway and the league's expansion czar, Larry Ryckman (was) in western Canada." The fact was that "no one in authority was near the League's Toronto office and a news release replete with spelling and grammatical errors hammered that point home."[1053] The reporter continued that with the League having expanded into the United States, with a game a week on ESPN2, the All Sports US cable network, with the publicity that the CFL craved emanating from the league and approved betting in Las Vegas, it was necessary for the league to "shed its Mickey mouse image."[1054]

It was an ironic choice of words. A meeting of the CFL Board of Governors was rescheduled from Toronto to Orlando for 7:30 AM, January 18. It was strongly suggested that a franchise would be awarded; a press conference for that purpose was scheduled for 11:30 AM. It had all the appearances of a "sure thing". The CFL had "planned to charter a plane to fly the Canadian sports media south, at least until it found out that most of the organizations wouldn't accept the trip.'[1055] On the evening of February 17, the league sent out a news release, including satellite coordinates so that television stations in Canada and elsewhere could carry the announcement live. Larry Smith told a reporter that "the only thing that needed to be tidied up was a bit of 'paperwork'"[1056] before Orlando was granted a franchise.

Not all agreed. Larry Guest, writing in the Orlando Sentinel, suggested: "Mayor Hood, Orlando, tell CFL to take a hike."[1057] There had been too many times in the past when "the reps of every gadget sports league" convene monthly at our City Hall" to tell how their organization would put Orlando on the "big league map". Guest's advice was: "Anything short of the NFL should be given directions to Valdosta."[1058]

The Governors' meeting dragged on for more than two hours; it was obvious that something was amiss. In a statement issued by the league, it was announced that the franchise for Orlando had been put on hold. The CFL was concerned with the lack of financing and a lease for the Citrus Bowl. Even so, some things didn't ring true. It appeared that while the league was prepared to accept 15 yard end zones, five less than the rules called for, city officials declared that the maximum end zone could only be 12 yards![1059]

Again, Mickey Mouse was an overworked metaphor to describe the situation. A scapegoat was sought. Rumours even circulated that the league was no longer enamoured with the Commissioner who, reportedly, had asked it to double his salary from $250,000 to $500,000 per year.[1060]"Business consultant", Bill Hunter, "hired by Smith to preside over potential expansion"[1061] was identified by others as the culprit. Fred Anderson, owner of the Sacramento team was particularly upset. His quarterback, David Archer, had travelled to Orlando to be part of the ceremonies. Orlando would have provided a boost to season ticket sales. So too would it have in Las Vegas where leaked news of the "expansion" to Orlando had become front page news.

"Mickey Mouse" was also a term used by Ottawa Rough Riders personnel director Mike McCarthy after it was announced that Ottawa would lose its first round draft pick. In an attempt to present as few roadblocks as possible to the new owners of the Riders, Smith had told them "that it should not be held accountable for the previous Glieberman ownership's exceeding the salary cap."[1062] Were these new approaches being made on the fly?

The reaction of the league's clubs was swift when an announcement was made that Ottawa would be treated as if it had been within the salary cap. "General Managers were unanimous in their outrage. . . asked the league's governors to address their concern".[1063] It was revealed that four Canadian clubs were over the cap: Toronto, Edmonton, BC and Ottawa. The CFL put a positive spin on the effect. Rather than announcing that the four would not participate in the first round, it declared that Hamilton, Saskatchewan, Calgary and Winnipeg would be allowed to choose first in what was termed a bonus round. Only Canadian based teams participated in the draft; American teams did not have any import/non-import restrictions. Hamilton's first pick was offensive lineman Val St. Germain from McGill University.

There were changes from teams trying to trim their budgets by allowing free agents to leave and from trades. Compounding the situation was the fact that there were an additional three American teams bidding for players and all starting from the ground up. Baltimore, especially, made a concerted effort to stock their team with players having CFL experience. Tracy Ham left the Argos to join the CFLers as did Jearld Baylis from Saskatchewan and O.J. Brigance from BC and Mike Pringle from Sacramento. The Roughriders also lost Jeff Fairholm to the Argonauts. Winnipeg lost Michael Richardson to Ottawa, Elfrid Payton to Shreveport and Greg Battle to Las Vegas, later to Ottawa. The Tiger-Cats lost Mike Jovanovich, an offensive lineman to Toronto and receiver Nick Mazzoli to Ottawa.

Complicating the issue was the relative value of Canadian and American currency. A contract for the same dollar figure would have a difference of 30% because of the higher value of the American currency. A case in point was Elfrid Payton. He had been selected as the Eastern Division Outstanding Defensive Player of 1993. Payton had a contract for $49,000 with bonuses capable of bringing in another $7,000.[1064] Winnipeg had offered him a new contract for $52,000. His team mate Greg Battle had signed with the Las Vegas Posse for $85,000 (US). Payton negotiated a contract with Shreveport which included: "$75,000(US), bonuses worth $7500 in cash and a percentage of all tickets sold for Shreveport home games. . . the club also agreed to allow him the use of a luxury apartment . . . year round.[1065]

Quarterbacks continued to move around. When Tracy Ham left Toronto to join Baltimore, it was assumed that Reggie Slack would inherit the position He was traded to Hamilton who needed a quarterback since high profile signing Timm Rosen-bach didn't live up to the club's expectations and was released. Don McPherson had moved on to Ottawa. Yet another "major" signing fell through, this one in Winnipeg where the Blue Bomb-ers, perhaps anticipating that Matt Dunigan would not return from his achilles tendon operation or that they could not afford his contract. They signed Todd Marinovich. The former NFL quarterback injured his knee the first day of training camp and left abruptly. The comings and goings caused Bruce Cheadle of the Canadian Press to dub it the Carousel Football League, es-pecially after a three team quarterback swap. Saskatchewan sent Kent Austin and offensive lineman Andrew Greene to Ottawa in return for quarterback Tom Burgess, defensive back Anthony Drawhorn, Linebacker Ron Goetz and Defensive tackle Ron Yat-kowski. When Yatkowski didn't pass the Saskatchewan physical, Ottawa took him back in return for first and second round picks in the 1995 draft.[1066] Ottawa then traded Austin to BC in return for Adam Rita favourite, Danny Barrett and defensive back Cory Dowder. A philosophical Barrett reacted: ""you join the CFL and you get the tour of Canada."[1067]

There were twelve teams in the CFL for 1994, six in each division. In the East were Winnipeg, Hamilton, Toronto, Ottawa, Balti-more and Shreveport. The West included Saskatchewan, Ed-monton, Calgary, British Columbia, Sacramento and Las Vegas. A change was made in the playoff structure. Four teams from each division were to continue in post season play. There was still an east-west format provided for the Grey Cup game and the possibility that two American based teams could be playing in it. Playoff money had been adjusted. Losing teams earned $1900; the winning club players received $2400 each. In the Grey Cup game, the winners were rewarded with $12,000, the losers $6,000 each.

Several records were set during the '94 season. Lui Passaglia of the BC Lions, the all time leading scorer in professional football, was noted as the "CFL career leader in games played".[1068] Ray Elgaard of the Saskatchewan Roughriders passed Rocky DiPietro in most career receptions. Calgary's Allen Pitts and Baltimore's Mike Pringle also set records in pass receiving and rushing; Pitts caught passes for 2036 yards and Pringle established a new CFL rushing total of 1972 yards.

During the Winnipeg Ottawa game, won by Winnipeg 46-1, there were charges of electronic eavesdropping. The game was broadcast on ESPN2. Producers had approached Cal Murphy, wanting to "wire him up" with a live microphone so viewers could be aware of plays that were being sent in from the bench. Murphy declined. Adam Rita, coach of the Rough Riders agreed. Winnipeg's director of player personnel, Paul Jones, was watching the game in Tennessee. He overheard Rita calling a set of plays, phoned the Bombers assistant general manager Lyle Bauer in the Winnipeg Stadium press box. Bauer, in turn, relayed the information down to Murphy who signalled in appropriate defences.[1069]

In Shreveport, the Pirates won their last three games to finish with a 3-15 record. Though relatively well supported by the public, the club was still seeking to have the taxpayers "guarantee a loan of up to $4.5 million. . . the Pirates (were expecting) to lose up to $2 million more than anticipated."[1070] The franchise in Las Vegas was all but finished and would relocate because of the poor fan support. One report headlined that Desert Flop takes to road: Posse to end its run in Edmonton.

A franchise was announced for 1995 to Memphis, Tennessee, and owner Fred Smith of Federal Express. Although the value of the next round of franchises was to be $6 million (US), the reported price paid by Memphis was $1.8 million(US).[1071] The CFL was most anxious to have him in the League because of his "deep pockets" and because he had been mentioned as one of the parties behind the proposed North American League which some wanted to begin as a rival to the NFL in the United States and pre-empt eligible American cities from being available for the CFL.

In the CFL playoffs, Calgary defeated Saskatchewan 36-3 and BC won over Edmonton on a last minute field goal by Lui Passaglia, 24-23. It had been set up by an interception by Charles Gordon of a Damon Allen pass thrown from the BC four yard line. He ran it back to the Eskimo 41 and might have run it all the way for a touchdown but for a hinted at bounty on the Edmonton quarterback. One block short of returning it for the major, he thought that linebacker Virgil Robertson would provide it "but he said that he was going to get Damon. They had a little bet going. If somebody got a good hit on Damon there was a little money involved."[1072]

In the Eastern Division, first place Winnipeg defeated Ottawa 26-16 while Baltimore, the first American team to make the playoffs, scored a 34-15 win over the Argos. It was the first CFL playoff game played outside Canada and drew an attendance of 35,223 to Memorial Stadium.

In division finals, Baltimore surprised Winnipeg 14-12 in a game played in frigid temperatures made more so by a howling wind gusting up to 60 Kms. per hour. In the west, Calgary fell short for the second consecutive year. The Stampeders lost to the Lions 37-36. BC scored a touchdown on the last play of the game; the four yard line again providing the setting. Amid a swirling snowfall, Danny McManus threw a pass to Darren Flutie. It was the winning score and provided the match up the League wanted, a Canadian team playing an American. There was the added bonus that the Lions would be playing before their home fans.

In Baltimore, more than 500 fans showed up at the airport to welcome back their "Colts For Life". The game with Winnipeg had been well received: it had drawn a "34 per cent share. . . an NFL rating in America"[1073] during the final 15 minutes of the game which was picked up by the local NBC affiliate. The CFLers advancement to the Grey Cup was hailed by the Baltimore Sun as a "symbol of an era passed by."[1074]Some in the Maryland city were concerned, referring to the "fresh round of anti-American hysteria" surely to be whipped up, referring to banners in Winnipeg which read "no Grey Cup in USA" and the flying of the American flag upside down.[1075] Baltimore coach Don Mathews saw it all simply as "the home team trying to rattle his players".

The BC Lions were also basking in the adulation of their fans. They were favoured because of home field advantage. In successive weeks, they had come from behind to score dramatic victories. There was some concern whether the "cost" had been too high. Some perceived that they were at a distinct disadvantage, "Canadian riddled",[1076] as one reporter described them tongue in cheek. They did have injuries at the quarterback position. Both Kent Austin and Danny McManus were hurting, the former with a slight shoulder separation, and the latter with a bruised thigh. The Vancouver Canucks' hyperbaric chamber, credited with speeding up healing during the Stanley Cup finals, was enlisted.

If in Baltimore, the Grey Cup was "just another ball game". . . (it had) turned into a referendum on nationalism in Canada."[1077] There was some good natured bantering taking place. Vancouver Sun reporter Pete McMartin commented: "This is not the first time a Baltimore team has met a Canadian team in a championship. They met once before. It was for the championship of North America in a series known as the war of 1812. The best Baltimore managed even with the home field advantage was a draw. Baltimore played a defensive game. We were on offence." The Baltimore Sun's Ray Frager replied in kind: "a draw? Oh yeah Mr Big Shot historian Pete McMartin. You don't even know how to spell offense. And you had to steal from Baltimore to get a name for your newspaper."[1078] The Vancouver Sun continued to play up the Canadian angle. It published a photo of Ian Sinclair, Donovan Wright, Glen Scrivener and Sean Foudie over the caption: On Guard For Thee.[1079]

The debate continued: Baltimore's coach Don Mathews was described as being 'freed from the traditional roster restrictions. . . finally able to recruit exactly the right types of athletes to play defence in the pass happy Canadian game."[1080] In the midst of all the hoopla, the question of "Canadian" kept surfacing. American owners seemed to prefer either a new name for the League or at the very least, playing down the "Canadian" aspect in order to refer to it as the CFL. CBC play by play man Don Wittman and co-worker Scott Oake both noted that the Canadian players would be "playing to save their jobs".[1081] The Toronto Star printed a cartoon showing a football player under the stars and striped letters CFL. Hanging from the L was a sign: "No Canadians Need Apply".[1082] Earlier, it had published a group of football players in an Iwo Jima-like pose planting a flag on top of "Lord Grey's Cup".[1083] Even the Prime Minister was brought into the debate. Asked by Canadian Press who would win the game, Chretien said that "he would be cheering for BC but the endorsement came only after the PM needed to ask who exactly would be playing for the 1994 Grey Cup."[1084]

When Gerald Wilcox of the Winnipeg Blue Bombers won the Outstanding Canadian Award, he "took the opportunity of his acceptance speech to say to a national television audience: 'I hope this isn't the last time we see this award.'"[1085]The Toronto Star gave his comment a laurel in its darts and laurels feature while proclaiming: "Our feelings too as the League continues to Americanize itself."[1086] Wilcox had been selected over Edmonton's Larry Wruck. Other awards went to Doug Flutie, chosen over Baltimore's Mike Pringle as the Most Outstanding. It was Flutie's fourth consecutive selection, a first in the League. Another Baltimore player, Shar Pourdanesh, was chosen the Outstanding Offensive Lineman over Calgary's Rocco Romano. Still another CFLer, linebacker Matt Goodwin, took the outstanding Rookie award over the Las Vegas kicker Carlos Huerta. Edmonton's Willie Pless, a linebacker, was chosen as the Defensive Player over Hamilton's Tim Cofield. Each winner received an original trophy, a custom designed ring from Jostens Canada, an original portrait from artist Tony Harris and a set of travel luggage from Chrysler Canada. Runners-up received $1,000 in electronic equipment. Norm Fieldgate, former BC player and director was presented with the Commissioners Award. Baltimore's Mike Pringle won the first ever Terry Evanshen Award, newly instituted to replace the Jeff Russel Trophy which was retired during the year by its board.

Although BC was listed as 3 1/2 to 4 1/2 point favourites, there were those who saw Baltimore as next to a sure thing. CBC analyst James Curry suggested that "Baltimore doesn't have any weaknesses at all from their coaching staff on down. Even their special teams guys are better than average players in the Canadian Football League."[1087] Others spoke of "Baltimore's massive offensive line. . . the Lions' defensive line and linebacking corps are vulnerable to Baltimore's rushing attack."[1088] Curry's sentiments were echoed by Matt Dunigan who thought that it was "Baltimore's game to win or lose" because of their huge offensive line led by Shar Pourdanesh. It would allow Tracy ham to "run around and create time for his receivers to get open. it'll be tough to get to Tracy."[1089] The team speed of Baltimore's defence plus their running attack of Pringle and Drummond behind its "oversized offensive line"[1090] going against the all Canadian three man front of the BC team, was pointed out as "keys" by many "objective" pundits.

Baltimore was concerned with other matters, crowd noise specifically. Don Mathews, as a former coach of the Lions, was well aware of the deafening obstacle to teams' being able to hear signals. The CFLers took specific aim at the BC Place "fan o meter" which gave a reading on the level of crowd noise while encouraging fans to increase it. Baltimore's operations director E.J. Narcisse pointed out that the contest was a league one as opposed to a home game for either side and as such "emphatically oppose(d) anything that would artificially stimulate the crowd."[1091]

The BC Lions defeated the Baltimore CFLers 26-23 before 55,097 highly charged and entertained fans. The margin of victory was a last play field goal by venerable Lui Passaglia, the first time in his 19 year career he had ever kicked a game winning field goal in a playoff game. There were a number of turning points. In the third quarter, BC stalled at the Baltimore 27 yard line. Passaglia was called in for a field goal. The holder, Darren Flutie, ran to his right to gain a first down. Later, with BC on the Baltimore one, BC gambled on a third down keeper by sore legged quarterback Danny McManus. It was a big play by the quarterback who entered the game in relief of Kent Austin after Baltimore had jumped into a 14 - 3 lead.

The unsung heroes of the game were the BC Canadian contingent. Ian Sinclair, Denny Chronopoulos, Rob Smith, Jamie Taras and Vic Stevenson, the "all Canadian offensive line, was savage in its treatment of Baltimore's front seven".[1092] Sean Millington along with Cory Philpot's 109 yards, were beneficiaries. Meanwhile the three man Canadian defensive line of Dave Chaytors, Andrew Stewart and Doug Peterson, gave the Baltimore offense all it could handle allowing its linebackers Newby, Robertson, Chatman and Snipes to harass Ham throughout the game. Safety Tom Europe, a winner of the Harry Jerome award in 1993 , was another who excelled with his defensive coverage and sure handed tackling. Emotions among all but especially the Canadian players was high. After the game was over, lineman Denny Chronopoulos "was one of the first to grab a Canadian flag and start waving and dancing on the field after the victory."[1093] In the stands, hundreds of fans, red maple leafs painted on their cheeks, roared with approval. Police, fearful of a repeat of the violence which marked the Stanley Cup end in June, were in the streets. But it was a good natured crowd. Some marched in the middle of Robson Street chanting "No Grey in the USA"; others were draped in Canadian flags or waving BC Lions standards.

The field was overrun causing the presentation of the Grey Cup to be made under the stands rather than for all to see outdoors. It might have contributed to the confusion in the awards presentations. Passaglia was named by CBC as the game's Most Valuable Player; Millington was the top Canadian.

Each was presented with his prize. Passaglia's was the key to a Dodge Ram truck, Millington's was a travel voucher worth $5,000. When the votes by the Football Reporters of Canada were counted, however, the five ballots showed that Baltimore's defensive back Karl Anthony, was the winner of the Outstanding Player and Passaglia the top Canadian. Anthony was not impressed saying that the league could stick the award "where the sun doesn't shine".[1094] Passaglia's team mates made the most of it in later presenting the kicker with a toy model truck. A group of six businessmen, perhaps practicing "ambush marketing", collaborated to present Passaglia with a Chevy pick-up. The allowed him to trade it in on a Chevy Blazer which more adequately suited Lui and his family of a wife and four children.

Not all were happy with the game. Baltimore players were upset with the officiating. Referee in Chief Don Barker, while not admitting that it had been a poor game and season for the officiating crew, blamed the problem on expansion from 8 to 12 teams and the use of part time officials who were earning from $300 to $625 per game. He suggested that it would be more difficult if the league moved to 14 clubs.

Football seemed to be thriving, however. The CBC announced that its coverage of the Grey Cup game peaked at 5.2 million for the half hour between 9 and 9:30[1095] and "drew an audience of 3.9 million viewers", up from 2.6 million in '93, 3.2 million in '92, 3.5 million in'91, 2.3 million in '90 and 3 million in '89. In the United States, the live presentation drew 145,000 on ESPN2 while the taped version on ESPN was viewed in 377,000 homes.[1096] In spite of the impressive numbers and the best case scenario for the game in Vancouver, it was still 4,000 seats short of a sell-out. The ratings for the Vanier Cup had also been the highest in history. It had attracted the largest crowd for football in the east in '94, 28,652, and 750,000 viewers on TSN, up 33% from the previous year.

Three amigos, Bruce McNall, John Candy,
Wayne Gretzky, 1991.

Raghib (Rocket) Ismai, 1991.

Michael Pinball Clemons, 1994.

Epilogue

Despite the success of the Grey Cup, 1994 was not a stable year for the League. Changes during and after the year would mean that it was a different group of owners and teams who would prepare for the new year. In Ottawa, team image, colours, ownership and logo changed earlier. The R was removed from each side of the helmet. In the heady days of the sixties, some had referred to their standing for Russ(Jackson) and Ronnie (Stewart). Prices of seats had risen dramatically. Disenchantment was the mood throughout the season. Even Isobel Firestone, mother of owner Bruce Firestone, was suing him for the $100,000 she said that she loaned him and he hadn't paid back.[1097] Ottawa's Bruce Firestone had announced his intention to sell. Sold it was, but only after long negotiations in '95. Chicago businessman Horn Chen bought the club. Unsecured creditors from the earlier regime settled for 14 cents on the dollar while a reported $1.25 million made its way to secured creditors, the League gaining $350,000 of that amount.[1098]

In Hamilton, that city was given an ultimatum to sell a minimum of 12,500 season tickets and attract over a million dollars in corporate sponsorship by December 23 or lose its franchise. Similar notices were given to Ottawa and Calgary: support the teams or lose them. Targets for season ticket sales and corporate sponsorship were set and met: Hamilton, 12,500 tickets and $1 million; Ottawa, 15,000 and $1 million; Calgary, 16,000 tickets.

Regina was named to host the 1995 game. The club and the Province had never held the Grey Cup game. It was a sentimental choice and yet, the club offered the league a tempting financial deal. Based on a projection of "$5.5 million from game and event revenue" and expenses of $3.5 million, the remaining $2 million profit would be shared by the CFL and Saskatchewan. "Cost overruns cutting into the $2 million profit would be shared by the two sides."[1099] It was the province's 90th birthday and the theme of the game would be a call for previous Saskatchewan residents to "Come Back". As early as March, 1994, phones at the 'riders offices were being answered with "Home of the 1995 Grey Cup".[1100] Plans were for only 5,000 tickets to be available outside the Province.[1101] To help make it a Saskatchewan year, the League announced that its draft would take place in Saskatoon as part of the Grey Cup preparations, the first time it would be held in a non CFL city.

Arrangements were also made regarding the 96 and 97 games, Hamilton and Baltimore, respectively, being selected. Initially, it appeared as if Baltimore would host the 96 game but "tax questions and revenue sharing"[1102] details were unclear. With the league "unable to decide between Hamilton and Baltimore for 1996. . . it went ahead and awarded the '96 and '97 games."[1103] it was a major coup for both cities. Hamilton had been all but written off by many as a viable franchise; Baltimore, in its first year was impressive in leading the league in attendance and was generating much enthusiasm for the CFL throughout the United States. Regardless, there was still that nagging worry as to what would happen if the NFL ever decided to return. Nonetheless, the Baltimore Governor moved to assist the CFLers in their attempt to improve Memorial Stadium. One hundred thousand dollars in the form of a grant and a $400,000 loan was to be made available by Maryland's Department of Economic and Employment Development.[1104]

Hamilton also had ownership problems. John Michaluk had resigned effective September 15 as President and CEO of the Ti-Cats. He had been under fire from a variety of sources for his approach in guiding the club's off field operation. Hamilton was a mix of community ownership and private investors. As with Ottawa, there had been an accumulation of debt. Retiring it seemed to be the key to attracting new ownership. A deal with unsecured creditors owed $2.2 million was made there too. They were to get 20 Cents on the dollar, 10 cents immediately and 10 cents within six months. Secured creditors, the CFL was owed $1 million and the Hamilton Wentworth Regional Government $750,000, were to be paid in full.[1105] The Club was sold to a group of investors headed by David Macdonald, the deal finalized in April, 1995.[1106] At the same time, efforts were being made to relocate the Las Vegas and Sacramento teams. While the Gold Miners relocated in San Antonio to become the Texans, the Posse, after a frantic and protracted attempt to move them to Jackson, Mississippi, folded. Their players were redistributed throughout the League in a dispersal draft on April 18, 1995.

All the while two new American franchises were welcomed into the league. Memphis, Tenn., known as the Mad Dogs and the Barracudas of Birmingham, Alabama.

The radical changes that the League underwent since it decided to expand to the United States had returned it to the issues which disturbed it 20 years previous.

Commissioners of the CFL had always held a Grey Cup news conference. Perhaps because of the expansion into the U.S., reporters had recently taken to all it the State of the League address, a not too subtle reference to the American President's State of the Union Address. At his "state of the league" address at the '94 Grey Cup game, Smith brushed off rumours that he would be fired, forecasted greater US content, spoke of league plans for a shift from the east-west to a north-south rivalry in a Grey Cup which could be played permanently in December.[1107] That concept moved towards more of a reality when the CFL announced its 18 game schedule for 1995 and a new North-South divisional alignment.[1108] All eight Canadian teams were placed into the North Division; the five American clubs were in the South. Playoffs among Division teams guaranteed a Canadian versus American Grey Cup game.

The league's argument for moving to more American players was said to have revolved around the fact that if a starter for a US team were injured, he could be replaced by an available and superior American player - not the case if a Canadian were injured on a Canadian team. Opponents of the proposal argued that of the four American teams, three had not even made the playoffs. Only Baltimore had demonstrated some success but it was suggested that was more due to the approach taken by the club to seek out players with CFL experience. There were others who proposed that another method of ensuring equality was to place restrictions on the area from which Americans could draw their talent pool, something which could also make for more local identification and acceptance.

With the collective bargaining agreement due to expire in June of 1995, it was necessary to attempt to have a new one in place for the '95 season. The League had already addressed the issue publicly. Initially, it wanted to remove the quota altogether; now it was saying that twenty spots on Canadian teams' rosters for non imports were too many. The number 10 was floated but Smith would only say that "our objective is not to eliminate the quota." It is interesting to note that the CFLPA was formed over the issue of the import ratio; thirty years later, the question was still one which had to be resolved. The issue of the place for the Canadian player in the Canadian game had been highlighted from the days of the forward pass and later the Designated Import regulation. It was now a focus of the league and the Players' Association discussions. If the CFL did in fact move towards an eventual target of ten Canadians, it would mean that all starters would be Americans. Canadians would no longer be developed to take over first string positions. It would be unnecessary.

The increasing influence of the American clubs was being felt in some "cosmetic" areas. The name of the league was being questioned; American owners, specifically Jim Speros of Baltimore, wanted the "Canadian" removed to de-emphasize the non American aspect. The CFL was also contemplating a change in logo to incorporate the new reality. The move had already been announced away from the Spalding football to the American made Wilson, although as a concession, the stripes would remain on the CFL ball. They were originally deemed necessary because of poor lighting in some of the parks. The talk of moving the Grey Cup game to a later date in December was tied directly to the fact that the American Thanksgiving holiday was at the end of November, the traditional Grey Cup time. End zones were in danger of being shrunk. Many American parks could not accommodate 20 yard goal areas and 110 yard playing fields. Prospective applicants had already been told that a shortened end zone wouldn't present any problem.

There were influences on more substantial aspects of the game too. After years of stability in the rules, of recognition that the game was a good one as it was, American owners were continually suggesting moving to 4 downs rather than 3 as a means of appealing more to American fans. While the business aspect of expansion was recognized as desirable by most Canadians, there was concern that like the NHL, control of the game would shift to the United States: more American than Canadian teams, a decline in Canadian players, the head office and the commissioner located in the United States.

Expansion of the Canadian Football League, controversial when it was announced, will continue to be the critical issue around which the health of the League will revolve. There has been a change from the original thought of expanding only to those areas which would not be considered for an NFL franchise. Aside from whether the NFL will respond by expanding into Canadian markets, there are other concerns for the league. Its decision to move to a North-South divisional alignment, rather than the traditional East-West, is part of that issue. Clearly, the CFL has always perceived and defined itself in terms of regions. The Grey Cup game played on the natural differences between East and West. The season culminated with one side's representative team gaining the bragging rights for the nation. Everyone knew it was artificial; the American players had more of a contributing role than Canadians but the essential feature was that all the cities in the league were Canadian. Civic, Provincial and national pride were all at stake.

Yet, with all of this, it was obvious that changes had to be made. Government support was diminishing. Revenues from television contracts and attendance fell. There were a multitude of other competing entertainment possibilities available. Perception of it as a "Big League" or "Major League" sport declined. The League needed a boost. It saw an opportunity to move into the huge American market. The Americans were seen to be starving for more football; there were television networks looking to fill programming time.

Expansion to the United States might ultimately solve some of the League's problems; it might also create more. With the South (American) and the North (Canadian) divisions, somewhere down the road the League will have to establish a presence in the United States, an aide to the Commissioner, an office to expedite American matters. Eventually, as the United States division strengthens and gains more clout, the possibility is there for the head office and Commissioner to be American.

One has to look at the motives of Americans for wanting to join the Canadian Football League. It is a different style from the American; it is an established League; it has a salary cap; it is spectator driven in terms of revenue, thus having more opportunities for growth; it is relatively inexpensive in terms of the cost of professional franchises. In short, there is good opportunity for profit. But all of these seeming advantages can quickly turn into disadvantages. Because the Canadian game is different, some Americans perceive it as not being "real football". The name "Canadian" verifies it in a land where "American" is a synonym for the best. There will be a tendency on the part of U.S. teams to Americanize the game, to make it more like "real football". The demands of the larger Canadian field on American stadia will contribute to that movement. Pressures to change the name of the League will continue, the object being to make it more pertinent to the American marketplace.

The salary cap also has the possibility for disharmony. At $2.5 Canadian and with the weakness of the Canadian dollar in relative terms, the American equivalent is much lower. One would think that with the huge talent supply in the United States, the cap is in everyone's interest. The reality is that among the American owners there are a variety of reasons as to why they have franchises. Some are in locales where they have been rebuffed by the NFL; that feeling of abandonment is cultivated in order to sell tickets. A "we'll show them" attitude is promoted. There are others who want to get into the NFL via the back door, using the CFL, wanting it to grow to compete with the NFL and later merge with the premier "real football" league. There is a very real fear that clubs will ignore the salary cap in an effort to attract high profile collegians or established NFL players in order to secure credibility with the U.S. public. This being the case, the possibility is there that the South Division will simply become an entity in itself, break away from the CFL and form its own league.

Maintaining the salary cap is critical to the Canadian aspect of the League. The CFL has already served notice that it wishes to do away with what it calls the "quota system" of Canadian players (It's interesting that normally quota systems are imposed upon products coming into the market as opposed to those already there. It is somewhat akin to Canadian players being defined as non-imports.) It wants access to the huge and inexpensive supply of talent in the American market. The League's Players' Association has stood firm. It has been demonstrated on the field that Canadian talent can play competitively with the Americans in the CFL. All recognize that the Canadian needs two years or so gaining experience and benefiting from the intensive practices to bring himself up to the level of the American collegians. The "quota system" allows that to occur. Without the "quota system", Canadian content would be minimal, since coaches would never have any reason for playing Canadians in starting positions. As an aside, if the North South divisions are to work, there might be more interest all around if a "quota system" of sorts was implemented in the United States. The same principle would see

American teams restricted to a defined number of players from their cachement area, i.e. a State or a number of States.

The whole area of "free agency" is another one which will continue to be a problem area unless the salary cap is maintained. Ever since the "gentlemen's agreements" were eliminated, players have been free to move to another team after playing out their option. In some ways it has served to create interest as established players left or joined a club. If the salary cap is enforced, the net effect would not allow any one team to corner the best players available. Owners being who they are, however, could find a way to circumvent the cap. Others would be forced to do the same or an imbalance would be created. In so doing, however, some teams would be forced to drop out, unable to afford the new reality.

Television will also play a role in the future CFL. In Canada, it appears necessary to attract more networks, especially CTV, to the bidding process. In the United States, there are a few obstacles. It's more likely that the American teams will be the ones to attract a network simply on the basis of public identification. The shortness of the CFL season remains one impediment. The Grey Cup game is traditionally played in the last week in November. There is a conflict with the American Thanksgiving weekend. As well, the last week in November is the traditional end of the College season. There is a void until the bowl games begin. Networks are looking for programming to fill in that space. The CFL's Canadian teams, especially in the Prairies, are unable to play later than the present (that is why the Grey Cup Game of 1995 in Regina was scheduled for the third week in November). There will be pressure on the United States teams to break away once their South division is established; or for the CFL to form a Spring - Fall league in order to compensate; or forego the lure of the big television contract from the American networks.

Franchises in Canada will continue to be important if the League wants to maintain the North-South division approach. Until television revenue increases, finances will have to be brought under control; community support for clubs will have to be increased. The "Canadian" aspect of the clubs, particularly in the North-South alignment will play a large role; expansion to Montreal and the Maritimes will be targeted.

It's interesting to speculate as to what will happen if American clubs, for reasons stated above, were to break away and start their own league. It would leave the North Division where it was prior to expansion. Perhaps the pass would be completed after a deflection. It would be interesting to note how many of the present owners would still have their clubs. Would it be an indication of future trends if some of the higher profile owners were to move out of the CFL? Are some owners tempted to sell their high profile American players to United States teams who have the cash available? Would bridges have been burned beyond repair? Would the Canadian Football League set itself on the road, once again, and if so, within or outside Canada?

The story continues in Canadian Football 1995-2014; Home Again

Endnotes

1   B.C. Lions 1984 Fact Book, p. 59.
2   Ibid.
3   Ibid. p. 60.
4   B.C. Lions 1984 Fact Book, p. 16.
5   CFL Minutes, May 3, 1983.
6   CFL Minutes, January 19, 1983.
7   Ibid. May 3, 1983.
8   Ibid.
9   Ibid. February 15, 1983.
10   Ibid. May 3, 1983.
11   Toronto Sun, February 16, 1983.
12   Ibid. February 15, 1983.
13   Ibid.
14   Ibid.
15   Ibid. February 15, 1983.
16   Ibid.
17   Vancouver Sun, May 6, 1983.
18   Ibid.
19   Ibid.
20   Ibid.
21   CFL Memo, February 28, 1983.
22   Ibid. January 25, 1983.
23   CFL Minutes, February, 1983.
24   Ibid.
25   Ibid.
26   Ibid.
27   Ibid.
28   Ibid.
29   Ibid.
30   Ibid. January 20, 1983.
31   B.C. Lions 1984 Fact Book, p. 60.
32   Toronto Sun, May 24, 1983.
33   Vancouver Sun, November 21, 1983.
34   Ibid. November 22, 1983.
35   Ibid.
36   Toronto Globe and Mail, November 24, 1993
37   Ibid.
38   Vancouver Sun, November 22, 1983.
39   Ibid.
40   Ibid.
41   Ibid. November 28, 1983.
42   Vancouver Sun, November 30, 1983.
43   Ibid. December 5, 1983.
44   Ibid.
45   Ibid. December 5, 1983.
46   Toronto Sun, February 18, 1983.
47   Toronto Star, February 16, 1984.
48   Ibid. March 8, 1984.
49   CFL Minutes, March 6, 1984.
50   Ibid.
51   Ibid.
52   Ibid. May 2, 1984.
53   Ibid. May 4, 1984.
54   CFL Minutes, November 7, 1984.
55   Ibid. November 7, 1984.
56   CFL Minutes, January 18, 1984.
57   Ibid.
58   Ibid. February 13, 1984.
59   Ibid. February 15, 1984.
60   Ibid.
61   Ibid.
62   Ibid.
63   Calgary Herald, May 4, 1984.
64   Toronto Star, February 14, 1984.
65   Ibid.
66   Calgary Herald, January 19, 1984.
67   Ibid.
68   Toronto Star, March 1, 1984.
69   Ibid. March 7, 1984.
70   Ibid. November 29, 1983.
71   Ibid.
72   Ibid.
73   Ibid. November 15, 1984.
74   Calgary Herald, May 6, 1984.
75   CFL Minutes, November 25, 1983.
76   Ibid.
77   Calgary Herald, May 6, 1984.
78   CFL Minutes, May 2, 1984.
79   Ibid. November 16, 1984.
80   Toronto Star, November 4, 1984.
81   Ibid. November 4, 1984.
82   Ibid. November 5, 1984.
83   Ibid.
84   Ibid. November 7, 1984.
85   CFL Facts and Figures, 1985, p. 9.
86   Toronto Star, November 7, 1984.
87   Ibid. November 8, 1984.
88   Ibid. November 18, 1984.
89   Ibid.
90   Ibid.
91   Ibid.
92   Ibid. November 12, 1984.
93   Ibid. November 19, 1984.
94   Ibid.
95   CFL Minutes, November 16, 1984.
96   CFL Minutes, January 16, 1985.
97   Ibid.
98   Ibid.
99   Ibid.

100 Ibid.
101 Ibid.
102 Ibid.
103 Ibid.
104 Ibid. September 24, 1985.
105 Ibid.
106 Ibid.
107 Ibid.
108 Ibid. October 7, 1985.
109 Ibid.
110 Ibid.
111 Ibid.
112 Ibid.
113 Ibid.
114 Ibid.
115 Winnipeg Free Press, July 28, 1985.
116 Ibid.
117 Ibid. July 29, 1985.
118 Toronto Star, November 5, 1985.
119 Ibid.
120 Ibid.
121 Ibid.
122 CFL Minutes, July 23, 1985.
123 Ibid.
124 Ibid.
125 Ibid.
126 Ibid.
127 Ibid.
128 Ibid.
129 Ibid.
130 Ibid.
131 Ibid.
132 Ibid.
133 Ibid.
134 Ibid.
135 Ibid.
136 Ibid. October 7, 1985.
137 Ibid.
138 Ibid.
139 Ibid.
140 Ibid.
141 Ibid.
142 Ibid.
143 Ibid.
144 Ibid.
145 Ibid.
146 Ibid.
147 Ibid.
148 Ibid.
149 Ibid. May 7, 1985.
150 Ibid.
151 Ibid.
152 Ibid.
153 Ibid. February 19, 1985.
154 Ibid.
155 Ibid.
156 Ibid.
157 Ibid. April 18, 1985.
158 Ibid.
159 Montreal Gazette, May 9, 1985.
160 Ibid.
161 Ibid. May 9, 1985.
162 Ibid. September 24, 1985.
163 Toronto Star, November 17, 1985.
164 Ibid. February 19, 1985.
165 Ibid.
166 Winnipeg Free Press, August 25, 1985.
167 CFLPA, NEWS, pg. 3, September 1985.
168 CFL Minutes, October 7, 1985
169 Ibid. October 7, 1985.
170 Ibid., May 9, 1985
171 Ibid.
172 Ibid.
173 Ibid.
174 Ibid. November 22, 1985.
175 Ibid.
176 Ibid.
177 Toronto Star, November 23, 1985.
178 CFL Minutes, November 22, 1985.
179 Ibid.
180 Ibid.
181 Ibid.
182 Ibid.
183 Ibid.
184 CFLPA News, June, 1985, p. 4.
185 Toronto Star, November 11, 1985.
186 Ibid.
187 Ibid. November 21, 1985.
188 Ibid.
189 Ibid.
190 Ibid. November 24, 1985.
191 CFL Minutes, February 11, 1986.
192 Ibid.
193 CFL Letter to GMs, March 13, 1986.
194 CFL Meeting, May 8, 1986.
195 Ibid. January 22, 1986.
196 Ibid.
197 CFL Minutes, February 19, 1985.
198 Ibid.
199 Ibid.
200 Winnipeg Free Press, April 29, 1986.
201 Ibid.
202 Ibid.
203 CFL Minutes, May 8, 1986.
204 Winnipeg Free Press, January 21, 1986.
205 Ibid.
206 Ibid.
207 Ibid.

208 Ibid.
209 Toronto Star, February 13, 1986.
210 Ibid.
211 Ibid. January 22, 1986.
212 Ibid.
213 Ibid.
214 Ibid. January 24, 1986.
215 Ibid. February 17, 1986.
216 Ibid. February 17, 1986.
217 CFL Minutes, May 27, 1986.
218 Toronto Star, February 17, 1986.
219 CFL Minutes, January 22, 1986.
220 Ibid.
221 Ibid.
222 Ibid.
223 Ibid.
224 Ibid.
225 Ibid.
226 Toronto Star, February 21, 1986.
227 CFL Meeting, April 29, 1986.
228 Ibid.
229 CFL Minutes, November 28, 1986.
230 Ibid.
231 Ibid.
232 CFL Minutes, April 29, 1986.
233 Ibid.
234 Ibid. May 8, 1986.
235 Ibid. June 11, 1986.
236 Ibid. May 8, 1986.
237 Ibid.
238 Ibid.
239 Winnipeg Free Press, January 24, 1986.
240 Ibid. April 26, 1986.
241 Winnipeg Free Press, January 18, 1985.
242 Montreal Gazette, May 10, 1985.
243 Toronto Star, December 1, 1986.
244 Ibid.
245 Ibid.
246 Ibid. November 26, 1986.
247 Ibid.
248 Ibid.
249 Ibid.
250 Ibid.
251 Vancouver Sun, November 22, 1986.
252 Ibid.
253 Ibid.
254 Ibid.
255 CFL minutes, February 20, 1987
256 ibid.
257 ibid.
258 ibid.
259 ibid.
260 ibid.
261 ibid.
262 CFL Minutes, January 5, 1988
263 ibid.
264 ibid.
265 ibid.
266 ibid.
267 ibid.
268 ibid.
269 ibid.
270 ibid.
271 ibid.
272 ibid.
273 ibid.
274 CFL Minutes, June 11, 1986.
275 ibid.
276 ibid.
277 ibid.
278 ibid.
279 Report on Roster Considerations for 1987, p. 1
280 ibid.
281 ibid
282 ibid.
283 ibid.
284 ibid.
285 CFL Minutes, November 28, 1986
286 ibid.
287 ibid.
288 ibid.
289 Winnipeg Free Press, January 10, 1987
290 CFL Minutes, January 7, 1987
291 CFL Minutes, February 17, 1987
292 ibid.
293 CFL Minutes, October 30, 1987
294 CFL Minutes, January 23, 1987
295 CFL Minutes, January 21, 1987
296 ibid.
297 ibid.
298 Winnipeg Free Press, January 28, 1987
299 CFL Minutes, January 23, 1987
300 Toronto Star, February 18, 1987
301 ibid.
302 Toronto Star, February 19, 1987
303 Winnipeg Free Press, May 13, 1987
304 ibid.
305 ibid.
306 ibid.
307 ibid.
308 Winnipeg Free Press, May 20, 1987
309 ibid.
310 CFL Minutes, February 20, 1987
311 ibid.
312 ibid.
313 ibid.

314   ibid.
315   ibid.
316   CFL Minutes, April 12, 1987
317   CFL Minutes, June 23, 1987
318   ibid.
319   ibid.
320   ibid.
321   CFL Minutes, September 17, 1987
322   ibid.
323   CFL Minutes, July 28, 1987
324   ibid.
325   ibid.
326   ibid.
327   ibid.
328   ibid.
329   ibid.
330   ibid.
331   ibid.
332   Toronto Star, February 21, 1987
333   ibid.
334   ibid.
335   Winnipeg Free Press, July 29, 1987
336   Toronto Star, November 24, 1987
337   CFL Minutes, September 17, 1987
338   Toronto Star. September 18, 1987
339   ibid.
340   Toronto Star, January 9, 1987
341   Winnipeg Free Press, July 28, 1987
342   CFL Minutes, January 23, 1987
343   CFL Minutes, October 30, 1987
344   ibid.
345   ibid.
346   Toronto Star, November 25, 1987
347   Toronto Star, November 25, 1987
348   Toronto Star, November 30, 1987
349   ibid.
350   ibid.
351   Calgary Herald, January 29, 1988
352   Toronto Star, January 8, 1988.
353   ibid.
354   Calgary Herald, January 29, 1988
355   ibid.
356   ibid.
357   CFL Minutes, March 2, 1988
358   CFL Minutes, January 29, 1988
359   CFL Minutes, March 2, 1988
360   CFL Minutes, June 9, 1988
361   CFL Minutes, January 8, 1988
362   CFL Minutes, January 5, 1988
363   CFL Minutes, January 26, 1988
364   ibid.
365   ibid.
366   ibid.
367   CFL Minutes, January 26, 1988

368   ibid.
369   CFL Minutes, January 5, 1988
370   CFL Minutes, January 8, 1988
371   ibid.
372   ibid.
373   ibid.
374   CFL Minutes, March 2, 1988
375   CFL Minutes, May 18, 1988
376   ibid.
377   ibid.
378   CFL Minutes, September 16, 1988
379   ibid.
380   Calgary Herald, November 25, 1988
381   ibid
382   ibid.
383   ibid, November 25, 1988
384   ibid.
385   interview with Matt Dunigan, May 1992
386   Calgary Herald, November 26, 1988
387   CFL Minutes, January 8, 1988.
388   Ibid. December 12, 1988.
389   Ibid.
390   Ibid.
391   Ibid.
392   Ibid.
393   Calgary Herald, December 13, 1988.
394   CFL Minutes, December 12, 1988.
395   Calgary Herald, December 13, 1988.
396   Calgary Herald, January 26, 1989.
397   Toronto Star, January 24, 1989.
398   Ibid. February 25, 1989.
399   CFL Minutes, February 23, 1989.
400   Ibid.
401   Ibid.
402   Calgary Herald, May 11, 1989.
403   CFL Minutes, December 12, 1988.
404   Toronto Star, May 23, 1989.
405   Ibid.
406   Ibid.
407   Ibid. October 14, 1989.
408   Ibid.
409   Ibid.
410   CFL Minutes, December 12, 1988.
411   Ibid.
412   Ibid.
413   Calgary Herald, December 13, 1988.
414   Ibid.
415   Ibid.
416   Ibid. January 10, 1989.
417   Ibid. June 8, 1989.
418   Ibid.
419   Ibid.
420   CFL Minutes, September 10, 1990.

421   Ibid.
422   Ibid.
423   Ibid.
424   CFL Minutes, January 25, 1989.
425   Ibid.
426   Calgary Herald, January 26, 1989.
427   Ibid.
428   CFL Minutes, February 24, 1989.
429   Ibid.
430   Ibid.
431   Toronto Star, February 25, 1989.
432   Hamilton Spectator, May 13, 1989.
433   Ibid. May 13, 1989.
434   CFL Minutes, February 24, 1989.
435   Ibid. July 16, 1989.
436   Toronto Star, July 17, 1989.
437   CFL Minutes, July 16, 1989.
438   Ottawa Citizen, July 27, 1989.
439   Ibid.
440   Ibid. July 27, 1989.
441   Ibid.
442   Ibid.
443   Ibid.
444   CFL Minutes, July 16, 1989.
445   Ibid.
446   Ibid.
447   Ibid. May 10, 1989.
448   Ibid.
449   Ibid.
450   Toronto Globe and Mail, November 25, 1989.
451   Ibid.
452   CFL Minutes, November 23, 1989.
453   CFLPA Newsletter, March 1990, p. 1.
454   Ibid. No names were given in the Players' Association reports which documented these cases.
455   Ibid.
456   Ibid. March, 1989, p. 3.
457   Ibid. March, 1990, p. 5.
458   Ibid.
459   Ibid. September 21, 1990.
460   CFL Minutes, January 25, 1989.
461   Ibid. February 24, 1989.
462   Ibid. January 25, 1989.
463   Toronto Globe and Mail, January 25, 1989.
464   Ibid. February 23, 1990.
465   Toronto Globe and Mail, November 24, 1989.
466   Ibid.
467   CFL Minutes, August 15, 1989.
468   Ibid. June 8, 1989.
469   Ibid.

470   Ibid. October 14, 1989.
471   Ibid.
472   Star Week, December 9, 1989.
473   Toronto Globe and Mail, November 24, 1989.
474   Ibid.
475   Ibid. November 27, 1989.
476   Ibid. November 27, 1989.
477   Ibid.
478   Ibid.
479   Ibid.
480   Toronto Star, November 28, 1989.
481   Toronto Globe and Mail, December 13, 1989.
482   Ibid.
483   Ibid.
484   Canadian Football League Financial Statements for the year ended December 31, 1989
485   Toronto Star, November 29, 1989.
486   Ibid.
487   Toronto Star, October 14, 1989.
488   Ibid., August 4, 1989.
489   Ibid.
490   Ibid., October 15, 1989.
491   CFL Minutes, November 24, 1989.
492   Vancouver Sun, January 6, 1990.
493   Ibid.
494   Ibid.
495   Ibid.
496   Ibid., January 23, 1990.
497   Vancouver Sun, January 23, 1990.
498   Ibid.
499   Ibid.
500   Ibid.
501   CFL Minutes, February 23, 1989.
502   Toronto Star, February 23, 1989.
503   Toronto Star, February 24, 1989.
504   Calgary Herald, January 25, 1989.
505   Ibid.
506   Ibid.
507   Ibid.
508   Ibid., January 24, 1990.
509   Toronto Star, March 30, 1990.
510   Ibid.
511   Ibid.
512   Ibid.
513   Ibid.
514   Ibid.
515   Ibid.
516   Ibid., March 29, 1990.
517   Ibid., March 30, 1990.
518
Toronto Globe and Mail, March 30, 1990

519   Ibid., February 21, 1990.
520   Toronto Star, May 25, 1990.
521   Vancouver Sun, February 24, 1990.
522   Ibid.
523   Vancouver Sun, May 19, 1990.
524   Ibid.
525   Ibid.
526   Winnipeg Free Press, May 10, 1990.
527   Ibid., May 19, 1990.
528   Toronto Globe and Mail, January 24, 1990.
529   Ibid.
530   Vancouver Sun, January 26, 1990.
531   Ibid., January 25, 1990.
532   Ibid.
533   Ibid., January 25, 1989.
534   Vancouver Sun, May 17, 1990.
535   Winnipeg Free Press, May 18, 1990.
536   Ibid., May 17, 1990.
537   Ibid.
538   Ibid.
539   Vancouver Sun, January 25, 1990.
540   Ibid.
541   Ibid.
542   Toronto Star, January 25, 1990.
543   Vancouver Sun, January 25, 1990.
544   Ottawa Citizen, September 25, 1990.
545   Ibid.
546   Ibid.
547   Toronto Globe and Mail, November 25, 1989.
548   Winnipeg Free Press, May 19, 1990.
549   Ibid.
550   Vancouver Sun, May 2, 1990.
551   Ibid.
552   Ibid.
553   Ibid., May 11, 1990.
554   Toronto Globe and Mail, September 13, 1990.
555   Ibid.
556   Ibid.
557   Ibid.
558   Ibid.
559   Ibid.
560   Ibid.
561   Ibid.
562   Ibid.
563   CFL Minutes, September 12, 1990.
564   Toronto Globe and Mail, September 22, 1990.
565   Ibid.
566   Ibid.
567   Ibid.
568   Ibid., September 20, 1990.
569   Ibid., September 12, 1989.
570   Toronto Globe and Mail, October 6, 1990.
571   Ibid., September 14, 1990.
572   Ibid.
573   Vancouver Sun, October 12, 1990.
574   Ibid., January 1, 1991.
575   Ibid., September 12, 1990.
576   Ibid., January 25, 1990.
577   Ibid.
578   Toronto Star, TV Guide, October 20, 1990.
579   Toronto Star, November 21, 1990.
580   Ibid., November 6, 1990.
581   Ibid.
582   Ibid., November 26, 1990.
583   Ibid.
584   Vancouver Sun, November 21, 1990.
585   Toronto Star, November 21, 1990.
586   CFL Financial Report, February 14, 1991.
587   Ibid., February 26, 1991.
588   Ibid.
589   Ibid.
590   Ibid., October 2, 1991.
591   Ibid.
592   Ibid.
593   Ibid.
594   Ibid., April 21, 1991.
595   Ibid., April 23, 1991.
596   Ibid., June 5, 1991.
597   Ibid.
598   Ibid.
599   Ibid.
600   Ibid., September 23, 1991.
601   Ibid., October 2, 1991.
602   Ibid.
603   Ibid., October 30, 1991.
604   Ibid.
605   Ibid.
606   Ibid.
607   Ottawa Citizen, July 27, 1991.
608   Ibid.
609   CFL Stabilization Fund, December 31, 1990.
610   CFL Financial Report, February 14, 1991.
611   CFL Minutes, July 26, 1991.
612   Ibid.
613   Ibid.
614   Ottawa Citizen, July 27, 1991.
615   Ibid.
616   Ibid.

617 CFL Minutes, September 23, 1991.
618 Ibid.
619 Ibid.
620 Toronto Sun, October 15, 1991.
621 Ibid.
622 CFL Minutes, October 18, 1991.
623 Ibid.
624 Ibid.
625 Ibid.
626 Toronto Globe and Mail, November 28, 1991.
627 Ibid.
628 CFL Minutes, July 26, 1991.
629 Ottawa Citizen, July 27, 1991.
630 CFL Minutes, September 23, 1991.
631 Ibid.
632 Ibid.
633 Ibid.
634 Ibid.
635 Ibid., May 15, 1991.
636 CFL Minutes, January 3, 1992.
637 Ibid.
638 CFL Minutes, January 29, 1992.
639 Ibid.
640 Ibid., July 26, 1991.
641 Ibid.
642 Ibid.
643 Ibid.
644 Ibid.
645 Ibid., September 23, 1991.
646 Ibid.
647 Ibid.
648 Ibid.
649 Ibid.
650 Ibid.
651 Ibid.
652 Toronto Globe and Mail, October 17, 1991.
653 Ibid.
654 Toronto Star, October 31, 1991.
655 CFL Minutes, November 22, 1991.
656 Ibid.
657 Toronto Star, January 11, 1991.
658 Ibid., January 24, 1991.
659 Ibid.
660 Toronto Star, February 1, 1991.
661 CFL Financial Report, 1990, February 14, 1991.
662 Toronto Globe and Mail, November 21, 1991.
663 Ibid.
664 ibid.
665
666 Ibid.

667 Ibid.
668 Ibid. November 20, 1991.
669 Ibid.
670 Ibid.
671 Ibid. November 21, 1991.
672 Ibid.
673 Ibid. November 2, 1991.
674 Ibid.
675 Ibid. November 23, 1991.
676 Ibid. November 21, 1991.
677 Ibid.
678 Ibid. November 22, 1991.
679 Toronto Star, November 23, 1991.
680 Ibid.
681 Ibid.
682 Toronto Globe and Mail, December 18, 1991
683 Ibid. Nov. 22, 1992.
684 Ibid. Nov. 27, 1991.
685 Ibid.
686 CFL Minutes, January 7, 1991.
687 Ibid.
688 Toronto Star, November 23, 1991
689 Toronto Globe and Mail, November 22, 1991
690 Toronto Star, November 23, 1991
691 Toronto globe and Mail, November 21, 1991
692 Ibid.
693 Toronto Globe and Mail, November 21, 1991
694 Ibid.
695 Ibid. Dec. 12, 1991.
696 CFL Minutes, April 29, 1992.
697 Toronto Star, January 7, 1992.
698 Ibid.
699 Ibid.
700 Toronto Globe and Mail, December 12, 1991.
701 Toronto Star, January 7, 1992.
702 Ibid.
703 Ibid.
704 Ibid.
705 CFL Minutes, January 3, 1992.
706 Ibid.
707 Ibid.
708 Ibid.
709 CFL Minutes, January 29, 1992.
710 Toronto Sun, February 28, 1992.
711 Ibid.
712 Toronto Globe and Mail, February 28, 1992.
713 Toronto Sun, February 28, 1992.
714 Ibid.

715 Ibid.
716 Ibid.
717 Ibid.
718 CFL Minutes, January 29, 1992.
719 Ibid.
720 CFL Minutes, February 27, 1992.
721 Ibid.
722 Ibid.
723 Ibid.
724 CFL Minutes, April 29, 1992.
725 Ibid.
726 Ibid.
727 Ibid.
728 Ibid.
729 Ibid.
730 ibid.
731 Toronto Globe and Mail, February 28, 1992.
732 Ibid.
733 CFL Minutes, January 29, 1992.
734 Ibid.
735 Ibid.
736 Ibid.
737 CFL Minutes, January 29, 1992.
738 CFL Minutes, January 29, 1992.
739 CFL Minutes, February 27, 1992.
740 CFL Minutes, February 27, 1992.
741 CFL Minutes, February 27, 1992.
742 Ibid.
743 Toronto Star, June 4, 1992.
744 Ibid.
745 Ibid.
746 Ibid.
747 Ibid.
748 Ibid.
749 Ibid.
750 CFL Minutes, June 29, 1992.
751 Ibid.
752 Ibid.
753 Ibid.
754 Ibid.
755 CFL Minutes, June 2, 1992.
756 Ottawa Citizen, June 13, 1992.
757 Ibid. July 4, 1992.
758 Ibid.
759 Ibid.
760 Hamilton Spectator, July 7, 1992.
761 Toronto Sun, January 7, 1992.
762 Toronto Star, February, 1992.
763 Ibid.
764 Toronto Sun, March 24, 1992.
765 Ibid.
766 Ibid.
767 Ibid.

768 Toronto Globe and Mail, March 25, 1992.
769 Toronto Star, July 22, 1992.
770 Toronto Star, July 22, 1992.
771 Ibid.
772 Ibid.
773 Toronto Star, August 27, 1992.
774 CFL Minutes, August 26, 1992.
775 Ibid.
776 Ibid.
777 Ibid.
778 Ibid.
779 CFL Minutes, September 4, 1992.
780 Ibid.
781 CFL Minutes, September 16, 1992.
782 Ibid.
783 Ibid.
784 Ibid.
785 Ibid.
786 Toronto Sun, September 24, 1992.
787 Toronto Globe and Mail, September 24, 1992,
788 Toronto Star, April 16, 1992.
789 Toronto Globe and Mail, May 8, 1992.
790 Ibid.
791 Ibid.
792 Ibid.
793 CFL Minutes, February 27, 1992.
794 Toronto Globe and Mail, January 25, 1992.
795 Ottawa Citizen, June 25, 1992.
796 Ibid.
797 Ibid.
798 Ibid.
799 Ibid.
800 CFL Minutes, January 29, 1992.
801 CFL Minutes, February 27, 1992.
802 Ibid.
803 CFL Minutes, June 2, 1992.
804 Ibid.
805 Ibid.
806 Ibid.
807 Ibid.
808 CFL Minutes, June 29, 1992.
809 Toronto Globe and Mail, November 27, 1992.
810 Ibid.
811 CFL Minutes, February 27, 1992.
812 CFL Minutes, April 29, 1992.
813 CFL Minutes, April 29, 1992.
814 Toronto Star, May 12, 1992.
815 Ibid.
816 Toronto Globe and Mail, October 30, 1992.

817   CFL Minutes, November 26, 1992.
818   Ibid.
819   CFL Minutes, December 3, 1992.
820   Ibid.
821   Ibid.
822   CFL Minutes, December 3, 1992.
823   CFL Minutes, June 2, 1992.
824   Ibid.
825   Ibid.
826   CFL Minutes, June 29, 1992.
827   Ibid.
828   Ibid.
829   Ibid.
830   Ibid.
831   CFL Minutes, October 19, 1992.
832   Ibid.
833   Ibid.
834   Ibid.
835   Ibid.
836   Ibid.
837   Ibid.
838   Ibid.
839   Ibid.
840   Ibid.
841   Ibid.
842   Ibid.
843   Toronto Globe and Mail, November 11, 1992.
844   CFL Press Conference, November 12, 1992.
845   Toronto Globe and Mail, November 14, 1992.
846   Toronto Globe and Mail, November 10, 1992.
847   Toronto Globe and Mail, November 11, 1992.
848   Ibid.
849   Toronto Star, November 29, 1992.
850   Ibid.
851   Ibid.
852   Toronto Star week, November 28, 1992.
853   Ibid.
854   Ottawa Citizen, November 28, 1992.
855   Ibid.
856   Ibid.
857   Toronto Globe and Mail, November 24, 30, December 7, 1992.
858   Toronto Globe and Mail, November 20, 1992.
859   Ibid.
860   Ibid.
861   Toronto Star, November 26, 1992.
862   Ibid.
863   Ibid.
864   Ibid.
865   Ibid.
866   Toronto Globe and Mail, November 19, 1992.
867   Toronto Globe and Mail, November 12, 1992.
868   Toronto Globe and Mail, November 26, 1992.
869   Toronto Globe and Mail, November 30, 1992.
870   Toronto Star, November 29, 1992.
871   Toronto Globe and Mail, November 14, 1992.
872   Toronto Star, February 25, 1993
873   ibid.
874   ibid.
875   Toronto Star, November 27, 1994
876   Ibid.
877   Toronto Globe and Mail, November 30, 1992.
878   Toronto Globe and Mail, November 27, 1992.
879   Ibid.
880   Toronto Globe and Mail, November 27, 1992.
881   Toronto Globe and Mail, October 5, 1992.
882   Ibid.
883   Ibid.
884   Ibid.
885   Ibid.
886   Ibid.
887   Ibid.
888   Ibid.
889   Toronto Globe and Mail, January 13, 1993.
890   Ibid.
891   Toronto Star, January 11, 1993.
892   Toronto Sun, January 13, 1993.
893   Ibid.
894   Ibid.
895   Toronto Star, January 13, 1993.
896   Toronto Globe and Mail, January 15, 1993.
897   Ibid.
898   Ibid.
899   Ibid.
900   Toronto Globe and Mail, January 28, 1993.
901   Ibid.
902   Toronto Globe and Mail, January 30, 1993.

903   Toronto Globe and Mail, February 2, 1993.
904   Toronto Star, February 6, 1993.
905   Toronto Globe and Mail, February 3, 1993.
906   Toronto Globe and Mail, March 4, 1993.
907   Toronto Globe and Mail, February 9, 1993.
908   CFL Minutes, November 26, 1992.
909   Ibid.
910   Ibid.
911   Ibid.
912   Toronto Sun, December 30, 1992.
913   Ibid.
914   Toronto Sun, December 30, 1992.
915   CFL Minutes, October 19, 1992.
916   Ibid.
917   Toronto Star, January 21, 1993.
918   Ibid.
919   Ibid.
920   Toronto Star, January 8, 1993.
921   Toronto Star, January 13, 1993.
922   Toronto Star, January 30, 1993.
923   Winnipeg Free Press, February 12, 1993.
924   Ibid.
925   Ibid.
926   Ibid. February 13, 1993.
927   Ibid.
928   Winnipeg Free Press, February 15, 1993.
929   Ibid.
930   Ibid.
931   Ibid.
932   Toronto Star, February 27, 1993.
933   Ibid.
934   Winnipeg Free Press, June 18, 1993.
935   Ibid.
936   Ibid.
937   Ibid.
938   Ottawa Citizen, July 7, 1993.
939   Ibid.
940   Winnipeg Free Press, July 19, 1993.
941   Ibid.
942   Ibid.
943   Ibid.
944   Toronto Globe and Mail, September 29, 1993.
945   Ibid.
946   Ibid. September 29, 1993.
947   Ibid.
948   Toronto Star, August 28, 1993.
949   Toronto Globe and Mail, September 9, 1993.
950   Ibid.
951   Ibid.
952   Ibid.
953   Toronto Globe and Mail, January 6, 1993.
954   Toronto Star, August 15, 1993.
955   Toronto Globe and Mail, July 6, 1993.
956   Toronto Star, March 6, 1993.
957   CFRB Interview, September 19, 1993.
958   Toronto Star, November 9, 1993.
959   Toronto Sun, November 2, 1993.
960   Toronto Star, November 9, 1993.
961   Toronto Star, November 19, 1993.
962   Toronto Star, November 23, 1993.
963   Ottawa Citizen, June 3, 1993.
964   Ibid.
965   Ottawa Citizen, July 12, 1993.
966   Ottawa Citizen, August 17, 1993.
967   Ibid.
968   Ibid.
969   Ibid.
970   Ibid.
971   Winnipeg Free Press, October 31, 1993.
972   Ibid.
973   Ibid.
974   Toronto Globe and Mail, October 30, 1993.
975   Ibid. November 10, 1993.
976   Ibid.
977   Ibid.
978   Toronto Globe and Mail, November 15, 1993.
979   Toronto Star, November 23, 1993.
980   Toronto Globe and Mail, September 30, 1993.
981   Toronto Globe and Mail, August 11, 1993.
982   Toronto Star, November 24, 1993.
983   Calgary Herald, November 12, 1993.
984   Calgary Herald, November 20, 1993
985   ibid
986   Toronto Globe and Mail, November 27, 1993
987   ibid., November 27, 1993
988   Calgary Herald, November 22, 1993
989   ibid. November 20, 1993
990   Toronto Globe and Mail, November 24, 1993
991   ibid.
992   Edmonton Journal, November 24, 1993

993 Toronto Globe and Mail, November 24, 1993
994 Toronto Sun, November 29, 1993
995 ibid.
996 Toronto Globe and Mail, November 27, 1993
997 ibid.
998 Canadian Press, cited in Calgary Herald, November 26, 1993
999 Toronto Globe and Mail, November 25, 1993
1000 Winnipeg Free Press, July 27, 1993.
1001 Toronto Globe and Mail, March 17, 1993.
1002 Winnipeg Free Press, July 27, 1993.
1003 Toronto Star, July 30, 1993.
1004 Toronto Star, August 7, 1993.
1005 Toronto Star, December 9, 1993
1006 CFL Minutes, Calgary, October 2, 1991.
1007 Toronto Globe and Mail, January 14, 1994
1008 Toronto Sun, January 24, 1994
1009 Ottawa Citizen, January 27, 1994
1010 ibid.
1011 ibid.
1012 Edmonton Journal, January 27, 94
1013 Ottawa Citizen, February 1, 1994
1014 ibid.
1015 Toronto Globe and Mail, February 17, 1994
1016 ibid.
1017 CFL Facts and Figures and Records 1994, p.26
1018 Toronto Globe and Mail. June 17, 1994
1019 ibid.
1020 Toronto Globe and Mail, September 20, 1994
1021 Baltimore Sun, January 23, 1994
1022 Winnipeg Free Press, April 8, 1994.
1023 Toronto Globe and Mail, April 28, 1994
1024 Toronto Globe and Mail, June 1, 1994
1025 Ottawa Citizen, August 23, 1994
1026 Ottawa Citizen, August 27, 1994.
1027 Toronto Sun, September 1, 1994.
1028 The Fan Radio, Toronto September 22, 1994
1029 Ottawa Citizen, July 20, 1994
1030 ibid.
1031 Winnipeg Free Press, October 22, 1994.
1032 Toronto Globe and Mail, January 11, 1994
1033 Toronto Globe and Mail, February 4, 1994
1034 ibid
1035 Toronto Globe and Mail, March 5, 1994
1036 Winnipeg Free Press, April 26, 1994
1037 Winnipeg Free Press, May 6, 1994.
1038 Toronto Globe and Mail. May 27, 1994
1039 Toronto Star, June 3, 1994
1040 ibid.
1041 Winnipeg Free Press, November 12, 1994
1042 Winnipeg Free Press, January 28, 1994
1043 Vancouver Sun, February 23, 1994
1044 Winnipeg Free Press, February 24, 1994
1045 Sean Foudie, interview December 10, 1994
1046 Winnipeg Free Press, April 9, 1994
1047 Ottawa Citizen, March 9, 1994
1048 Winnipeg Free Press, March 8, 1994
1049 ibid, October 16, 1994
1050 Toronto Globe and Mail, November 10, 1994
1051 Toronto Globe and Mail, January 6, 1994
1052 ibid.
1053 ibid.
1054 Ibid.
1055 Toronto Globe and Mail, January 18, 1994
1056 ibid.
1057 Orlando Sentinel, January 17, 1994
1058 ibid.
1059 Orlando Sentinel, Jan. 19, 1994.
1060 Toronto Globe and Mail, January 21, 1994
1061 ibid, January 20, 1994
1062 Toronto Sun, March 4, 1994
1063 ibid.
1064 Winnipeg Free Press, March 16, 1994
1065 Toronto Globe and Mail, April 1, 1994
1066 Ottawa Citizen, November 6, 1994
1067 Toronto Globe and Mail, March 15, 1994
1068 Ottawa Citizen, July 23, 1994
1069 Ottawa Sun, August 19, 1994
1070 ibid, October 15, 1994
1071 Winnipeg Free Press, November 18, 1994
1072 Toronto Globe and Mail, November 14, 1994
1073 Toronto Globe and Mail, November 22, 1994

1074   Toronto Star, November 22, 1994
1075   ibid.
1076   Toronto Globe and Mail, November 30, 1994
1077   Baltimore Sun, November 23, 1994
1078   Vancouver Sun, December 1, 1994
1079   Vancouver Sun, November 23, 1994
1080   Toronto Star, November 26, 1994
1081   Toronto Globe and Mail, November 25, 1994
1082   Toronto Star, November 27, 1994
1083   ibid, November 24, 1994
1084   Toronto Globe and Mail, November 26, 1994
1085   Toronto Star, November 24, 1994
1086   ibid.
1087   Toronto Globe and Mail, November 26, 1994
1088   ibid.
1089   Toronto Star, November 27, 1994
1090   ibid.
1091   Toronto Globe and Mail, November 26, 1994
1092   Toronto Globe and Mail, November 28, 1994
1093   ibid.
1094   Vancouver Sun, November 30, 1994
1095   Toronto Globe and Mail, December 8, 1994
1096   Toronto Globe and Mail, December 1, 1994
1097   Toronto Globe and Mail, September 20, 1994
1098   Toronto Globe and Mail, March 15, 1995
1099   Winnipeg Free Press, March 4, 1994
1100   ibid.
1101   Larry Smith, Inside Sports, TSN, January 31, 1994
1102   Ottawa Citizen, July 12, 1994.
1103   ibid., August 10, 1994
1104   Winnipeg Free Press, October 19, 1994
1105   Toronto Star, February 4, 1995
1106   Toronto Globe and Mail, April 13, 1995
1107   Toronto Globe and Mail, November 24, 1994
1108   CFL Media Release, April 25, 1995

Made in the USA
Monee, IL
05 November 2023

45840066R00169